WHAT YOUR COLLEAGUES ARE SAYING . . .

Problem solving has long been a challenge for students—until now! This book provides teachers with a bank of routines to engage students in thinking, reasoning, and sense making. Everything you need to teach students to be effective problem solvers is in your hands right now!

Marissa Walsh
Elementary Math Coach, Blue Springs School District
Blue Springs, MO

John J. SanGiovanni has written yet another masterful book on routines focused on problem solving. My mentor once told me the way you get better at solving math problems is making sense and solving more math problems. Many students typically shy away from problem solving, yet in this book SanGiovanni has developed culturally relevant problems students can engage in to help build their problem-solving skills. He has brilliantly put together a book of problem-solving routines to help all students be more successful. If we want equitable mathematics classrooms, ALL students must be engaged in daily problem solving and *Daily Routines to Jump-Start Problem Solving* is a resource to ensure that!

Georgina Rivera
NCSM Vice President
Principal, Charter Oak International Academy
West Hartford, CT

I have been using resources from John J. SanGiovanni since 2018! His strategies have helped propel thinking and student engagement in my classroom as well as classrooms across my district. His activities and routines have increased students' enjoyment of mathematics concepts, which has led to higher scores across the district.

Milton Leathers
Supervisor of Mathematics, Prairie-Hills Elementary School District 144
Markham, IL

Teachers often say, "My students can solve math equations, but not word problems." With SanGiovanni's *Daily Routines to Jump-Start Problem Solving*, teachers can ensure students develop the confidence to solve word problems without using hazardous tricks and gimmicks. Students will be encouraged to think about the mathematics behind the problem. The ideas in this book should be part of every mathematics class.

Lorie Huff
Director of K–12 Mathematics
Fayetteville, AR

Instead of "cookbook" problem-solving prompts, SanGiovanni provides teachers with step-by-step guidance on implementing problem solving through the use of classroom-ready instructional routines that allow students to engage in rich problem-solving experiences and promote reasoning. Additionally, this book encourages productive discourse, facilitates "just in time" scaffolds, and supports existing high-quality curriculum materials.

Latrenda Knighten
Mathematics Content Trainer
Baton Rouge, LA

The routines in this book are easy to follow and help set the stage to spark student engagement and discourse in any math class. As a math coach, I am always looking for ways to support teachers in helping students to be better thinkers and to reason with math, and these quick bursts of quality practice are an amazing resource. The graphic organizers provided to support the routines help ensure all students have an entry point to problem solving.

Cortni Muir
Math Instructional Coach Grades 3–5, New Milford Public Schools
President, Associated Teacher of Mathematics in Connecticut (ATOMIC)
New Milford, CT

Daily Routines to Jump-Start for Problem Solving offers a plethora of problem-solving routines to promote reasoning and critical thinking skills. A resource for administrators, instructional coaches, and math teachers, each protocol has a "Something to Think About" section, images and examples that encourage productive discussions, and variations of each routine to meet all students' needs.

Gail Donahue
Director, Academy of Catholic Educators
Notre Dame of Maryland University
Baltimore, MD

Daily Routines to Jump-Start Problem Solving is truly a game changer for K–8 educators. Every problem-solving situation embodies critical thinking and comprehension, thus building student self-efficacy. SanGiovanni provides practical tools and support to breathe new life into math language routines, promoting equitable problem solving for all students. Routines showcased in this book allow students to take the driver's seat as they engage in real-world problem solving.

Kimberly K. Jones
Math Consultant, Region 10 Educational Service Center
Richardson, TX

As math educators and leaders, we have all been waiting for a book like this to aid in facilitating rich discussions centered on problem-solving, all in the first few minutes of daily instruction! SanGiovanni provides 20 research-based strategies to help students become problem-posers and problem-solvers while building their confidence, agency, and identity. This book is truly a gift to the math education community.

Andrea Wood
Math Instructional Facilitator, Mid-Del Schools
Midwest, OK

SanGiovanni shares a creative collection of quick, high-quality practice opportunities that will help students sharpen their problem-solving skills. Teachers have been longing for purposeful activities like these to engage their students in thinking and sense-making as they strive to develop confident problem solvers in mathematics. This book will become one of teachers' best-loved instructional resources!

Susie Katt
K–2 Mathematics Coordinator, Lincoln Public Schools
Lincoln, NE

Daily Routines to Jump-Start Problem Solving should be on every elementary mathematics teacher's desk! These routines include practical approaches that will support all students in developing problem-solving strategies and skills. There is also substantial background information for teachers to deepen their own pedagogical understanding of how to further student success in approaching and solving problems.

Linda Gojak
Past President, National Council of Teachers of Mathematics
Willowick, OH

SanGiovanni does an excellent job empowering teachers to bridge the gap between some of their favorite math routines and problem solving. He provides a roadmap that will walk alongside teachers as they look to engage students and improve thinking beyond the first 15 minutes of math class.

Graham Fletcher
Math Specialist
Atlanta, GA

Daily Routines to Jump-Start Math Class, Grades K–8
THE BOOK AT-A-GLANCE

A quick-reference table provides you with a brief description of each task, along with the corresponding task purpose.

JUMP-START ROUTINES AT-A-GLANCE

	TITLE	BRIEF	TARGETED PROBLEM-SOLVING SKILL
1	I Would Say	Students practice restating problems in their own words.	Making Sense: Retelling
2	3Qs	Students practice with a variety of questions so that they can determine how to make sense of a problem, identify the question, and think about a strategy for solving it.	Making Sense: Asking Questions
3	Asked and Answered	Students learn to think carefully about a question by grappling with questions that can, and cannot, be answered.	Questions: Understanding the Question
4	What's the Question?	Students practice problem solving by creating questions and problems that yield a given solution.	Questions: Identifying Questions
5	Same Data, Different Question	Students practice thinking and reasoning as questions change from day to day.	Questions: Identifying Questions
6	How Do You . . .?	Students are presented with situations and then a question. Students determine how they would find the solution.	Reasoning: Solution Pathways
7	Same and Different	Students compare and contrast two problems to analyze the changing nature of contexts, numbers, and questions.	Making Sense: Problem Elements
8	What's the Sitch?	Students develop a process for analyzing different problem-solving situations (structures).	Making Sense: Analyzing Problems
9	They Did What?	Students examine strategies and solutions of worked examples.	Reasoning: Reasonable Solutions/ Pathways
10	This Number, That Number	Students practice the strategy of solving a simpler problem by working with identical problems that have different number complexities.	Reasoning: Simpler Problems
11	Imagine That	Students practice visualizing problems and generating useful representations to solve them.	Making Sense: Representing
12	Match the Equation	Students practice representing problems with equations.	Making Sense: Representing

3QS (QUESTION, QUESTION, QUESTION)

About the Routine

How do you know what question to ask yourself when you are solving a problem? After all, there are so, so many questions you could ask. Is it your experience solving problems that has helped you know what to look for? Do you monitor your own progress through the problem, thinking about what you know and don't know? Do you always ask yourself questions, or are there situations in which you simply move through the problem with little to no thought because you just "know what to do?" Do you ask questions to help you get unstuck? 3Qs (Question, Question, Question) is a routine that aims to provide students with experience asking all sorts of questions. The goal is to help students develop metacognition about the questions they ask themselves to be productive problem solvers. To do this, you pose a problem and present different questions for students to talk about.

Before you get into how the routine works, take a moment to think about the variety of questions one might ask while solving a problem and the purpose those questions serve.

Problem solvers metacognitively monitor their progress with questions in the three phases of problem solving (before, during, and after) as shown in the chart on page 34. Within those phases, there are essential questions like "What is the problem about?" and "What do I need to do?" These essential questions are the essence of problem solving, and each serves a specific purpose along the way.

37 cookies were given out at a restaurant. 26 were eaten. How many were left?

Credit: PicturePartners/istockphoto.com

What is important?

What is happening?

What am I trying to figure out?

Credit: Michael Burrell/istock.com

How This Routine Helps With Problem Solving

This routine builds problem-solving skill by providing opportunities for students to

- take time to read questions,
- determine whether a question can be answered with information presented,
- shift their approaches from grabbing numbers and doing something with them to focusing on the information and the question,
- recognize that questions can't always be answered from the given information,
- identify important information presented in problems or data charts,
- practice ignoring unnecessary information,
- experience problems with quantities presented in tables (i.e., not standard story or word problems),
- justify their thinking, and
- take ownership of the problem-solving process.

What to Do

1. Pose data for students to observe for a few moments. Optional: Have students turn and talk about the information by having them describe what it is about in their own words.

2. Pose three or four questions related to the data.

3. Have students think about which questions can be asked and answered with the data.

4. Have partners discuss their ideas about the questions.

5. Bring the class together to discuss their selections. During discussion, any question that probes their thinking is a good question. For this example, some questions you could ask include:

   » How could a question with a number that isn't in the table be asked and answered? (question D)

   » How did you know that question B couldn't be asked and answered?

   » Questions A and C both compare things. How did you know that question A could be answered but question C couldn't be answered?

   » What more information would you need to answer question B?

   » How would the equations for question A and D be similar?

6. Optional: After discussion, have students create new questions that can or can't be answered by the data. You can have each student generate one of each. Or you can have students pair with a classmate with one partner creating a question that could be asked and answered and the other partner creating something that can't be answered. If time permits, some student creations could be shared. Alternatively, they can be written down and saved for the next day.

Something to Think About: Where Do You Get the Data?

You might find yourself creating easy, contrived, trivial examples like survey results about favorite ice cream flavors. Instead, you want to use contexts that are interesting and meaningful to your students. But finding data appropriate for elementary students for lessons, let alone a routine like this one or Routine 5: Same Data, Different Question (page 57) can be quite the challenge. Your curriculum resources likely are a good place to start your search, but be sure to enlist your students and your colleagues.

One way to do this is to make it a homework assignment. Give an example or two of the types of data tables and graphs you want your students to create. Have students work with caregivers to create a table or graph relative to a source in their home like a newspaper, nutrition label on a food package,

Variations on each routine are provided to further deepen student understanding and provide ways to meet the varied needs of your learners.

HOW DO YOU . . . ? (VARIATIONS): CHANGING THE PROCESS

There is no wrong way to go about any routine. This one centers on the question, "How do I solve this?" It is shown with two problems, but you might find that you need to focus on just one with your students first as shown in the first variation. Your students might need numbers to help them think about the problem. You might find that posing three problems is a good challenge for your students. You could even use three problems of the same operation in which two have a common situation and the third doesn't (e.g., two take away subtraction problems and a subtraction comparison problem). Look at some of the following ideas. Use them and improve on them to yield the best results for your students.

Variation A: Single Problem (Focused Example)

Using one problem is a good place to begin with students, especially primary students. Here, they can focus on this context and a single question. In this example, discussion is about the group of rubber ducks floating down the river and the comparison between ducks who finished and didn't finish the race. Students might ask about why they didn't finish the race—which is fine. It shows they're trying to understand the problem. After discussing the single problem, you can end the routine or introduce a new question with the same context.

A

Rubber ducks were raced down a river. How do you find out how many didn't finish the race?

Credit: Heike Faber/istockphoto.com

NOTES

_____

_____

_____

_____

_____

_____

_____

_____

_____

_____

_____

_____

_____

DAILY ROUTINES to JUMP-START PROBLEM SOLVING

GRADES K-8

DAILY ROUTINES to JUMP-START PROBLEM SOLVING

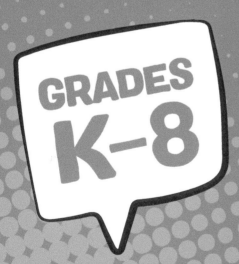

GRADES K-8

JOHN J.
SANGIOVANNI

CORWIN Mathematics

FOR INFORMATION:

Corwin
A SAGE Company
2455 Teller Road
Thousand Oaks, California 91320
(800) 233–9936
www.corwin.com

SAGE Publications Ltd.
1 Oliver's Yard
55 City Road
London, EC1Y 1SP
United Kingdom

SAGE Publications India Pvt. Ltd.
Unit No 323-333, Third Floor, F-Block
International Trade Tower Nehru Place
New Delhi - 110 019
India

SAGE Publications Asia-Pacific Pte. Ltd.
18 Cross Street #10–10/11/12
China Square Central
Singapore 048423

President: Mike Soules
Vice President and Editorial Director:
  Monica Eckman
Associate Director and Publisher, STEM: Erin Null
Senior Editorial Assistant: Nyle De Leon
Production Editor: Tori Mirsadjadi
Copy Editor: Heather Kerrigan
Typesetter: Integra
Proofreader: Dennis Webb
Indexer: Integra
Cover and Interior Designer: Scott Van Atta
Marketing Manager: Margaret O'Connor

This book is printed on acid-free paper.

23 24 25 26 27 10 9 8 7 6 5 4 3 2 1

CONTENTS

Acknowledgments   xv

About the Author   xvii

PART 1: WHY JUMP-START ROUTINES FOR PROBLEM SOLVING?   1

What Is Problem Solving and Why Is It Difficult?   2

Problem-Solving Routines Develop Reasoning and Address Challenges   6

Implementing Jump-Start Routines for Problem Solving   11

What's Next?   19

PART 2: THE JUMP-START ROUTINES FOR PROBLEM SOLVING   23

Routine 1: I Would Say   24

Routine 2: 3Qs (Question, Question, Question)   33

Routine 3: Asked and Answered   41

Routine 4: What's the Question?   50

Routine 5: Same Data, Different Question   57

Routine 6: How Do You . . . ?   68

Routine 7: Same and Different   76

Routine 8: What's the Sitch?   86

Routine 9: They Did What?   94

Routine 10: This Number, That Number   103

Routine 11: Imagine That   111

Routine 12: Match the Equation   118

Routine 13: And Then . . .   126

Routine 14: Another Question   136

Routine 15: TMI   143

Routine 16: It Can't Be   150

Routine 17: Is It Reasonable?   158

Routine 18: Sticky Patterns   165

Routine 19: Lots and Lots   174

Routine 20: The Swap   182

PART 3: WHERE TO GO NEXT 189

Make a Plan 189

Adjust to Their Adjustments 191

Further Modify Routines 192

Design Your Own Routines 192

Work Collaboratively and Share the Load 192

Use Jump-Start Routines for Professional Learning or PLCs 192

Jump-Start Mathematics Engagement 194

Appendix 195

References 199

Index 202

 Visit the companion website at https://qrs.ly/3cemjnt for downloadable resources.

ACKNOWLEDGMENTS

Each and every project is a collaborative effort with so many to thank. I want to thank Corwin (yet again) for making this book a reality. There is no better publishing team to work with than the Corwin Mathematics team. I am lucky to be a part of that team. I offer a special thanks to Editor and Publisher Erin Null for her enthusiasm, partnership, insight, and friendship.

My work in mathematics education is possible because of the greatness of so many mathematics educators, both nationally and locally, who have paved the way not only for me but countless others. They do more than teach. They inspire. There are too many to mention. But I would be remiss if I didn't mention two. I am grateful to Skip Fennell for his contributions to our field, his advice, and most importantly his friendship. I am grateful to Kay Sammons who through the many years has provided insight, council, perspective, support, and opportunity.

During this project I have thought quite a bit about my own problem solving. For much of my life, I have assumed that I am, by nature, curious about all things and apt to solve problems. I am realizing that opportunity and access have been the true culprits. My parents talked with me about solving problems without solving them for me. They played games with me and did what they could so that I could have experiences and resources (like puzzles and LEGO) to stoke my creativity and thinking. I thank them. My kids, likewise, have taught me all sorts of things about problem solving and I thank them too.

Problem solving grows through play, reasoning, exploration, and discussion. It doesn't end in childhood. This leads me to my final, and most important, acknowledgement. My wife Kristen's support and encouragement are unwavering. She too has grown my problem-solving skills because we play games together. We talk about problems together. I cherish those opportunities and conversations.

PUBLISHER'S ACKNOWLEDGMENTS

Corwin gratefully acknowledges the contributions of the following reviewers:

Jozette Black
Teacher, American School Foundation of
    Guadalajara
Guadalajara, Jalisco, Mexico

Gail Donahue
Director, Academy of Catholic Educators (ACES),
    Instructional Coach, Notre Dame Maryland
    University
Ellicott City, MD

Monica Tienda
Fourth-Grade Educator, Oak Park School
    District (day job) & PCMI Teacher Leadership
    Program Co-Director (summer job)
Royal Oak, MI

Latrenda Knighten
Mathematics Content Trainer
Baton Rouge, LA

Karen Brooks
Elementary Math Academic Coach, Chandler
    Unified School District
Chandler, AZ

ABOUT THE AUTHOR

John J. SanGiovanni is a nationally recognized leader in mathematics education. He works as a mathematics supervisor in Howard County, Maryland, leading mathematics curriculum development, digital learning, assessment, and professional learning. John is passionate about developing new mathematics leaders in his district and in his work at McDaniel College. He is an author of more than two dozen professional development books on math education, and an international consultant for mathematics curriculum development and professional learning. John is a frequent speaker at state and national conferences. He is active in mathematics professional organizations, having served on the Board of Directors for the National Council of Supervisors of Mathematics, the National Council of Teachers of Mathematics, the Maryland Council of Supervisors of Mathematics, and the Maryland Council of Teachers of Mathematics.

Look for other Corwin Mathematics titles by John J. SanGiovanni

- *Mine the Gap for Mathematical Understanding, Grades K–2: Common Holes and Misconceptions and What to Do About Them*
- *Mine the Gap for Mathematical Understanding, Grades 3–5: Common Holes and Misconceptions and What to Do About Them*
- *Mine the Gap for Mathematical Understanding, Grades 6–8: Common Holes and Misconceptions and What to Do About Them*
- *Daily Routines to Jump-Start Math Class, Elementary School: Engage Students, Improve Number Sense, and Practice Reasoning*
- *Daily Routines to Jump-Start Math Class, Middle School: Engage Students, Improve Number Sense, and Practice Reasoning*
- *Daily Routines to Jump-Start Math Class, High School: Engage Students, Improve Number Sense, and Practice Reasoning*
- *Productive Math Struggle: A Six-Point Action Plan for Fostering Perseverance*
- *Figuring Out Fluency in Mathematics, Grades K–8: Moving Beyond Basic Facts and Memorization*
- *Figuring Out Fluency—Addition and Subtraction With Whole Numbers: A Classroom Companion*
- *Figuring Out Fluency—Multiplication and Division With Whole Numbers: A Classroom Companion*
- *Figuring Out Fluency—Addition and Subtraction With Fractions and Decimals: A Classroom Companion*
- *Figuring Out Fluency— Multiplication and Division With Fractions and Decimals: A Classroom Companion*
- *Figuring Out Fluency—Operations With Rational Numbers and Algebraic Equations*

PART 1

WHY JUMP–START ROUTINES FOR PROBLEM SOLVING?

> **There are 125 sheep and 5 dogs in a flock. How old is the shepherd?**

A famous study posed this problem to elementary students. The shared findings were (and still are) shocking (Merseth, 1993). Three out of four students gave an answer! When you pause and think about it, the results might not be that shocking after all. In mathematics classrooms, students often feel compelled to give an answer, any answer, when confronting a problem. They might even think it's best to find it quickly, giving little thought about what to do. They grab the numbers and "do something with them," choosing the first operation that comes to mind. And when confused by the context, the numbers, or the question, they might assume that it's probably a problem with a more "challenging" operation (e.g., subtraction or division). As you think about all the reasons a student might give an answer to the sheep problem, ask yourself, "How many of my students would answer it too?"

Do you cringe when it's time to teach and practice word problems? Have you thought, "There has to be a better way"? Have you ever wondered what a Number Talk or number routine might look like for problem solving? Are you looking to spark student engagement and discussion? These jump-start routines for problem solving take aim at each of those questions, giving you a rich resource to nurture skilled problem solvers. More right answers aren't guaranteed, but better thinking and reasoning is. At the very least, you can be sure there will be fewer "problem-solving robots" in your classroom.

WHAT IS PROBLEM SOLVING AND WHY IS IT DIFFICULT?

Problems are tasks that provide intellectual challenge and promote students' mathematical development (NCTM, n.d.). Problems require higher-level thinking, can be solved in different ways, elicit skillful use of mathematics knowledge, promote engagement, encourage discourse, and provide practice of important skills. So, then problem solving is about making sense, identifying questions, determining a strategy, monitoring progress of that strategy, adjusting an approach, and determining the reasonableness of a result. Problem solving is not a procedure; it is an experience. It is the experience of challenge, anticipation, exploration, discussion, success, and even failure.

To be clear, word problems are not the only form of problems. But word problems are a regular feature of elementary and middle school mathematics. Skills developed through them transfer to most, if not all, other problem-solving situations in math class and beyond. For many, word problems are a formative experience about thinking, reasoning, and doing mathematics. Those early experiences forge dispositions about the meaning and purpose of math as well as dispositions about one's math identity—their deeply held belief about their ability to solve problems or do math. For many, problem solving is confusing and frustrating. Failed attempts to mimic someone else's approach undermines their agency. In short, problem solving is just plain hard.

Why is it hard for students to solve word problems? Take a moment to think about the challenges your students have shown when they work to solve word problems. Some of the most frequent responses to the question are captured in the table. It may not be a complete list, but it's highly likely that it includes a few of the challenges you thought about.

STUDENT DIFFICULTY	WHAT IT IS/WHY IT HAPPENS
Understanding the Context (Making Meaning of the Problem)	Reading skills that are still developing can contribute to this challenge, but not always. Sometimes the context or particular vocabulary is simply unfamiliar to a child. Sometimes the context or topic isn't relevant to students' culture or experience. And don't forget that some students just don't read the problem (like adults with directions for putting together furniture).
Understanding the Question	Students may not understand what a question is asking for a variety of reasons. It could be a reading issue, but it likely stems from instructional practices that focus on identifying keywords to select an operation or that are overly procedural and centered on question identification more than making sense of questions.
Skill Association	Skill association happens when students simply apply the operation that they have learned or used most recently or most frequently. They are often conditioned to this when asked to solve the word problems at the bottom of the textbook page as "applications" of the procedures or skills taught in the lesson or at the top of the page.
Connecting the Question to an Action or Operation	This challenge is connected to the student's conceptual understanding of an operation or inexperience with different problem structures or situations (see page 12). For example, they might only understand subtraction as taking away. So, then they are challenged when trying to solve comparison problems.

STUDENT DIFFICULTY	WHAT IT IS/WHY IT HAPPENS
Multiple Steps	Having to complete more than one step to solve a problem is not always intuitive to students. This challenge is compounded when problem solving is distilled into specific, sequenced actions. In other words, students conditioned to find numbers and select an operation have difficulty realizing that more than one action is needed. It's also difficult when a certain quantity (the result of one step) isn't presented in the problem directly.
Strategypalooza	Strategypalooza is the result of teaching many different strategies in a short amount of time and then having students solve a given problem with more than one strategy to show competence with the different strategies. When on their own, students then have difficulty choosing among different strategies, let alone carrying them out.
Making Sense of the Answer	It's hard for students to make sense of their answer for a few different reasons. One is due to their developing number and operational sense. Another is a lack of experience with real-world situations. A third is the overemphasis of procedural approaches often seen in core instruction and curricular materials.
Perseverance	Students struggle with a problem and don't know how to get unstuck and/or persevere. This can be attributed to past experiences that fraudulently presented problem solving as a quick and easy endeavor. Or, more likely, students don't know what questions to ask themselves when stuck while solving a problem.
Fear of Incorrect Answers	Lack of confidence and anxiety are all too familiar aspects of learning and doing math. They infiltrate the problem-solving process as well. When challenges with basic fact recall don't stir these feelings, word problems often do. And there is often anxiety around both.
Overwhelmed by Numbers, Words, or Context	Students can't get started with a problem because the numbers (e.g., size of numbers, types of numbers, complexity of numbers) seem hard. Sometimes the length (e.g., number of words) overwhelms students before they begin.
Unsure How to Start	This isn't that a student can't read and comprehend a problem. Instead, they don't know where to begin. They aren't sure what to do and haven't developed metacognitive questions for retelling or representing the problem.
Overly Complicated Representations	In short, creative students make intricate, overly detailed drawings or diagrams. The complexity of and time spent on their creativity undermines problem solving, possibly causing it to grind to a halt.
Writing Equations	Drawings and representations are good approaches to solving a problem. However, students also need to be able to write and use equations to solve problems. When they can't, problems with large numbers or complicated situations become very difficult to complete.
Incomplete Progress Monitoring (Metacognition)	This challenge is about a student moving through a problem mechanically and not thinking about what steps are being taken, why they are being taken, or if the steps being taken are moving toward a solution. Thinking about one's thinking (metacognition) is at the heart of problem solving and possibly the most difficult to develop. Though it can be modeled and discussed, it cannot be done for students.
Identity and Agency (Confidence)	Problem solving alone is hard. It's even more challenging when one tries to carry out steps that aren't understood or that are even counterintuitive to the individual. Failure results. Failing over and over again damages a student's identity and their agency, leading to lack of confidence.

As you know, each of your students is unique, and so their challenges with problem solving aren't all the same. Some students might show more than one challenge or may show different challenges with different problems. Factor in 20 or more students in a classroom, and it's easy to see why teaching problem solving can feel overwhelming.

Problem-Solving Hazards

Every teacher wants their students to be successful. They work hard to make math enjoyable. They are keenly aware of the challenges mentioned and look for all sorts of ways to navigate around them. In an effort to make the problem solving easier, or at least to ensure correct answers, teachers can resort to instructional practices or teaching moves that seem to make sense in the short term. Sometimes teachers use shortcuts like keywords, mnemonics for problem-solving steps, or using attention-grabbing but imprecise vocabulary like "the flip flop property" to describe the commutative property. Such tricks and instructional approaches are the outcome of a well-intended desire for student success and to make math enjoyable; but they set the stage for setbacks, an apparent loss of retention, and, ultimately, frustration. They become problem-solving hazards that lead to less success when new problem types and classes of numbers are introduced, or when the number of steps in a problem increases (Karp et al., 2014).

In some schools, some of these teaching moves have been employed for many years, yet student success with problem solving remains inconsistent and elusive. Ironically, it turns out that these common instructional solutions to problem solving actually factor out the most essential part of problem solving, which is the thinking! Let's look more in depth at a few examples.

Hazard: C-U-B-E-S and Other Mnemonics

You may not be familiar with "C-U-B-E-S" but you probably have experience (as a student or a teacher) with something very similar. In short, C-U-B-E-S is a mechanical process to solving a problem.

C – Circle the numbers

U – Underline the important information

B – Box the question

E – Eliminate unnecessary information

S – Solve and check

While the overarching process of looking for important information, identifying the question to be answered, and thinking about a solution path is useful, the result of using a method like C-U-B-E-S is that it distills student thinking into a series of steps. Finding the numbers and question makes sense but doesn't help much when one doesn't understand the question or the context of the problem. Without understanding, it's hard to determine what is and isn't important information. And the "check" element is about checking calculations rather than determining reasonableness of a solution.

C-U-B-E-S is comparable to other poor instructional practices in mathematics like DMSB ("Does McDonald's Sell Burgers," a.k.a. divide, multiply, subtract, bring down) for division with a standard algorithm or "five and above, give it a shove" for rounding. Each approach seems clever and foolproof until the student encounters a situation for which they need to think and reason.

Hazard: Keywords

A keyword "strategy" to problem solving asks students to look for a word that "tells them what to do" in the problem. For example, "altogether" means to add, "left" means to subtract, "times" means to multiply. When "solving" a problem, students scan the problem for numbers and use the keyword to determine what operation they should use to solve it. This approach is even more problematic than C-U-B-E-S because it looks to fully remove thinking from the problem-solving process. A keyword approach is faulty and unreliable (Karp et al., 2014). It leads to wrong answers, confusion, and frustration while compromising confidence and agency.

Take a look at these three problems:

A.	B.	C.
The Grade 3 class left 12 jackets on the playground and the Grade 4 class left 9 jackets on the playground. How many jackets were left on the playground?	Emmett practiced piano 18 times last week and 3 times this week. How many times did Emmett practice?	How many legs do 13 elephants have?

The three problems shared are good, though unextraordinary, examples of the why keywords don't work. In the jacket problem, the word left signals subtraction, but the question is asking about how many jackets were left, in total, on the playground. The problem requires addition. In the piano problem, with a keyword approach, "times" would signal multiplication, but again the question is how many hours are practiced in total in the two weeks—again, addition is needed. Last, the elephant problem has no keyword but should be a very simple problem to solve by doing nothing more than drawing a picture to help see that multiplication is an efficient operation. If any of those three problems were two-step problems, it's easy to imagine how poorly a student relying on keywords might do.

The C-U-B-E-S approach isn't much better. Look again at problem A. Other numbers appear in the problem, but they have nothing to do with what needs to be computed. Circling (C) them does no good and potentially leads to computing the wrong numbers. Compared to the other problems it looks long, implying that there is something to eliminate (E). But there isn't. How would C-U-B-E-S play out with problem C? There's nothing to eliminate. There aren't two numbers. What should you underline? Yet it's a problem that should be in the "problem-solving wheelhouse" of an elementary student.

Hazard: Problem-Solving Friday

In an attempt to make problem solving a routine feature of mathematics instruction, some have created entire days dedicated to word problems. Those days are dubbed "Problem-Solving Fridays," "Thinking Thursdays," or "Wordy Wednesdays." They are messaged as a "break" from doing math so that students can do . . . harder math! The intent to feature problem solving is good, but the idea misses the mark completely. It implies that word problems are something separate and distinct from doing the "everyday" calculating on naked numbers. This would be like making a distinction that subtraction with regrouping is something different than subtraction. It insinuates that solving word problems is uniquely hard and that word problems themselves are the only form of problem solving. It sets up falsehoods and perpetuates misunderstandings about what math really is. It fails because problem solving, thinking, and reasoning must be at the heart of every mathematics lesson (NCTM, 2014).

Hazard: Notice and Wonder Done Poorly

Notice and Wonder is a great way to introduce a concept, task, or problem. It taps into student observation and curiosity. When done well, it positions students to be the catalysts of doing math in the classroom. To do it well, a picture or context is provided, and students describe things they notice about it. Then, they are asked what they wonder about it. Often, their wonderings spark the prompt or task that the teacher intended for the lesson. Unfortunately, Notice and Wonder can often devolve into another layer of procedure complete with recording sheets and "rules." Worse yet is when it is portrayed as a problem-solving strategy. It is not. It is perfect for getting students excited about math and engaging them in doing it. But the act of problem solving goes further. This doesn't mean that Notice and Wonder shouldn't make it into problem-solving situations. It should, just like predicting and anticipatory sets should be part of the reading process. But it should not be considered a problem-solving routine or strategy on its own.

Hazard: Gradual Release of Problem Solving

Rote, procedural skills are sometimes taught through a gradual release of responsibility model (I Do, We Do, You Do). It is an instructional hazard for teaching problem solving. Problem solving is about making meaning or Mathematizing (Freudenthal, as cited in Fosnot & Dolk, 2001). Like comprehension, problem solving is about thinking and reasoning. You cannot think for someone. You can model good thinking and metacognition and you can help them learn to think, but thinking itself can't be "delivered."

PROBLEM-SOLVING ROUTINES DEVELOP REASONING AND ADDRESS CHALLENGES

Possibly the biggest issue with those instructional hazards (with the exception of Notice and Wonder) is that they circumvent what it takes to solve problems, and also fail to develop 21st Century Skills. Those are the skills our students need to be successful in the information age (Stauffer, 2022). Problem solving calls on critical thinking. Rich, discussion-laden problem-solving experiences expose students to new ideas, which stimulates their ingenuity and creativity. Opportunities to work together nurture collaboration. Explaining, justifying, and critiquing others' reasoning is the core of 21st century communication. The idea of teaching all of this feels daunting. But what if you practiced them, chipped away at them, little by little? What if you were able to rehabilitate faulty approaches and unproductive dispositions about word problems and doing math in general? What if a burst of rich problem solving, flush with engagement and discussion, was a routine feature of your mathematics instruction?

What Is Meant By a Problem-Solving Routine?

A routine is an activity that is done, well, routinely. It is familiar to students once established, and it is adaptable to practice different skills and concepts or, in this case, different types of problems (Bay-Williams & SanGiovanni, 2021). Routines aid classroom management while fostering positive relationships within a mathematics community (Berry, 2018). Routines become an instructional habit, maximizing precious time for greater learning opportunity. Teachers can use a variety of routines, including those to develop mathematical language, number sense, and mathematical fluency.

You may be familiar with Number Talks (Parrish, 2014), number routines (SanGiovanni, 2020), or fluency routines (Bay-Williams & SanGiovanni, 2021). In some schools or districts, routines may be recognized as "math talks." Those routines are used for developing number sense and computational fluency and give students an opportunity to play with and discuss numbers. The routines in *this* book go after problem solving. They target specific components of problem solving, including making sense of the context, identifying the question being asked, finding ways to represent the situation, and determining reasonableness of a solution. Like other routines, these intend to engage students in reasoning and discussion. They are meaningful, high-quality practice.

Jump-Start Routines for Problem Solving

The routines in this book are designed to "jump-start" problem solving. They are engaging opportunities for students to work with and discuss how they understand problems. They are designed to develop students' reasoning, critical thinking, and sense making. They can provide quality practice at the beginning of class or any other time during the math block and can repair or instill mathematics confidence in your students, shaping their productive dispositions and positive mathematical identities. These routines are also exceptional opportunities for building student agency with problem solving and doing mathematics in general.

These routines are

- practical and easy for teachers to implement each day,
- meant for quick five- to seven-minute engagements—typically at the start of math class,
- thinking exercises meant to ignite thinking and reasoning skills,
- open and flexible in nature, and
- modifiable to work with any problem type and most any content.

These routines create an environment in which the Standards for Mathematical Practice or SMPs (NGA Center & CCSSO, 2010) come to life. Though specific practices are linked to each routine throughout the book, in general students

- make sense of problems and persevere (SMP 1),
- reason abstractly and quantitatively (SMP 2),
- construct viable arguments and critique the reasoning of others (SMP 3),
- model with mathematics (SMP 4),
- use appropriate tools strategically (SMP 5),

- attend to precision (SMP 6),
- look for and make use of structure (SMP 7), and
- look for and express regularity in repeated reasoning (SMP 8).

How Does a Jump-Start Problem-Solving Routine Work?

These routines are quick bursts of quality practice. You pose a problem. Students are given a few moments to think about it. Students talk with partners about their thoughts and ideas. You bring the class together for students to share ideas and ask questions of others. You work to facilitate the discussion, poking at their ideas with questions, probing their reasoning, connecting statements to the problem or to others' ideas. You want to withhold how you think about the prompt or how you would solve it until they have had ample opportunities to share their thinking first. And again, these are quick bursts. A routine typically takes 5 to 10 minutes at most.

How Problem-Solving Routines Build Reasoning

Reasoning can be thought of as the process of drawing conclusions based on evidence or stated assumptions. Although reasoning is an important part of all disciplines, it plays a special and fundamental role in mathematics. In middle and high school mathematics, reasoning is often understood as engaging in *formal reasoning*, or formulating proofs, in which students are drawing conclusions logically deduced from assumptions and definitions. However, mathematical reasoning can take many forms, ranging from informal explanation and justification to formal deduction, as well as inductive observations. Reasoning begins in the earliest grades. It starts with explorations, various conjectures, false starts, and partial explanations before there is ever a result.

Reasoning is compromised as students accept rules and procedures without investigation of "why." They then practice these rules and procedures so much that the mathematics and reasoning within them fades away. Their task at hand becomes nothing more than completing a collection of problems. Over time, they generalize that *this* is what it means to do mathematics and solve problems.

Problem solving is more than the pursuit of a right answer. It includes critical thinking, reasoning, and determining reasonableness. Mix those with communication, explanation, and justification and you find the traits of individuals that are more desirable for Fortune 500 companies than calculation and procedural skill (Boaler, 2015). Problem-solving routines captured in this work can help your students develop these complex skills through daily, engaging activities. The strategies, approaches, and reasoning that they develop in your classroom during these routines will serve them for a lifetime of everyday mathematics.

Routines Provide Bursts of Quality Practice Over Time

Problem solving is obviously critically important. But it isn't something that is developed in a single unit of study or a handful of lessons over the course of a year. Problem solving evolves. Students develop their skill and understanding over long periods, through frequent experience, exposure to different ideas, and application in varied situations. Daily routines for problem solving provide opportunities for all of these to grow.

In his book *Outliers*, Malcolm Gladwell (2008) suggests that a person needs 10,000 hours of deliberate practice to master something. Though one might argue the exact amount of time, it is logical that the more people do something—the more they practice and experience something—the better they can understand and apply it. Consider playing an instrument. Passing a written test about the parts of the instrument, the way to hold it, and the meaning of recorded notes doesn't mean someone is proficient with the instrument. Instead, it shows that they understand how the instrument works and the basics of how music is recorded on paper. Their ability to play the instrument, and to play it well, is improved and enhanced as they play it more and more.

This analogy could be applied to problem solving and reasoning. The theory here is that with foundational understanding and frequent, plentiful opportunities to practice, students can increase their number sense and reasoning and justification skills. You might note that 10,000 hours seems impossible with limited instructional time and considerable skills and concepts already identified in your curriculum. However, with routines, students can achieve a great number of *hours on the road* in just a few minutes a day. Consider this: Through a daily, five-minute routine, students could access 900 minutes of problem-solving practice in one academic year (180 days). Over the course of their time in elementary grades, that adds up to more than 5,000 minutes or about 90 hours of practice for just problem solving!

Routines Satisfy the Need for Quality Practice

Quality practice is not defined by the number of problems students complete, the speed at which they calculate or recall, or the number of hours they spend doing mathematics. It is defined by what students do and how they are engaged. Quality practice should engage students in thinking. Quality practice focuses on a skill, varies how students engage, gives opportunity for processing what is being done, and highlights how something being done connects with something that has been done or has been learned (Bay-Williams & SanGiovanni, 2021). The problem-solving routines in this book provide quality practice. They are unique, engaging, and diverse experiences that will help students develop their thinking skills. They are neither repetitive nor mundane. They are not mindless drills. They are the quality practice that can help students perform better in class, outside the mathematics classroom, and even better on standardized tests.

Routines Frame a Growth Mindset and Build Confidence

The idea of consistent, engaging practice to develop students' problem solving promotes other prominent ideas about teaching and learning mathematics. One of those is a growth mindset. A growth mindset is an approach to teaching and learning mathematics that emphasizes that mindset is more important than initial ability in determining the progress students can make in their mathematical understanding (Dweck, 2006). Students with a growth mindset find agency in doing mathematics. For them, learning with a growth mindset means

- believing that problem-solving skills can be developed and great abilities can be built over time,
- viewing mistakes as an opportunity to develop understanding how to solve new problems,

- being resilient by finding ways to get unstuck and work through a problem when the solution path isn't clearly apparent,

- believing that effort builds skill and creates success, and

- reflecting about how one approaches new problems and learns to solve them.

Carol Dweck's work establishes that a growth mindset benefits students by empowering them to develop skills through engagement and effort. It positively shapes both their mathematics identity and agency. To realize this, teachers must provide worthwhile opportunities to participate in and discuss mathematics. Regular experience with interesting activities for building problem-solving skill naturally complements the facets of a growth mindset. Routines reinforce that students' ability can be developed through continued practice and effort. They can undercut any students' notion that their mathematical ability is fixed.

These routines help students build confidence. Confidence becomes part of students' mathematics identity and agency. Yet, some traditional, rule-based approaches to solving problems have done the exact opposite. Blindly applying rules to mathematics and problems without understanding can undermine a student's confidence (Van de Walle et al., 2019) as they rely on disconnected steps without understanding. Stalled progress erodes confidence. Perceptions of failure associated with making mistakes in mathematics or perceptions of *not having a math gene* damage student confidence. Infrequent, disengaging, or disconnected practice challenges confidence. Yet, jump-start problem-solving routines can counter each of these challenges and, in time, enhance students' confidence in themselves and mathematics in general.

Routines Prevent or Rehabilitate Number Pluckers

One might say that traditional approaches to mathematics instruction have created a *bunch of pluckers*. These pluckers are students who pluck keywords or numbers from problems without thinking. They just do something with numbers sometimes finding success and sometimes not. Their work can be inconsistent. It can be hard for them to explain or justify their thinking.

Not all are pluckers, yet a good number do simply highlight words (sometimes all of the words), circle the numbers, focus on labeling their answers correctly, and so on. They blindly carry out steps with little thought, using strategies that they don't understand well because they think they "have" to. This is not their fault. These "problem solvers" come about when instruction is overly procedural, centered on the pursuit of answers, and void of exploration, inquiry, and discussion. Their behaviors are reinforced over and over again on many worksheets of practice. To be clear, they are not at fault for their approaches!

Success can be fleeting for many, if not all, of the pluckers and others. Their ability to complete a procedure or solve a problem without understanding can be, and often is, lost without considerable practice, maintenance, or review. Even then, proficiency can fade. And though they may show skill with certain problem types, their "skills" are compromised when the structure of a problem changes or a reliable keyword doesn't show up. All of this adds up to damaged math dispositions.

Yet, thinking, reasoning, and understanding are never lost. Better yet, they are transferred to new concepts and new problem situations. Those come about when students can build on their current understanding, when they connect ideas, and refine them by talking about them. Discussion helps students acquire new strategies proposed by others. Routines can help students become independent doers of math who think and reason instead of mimicking the approaches of their teacher.

IMPLEMENTING JUMP-START ROUTINES FOR PROBLEM SOLVING

The routines in this book are intended as practical ideas for jump-starting your problem-solving instruction. You can (and should) modify them in all sorts of ways. You can adjust them to fit different amounts of time (from five to 10 minutes) that you allocate for them. Know that the first few times you use a new routine will likely take a bit longer until students understand the process. These routines will become a rich opportunity for meaningful discourse in mathematics and windows into student thinking.

Before You Begin, What Your Students Should Know

If you're familiar with using Number Talks and number routines, you know they're best done *after* you have provided a good amount of instruction relative to the skills and concepts those routines intend to strengthen. For example, students must learn strategies for adding two-digit numbers before reinforcing them with a Number Talk. And while it's generally true that students must learn some basic skills of solving problems before working with a routine, the amount of time and experience is less because these routines teach and develop skills through the actual activity. For example, a routine like I Would Say (page 24) practices retelling what a problem is about. You should teach what retelling is before using the routine, but students don't need to master retelling before starting routines, because the routine itself helps them become good at that skill.

Further, you want to be sure that students conceptually understand the operations you will include in your routines. For example, they should already know that subtraction can mean take away (e.g., number of candy bars eaten) but it can also describe the difference between things (e.g., how much faster someone runs or how much longer something is). In later grades, students understand that multiplication is about equal groups, arrays, area, or comparison. Those same students should know that division finds the number of groups or the group size.

You do want to be sure that students understand what problems are, how they can represent problems, and how operations are used to solve those problems. You want to make sure that you introduce different problem structures or situations before you begin to include them in your routines. A deep conceptual understanding of operations come from experiences with diverse problem-solving structures.

Before You Begin, What You Should Know

Using diverse problem structures is an important aspect of these routines because problems come in different constructs and students are expected to successfully work within each of them. Before we take a look at those structures, take a moment to jot down a word problem for any one of the operations on an index card, your notebook, or even right here in the margin. After you write it, set it aside and continue reading.

There are common word problem structures, which are referred to as problem-solving situations or problem types, and they are captured in Figures 1.1 and 1.2 (Carpenter et al., 2014; Moore et al., 2020; NGA Center & CCSSO, 2010). You can think of structure as the form a problem takes relative to the operation needed to solve it and what is known or unknown in the problem. In other words, are two things being combined, taken apart, or compared? Is the start of the situation, the change in the situation, or the result of the action known? Take a few moments to review them (Figures 1.1 and 1.2). Are they familiar to you? Which do you find more difficult to teach? Which seem to be more difficult for students to solve?

Figure 1.1 Addition and Subtraction Situations

	Join Situation is about putting together	Separate Situation is about separating or taking from		Compare Situation compares quantities	Part-Part-Whole Situation combines parts creating a "whole"
Result Unknown	There were 9 turtles in a pond. 4 more jumped in. How many turtles were in the pond?	There were 16 meatballs on a plate. Jake's family ate 12. How many meatballs were left?	**Whole Unknown**	9 inches of snow fell on Monday and 14 inches fell on Tuesday. How many more inches fell on Tuesday?	A third-grade class has 17 boys and 11 girls. How many students are in the class?
Start Unknown	There were some turtles in a pond. 4 jumped in and now there are 13 turtles. How many were in the pond before the 4 jumped in?	There were some meatballs on a plate. Jake's family ate 12 and now there are 4 left. How many meatballs were on the plate before dinner?	**Part Unknown**	Some snow fell on Monday and 14 inches fell on Tuesday. Tuesday was 5 more inches than Monday. How many inches fell on Monday?	A third-grade class of 28 students has 17 boys. How many girls are in the class?
Change Unknown	There were 9 turtles in a pond. Some jumped in and now there are 13. How many jumped in the pond?	There were 16 meatballs on a plate. Jake's family ate some for dinner. Now there are 4 meatballs left. How many did Jake's family eat?	**Part Unknown**	9 inches of snow fell on Monday. That was 5 fewer inches than what fell on Tuesday. How many inches fell on Tuesday?	There are 11 girls in a third-grade class that has 28 students. How many boys are in the class?

Figure 1.2 Multiplication and Division Situations

	Equal Groups Problem is about same-sized groups	Area/Array Problem is about equal-length rows (or columns)	Comparison Problem compares two quantities multiplicatively
Unknown Product	10 pieces of gum are in a pack. How many pieces are in 6 packs of gum?	A full parking lot has 5 rows of 8 cars. How many cars are in the full parking lot?	Brooke's paper airplane flew 3 feet. Diana's airplane flew 4 times farther. How far did Diana's airplane fly?
Number of Groups Unknown	There are 10 pieces in each pack of gum. There are 60 pieces of gum. How many packs of gum are there?	There are 40 cars in a full parking lot. Each row has 8 cars. How many rows are there?	Diana's airplane flew 12 feet. Brooke's airplane flew 3 feet. How many times farther did Diana's plane fly?
Group Size Unknown	There are 60 pieces of gum. There are 6 packs each with the same number of pieces. How many pieces are in a pack?	There are 40 cars in a full parking lot. There are 5 rows with the same number of cars. How many rows of cars are there?	Diana's airplane flew 12 feet. That was 4 times farther than Brooke's airplane. How far did Brooke's airplane fly?

Often, start and change unknown problems are perceived to be more difficult to teach and learn. Multiplicative comparison problems can be challenging, and one of the two division problems is sometimes more problematic. Why does this seem so? Well, take a look at the problem you wrote earlier. What type of problem is it? If you wrote an addition or subtraction problem, you likely wrote a result unknown problem. If you wrote a multiplication problem, you likely wrote an equal groups problem. And if you wrote a division problem, you likely wrote one that asks about the number groups.

Why does the problem you wrote matter? It's possible that you have a bias when writing word problems on your own. That is, there are certain constructs that you gravitate to. They are likely the types you write "on the fly" in math class. They might be the type that you tend to feature more often in your instruction. The outcome is that your students experience one or two types more often than others. They practice one type more than others. It's not that those other structures are necessarily more challenging, they're simply practiced less often. These problem-solving routines are excellent opportunities for your students to work with many different problem types. Again, they don't have to master them before you include them in your routines, but you do want to make sure that your students have been exposed to all the various situations.

Classroom-Ready Routines for Flexible Use

As you plan to use these routines, know that they support high-quality mathematics instruction. They can complement any curriculum or textbook program that you use. There are no specific requirements for how you use them. You can adjust the time allotted to a routine. You can adjust the number of prompts. You can use any routine, in any order, on any day. Routines provided throughout the book are ready-for-use. You'll find examples of specific numbers and problem types along with implementation guidance, and for each routine, you'll see a list of problem-solving skills each routine supports, including what mathematical processes and practices (SMPs) they encourage, and how they help build identity and agency. These are followed by variations and ideas for how the routine might be modified to meet the needs of all elementary content. Each routine is available as a downloadable, editable set of PowerPoint slides. The slides can be used in face-to-face, virtual, or hybrid instruction.

> **online resources** All routines can be downloaded for your use at
> https://qrs.ly/3cemjnt

Timing of Routines: How Long? When?

You can manage how long routines last by adjusting the number of questions you ask or the number of student approaches you investigate. In some cases, you can limit the number of problems or situations that students encounter. You can modify the complexity of the mathematics you present. You can cut or extend the amount of time students have to share their thinking with partners. Essentially, *you* control the amount of time allocated to your routine. Directions for specific routines are described in that section of the book. The general shape of a routine is that

- students work with the prompt independently (about one minute),
- students discuss their reasoning with a partner or triad (about two minutes), then
- the teacher facilitates class discussion about strategies and reasoning (about three to four minutes).

That said, here are a few basic guidelines:

1. These routines are intended to be quick, engaging activities that foster problem solving and reasoning. Typically, they should be no more than a few minutes. Most days they should last about five to seven minutes. Other days, they may be a bit more than five minutes. Occasionally, the discussion may be so vibrant and engaging that you find your class spending 10 minutes with the routine. The latter may not be ideal due to time and schedule challenges. However, it's important to note that it may happen from time to time. It's also important to note that these rich discussions are exactly what you want for your students, so spending a few minutes more with them shouldn't be thought of as time lost or wasted.

2. Routines are likely best situated at the beginning of the mathematics class. You can establish protocols for students to enter class and prepare for the opening routine. In this way, they naturally replace mundane warm-ups or review of homework. However, you can flexibly position routines throughout the class as well. In longer classes (75 minutes or more), you may decide that they are best used in the middle of the block as an opportunity for rekindling students' energy and engagement. In other cases, you may find that routines can be useful when offered at the end of the class. If you select the end of class, you must be sure to close instruction for the period early enough for the routine to take place. There is an obvious challenge of running out of time when planning for routines at the end of class.

3. Routines may take longer at first. For some students, this is the first time they are consistently challenged to think about mathematics in their own way. For others, discussing their reasoning may be problematic. For you, facilitating and investigating without lingering too long will take some practice. A routine will become more fluid the more you use it. You might experience a "time bump" each instance in which you introduce a new routine. It's important to keep in mind that you control the first minutes of mathematics class. You can extend or limit prompts and discussion to meet the needs of your students and/or the timelines of your lessons.

Which Routines and Problems to Use?

There is no suggestion of which to use, when to use it, or how to order the routines in this collection. There is no requirement for how long to use any routine or how many times you should use it during a unit, quarter, or semester. The recommendation is to use routines that are most comfortable to facilitate and most interesting for your students to investigate. Pick the ones that develop skills your students need to practice. Select a routine and use it for a few days or weeks, possibly two weeks, before moving to another. Circle back to a routine after you move on to others as you see fit. Remember that any routine can become stale with too much use. So, make subtle adjustments to a routine to keep it fresh. Even then, it will be wise to change out routines as needed.

The Routines At-a-Glance section on page 20 offers a table of routines that notes a brief description of the routine and its problem-solving *purpose*. Regardless of the focus or purpose, there are complementary skills every routine incorporates. And, as mentioned, you can adjust a routine to alter the purpose as needed.

Every class is different, so it is difficult to say which routines are *best* to begin with. That being said, routines that focus on summarizing or retelling might be a good place to start. Your students are also learning to read. That does add to the challenge of solving word problems. You'll notice that each routine includes an image related to the context of the problem. This is a simple, yet powerful way for students to recognize the context of a problem. It might be wise for you to simply show the image and have students discuss ideas about the context the image represents as a prereading strategy before introducing the problem. This improves access for students who may not have experiences with a certain topic.

You might also be wondering about how you'll ever find enough problems for your routines. First, know that every example and variation in this book works for you! All you need to do is edit a problem so that it works for your students. You can change the number type or the size of the number. You can change the unknown or the phrasing of the problem. You can change the context altogether if you find the example presented to be a problem of relevance for your students. And, if you still need more problems, you can take those in your textbook series or other curriculum resources and import them into your routines. You'll also notice that there are ideas throughout about how you can enlist your students and their creativity for generating more problems.

Plan for the Routine

While you should focus most of your planning energy on the core skill and concepts of the main lesson, you can incorporate routines easily because they are designed for low-intensity planning. You can use them over and over again by simply changing out the problems. You should be able to change them out with little effort. However, there are some things to keep in mind when selecting and planning the routine.

Select the Routine and the Content or Concepts

Obviously, you need to know how to facilitate the routine and the basic tenets of it. You must also select problems and numbers that are appropriate for your students. Your experience with your students will help you. Take cues from class discussion, student work, or test results about the topics and ideas that need to be developed.

Provide Scaffolding That Supports Routines

Routines are intended to be mental problem-solving activities. Occasionally, students might need to write something. Students should have background understanding before they practice. You can provide tools to support students as needed. At the least, you and your students can use tools to support discussion and confirm accuracy of calculations and reasoning. Tools you might consider providing include

- calculators for students to confirm accurate calculations and explore patterns;
- number charts for students to confirm accurate calculations and explore patterns;
- fact charts for students to make accurate calculations when recall isn't fully established;
- base ten models, including, but not limited to, base ten blocks and ten frames, to anchor student understanding and support justifications;
- anchor charts for students to access so that they can be reminded of learned strategies, relationships, or representations; and
- personal dry erase boards, sticky notes, or journals for students to record their thinking and to use to support them when communicating ideas.

Support Language and Discussion

Student reasoning and conversation can be buoyed by anchor references during routines. These charts are tools that help them organize their thinking and frame their arguments. Most routines come with suggested questions. You might add those to anchor charts so students can think about them before the whole-group discussion.

Anchor charts can also capture vocabulary and sentence starters to help students make arguments or rebut classmates. Vocabulary anchor charts might be situated near the projection of the routine so that statements can be made with precise mathematical language. Keep in mind that posting the charts alone will not ensure that students use the language. Instead, take student statements and inject the accurate vocabulary while referring to the chart.

Sentence starters are familiar tools in elementary schools. They help students make clear statements and complement vocabulary charts well. These starters help students think about how to begin their declarations. They can also help students respond to statements of classmates and their teachers. There is no one set of starters that is better than another. Below are some helpful examples. You might edit these prompts, add to them, or eliminate some altogether. Help starters include:

- I think that ____ because . . .
- I decided that . . .
- I chose ____ because . . .
- I agree with ___ because . . .
- I disagree with ___ because . . .
- I think ___'s idea will always work because . . .
- The pattern I noticed was . . .
- My thinking will always work because . . .
- I want to change my answer because . . .

"Listen for" charts are anchor charts that help students determine what to listen for in someone's argument. They might be single words or indicators such as *clarity*, *vocabulary*, or *make sense*. Listen for charts might also be questions or prompts that ask the listener questions, such as *is the argument clear*, *are math words being used*, or *does the idea make sense*? These listen for charts also help students think about what they might say before they say it.

Students might have personal tools like hundreds charts, addition charts, multiplication charts, or calculators that support their accuracy. They may be used for students who are still mastering basic facts or in cases where students are developing proficiency with adding two-digit numbers. These accuracy tools may be needed for two important reasons. First, and most obviously, they help provide checks and balances to ensure accuracy. They also help some students access rich problems within the routines. Brains are challenged to do more than one complex thing at once. The reasoning needed for these routines competes with the need to calculate. These tools can alleviate some of that challenge. As students' accuracy and precision grows, you can begin to limit or remove these tools. Even so, they should always be available to confirm that strategies and approaches are accurate.

Other personal tools might include paper and pencil or personal whiteboards or lapboards. These tools are fine for students to jot down ideas, sketch models of problems, and so on; however, providing these tools upfront can send the message that they must be used, which can distract from purpose of the routine. Instead of making these tools available initially, you might choose to direct your students to them when you misjudged the numbers, concepts, or reasoning in a routine and students need support to work through it.

It is important to keep a few things in mind about scaffolds like anchor charts and math tools. First and foremost, students need explicit instruction about the ideas on the charts and how the charts can help them. Anchor charts about concepts or discussion techniques should be developed *with* students instead of simply displayed *to* students. Students must understand how the mathematics tools work. Students should discuss when it is a good idea to use a tool or refer to a chart.

Setting the Stage for Meaningful Discourse

In a routine, the teacher poses prompts, which students then engage in. Students share ideas with partners so that all have an opportunity to talk. Then, the teacher leads a group conversation. During that time, every student does not have to share out. You don't have to explore every strategy. You don't have to discuss every solution. You make choices about what to explore, where to linger, and when to move on during the debrief. You facilitate discussion. You ask questions. From time to time, you will have to insert an idea or strategy. However, routines aren't intended to be mini-lessons or mini-lectures on a procedure that students are to carry out and practice. Conversation during routines is an opportunity for meaningful discourse.

Because discussion is such a critical component of the routines in this book, Smith and Stein's (2018) five practices for orchestrating productive mathematical discussions naturally connect with how you can orchestrate discussion about problems. These practices remind us to anticipate, monitor, select, sequence, and connect.

1. *Anticipate What Students Might Do During the Routine*

   Anticipating what students might do helps you consider how you will respond intentionally rather than randomly. Considering student ideas and misconceptions can also help you think about other prompts you might pose through the routine in subsequent days. You can start anticipating simply by thinking about how you would find the solution to the prompt.

2. *Monitor Student Discussions During the Routine*

   Monitor means that you listen to students as they discuss their thinking with partners. Granted, it is unlikely that you can listen to every student conversation. However, you can be strategic about the discussions you monitor. You may monitor the discussion of students who have understanding that you are concerned about. You may plan to monitor different groups on different days to balance whose conversations you listen to and focus on.

3. *Select Strategy and Reasoning to Promote During the Routine*

   As with discussions during your core lesson, you have to be careful to avoid randomly selecting students for discussion during routines as much as possible. A random selection may compromise the discussion. Anticipating what students might do or think during the routine can help you think about the conversations or ideas that you want to listen for when monitoring. This coupled with considering the strategies, reasoning, or possible misconceptions that we want to highlight can help us select students for sharing during whole-group discussion of the routine.

4. *Sequence Ideas During the Routine*

   Sequencing student ideas in a logical way helps advance student understanding. Sequencing may be quite challenging during a routine. In fact, careful, deliberate sequencing of ideas during a routine may be impossible due to the time constraints or inability to monitor every discussion in the short amount of time. You may be able to offset some of the sequencing challenge with your questions. To do this, pose questions that help students make connections between strategies, reflect on efficiency, and make use of structure and patterns within prompts. These questions include:

   • How is ____'s strategy similar to ____'s?

   • How is ___'s strategy different from ___'s?

   • How does this idea connect to something we have discussed recently?

   • Will this approach always work?

- If we think about efficiency, how do these strategies compare?
- What patterns do you notice in the expressions?
- How did you use patterns to help you find your solution?

5. *Connect Strategies and Concepts During the Routine*

   Questions during routines should help students connect solution paths and different ideas and reasoning. Your questions should help students see connections between concepts. Help them make connections between problems, numbers, operations, and representations.

WHAT'S NEXT?

It's time to get started. There are 20 routines waiting for you. Take time to get to know them. Use them to complement who you are as a teacher and what your students need. Modify them to make them your own. Use them as formative insights into who your students are and how they think about problem solving. Be committed and creative. It's possible that the first few times you use a routine you find the activity to be clunky. This is natural. Try to give the routine some time before cutting ties with it. Reflect on how you can make it better or how you might modify the content or process to improve its effectiveness. Be mindful, too, that reasoning, communicating about reasoning, and working with mathematics mentally may be new to your students. Because of this, it may take some time for them to get comfortable with a routine.

JUMP-START ROUTINES AT-A-GLANCE

	TITLE	BRIEF	TARGETED PROBLEM-SOLVING SKILL
1	I Would Say	Students practice restating problems in their own words.	Making Sense: Retelling
2	3Qs (Question, Question, Question)	Students practice with a variety of questions so that they can determine how to make sense of a problem, identify the question, and think about a strategy for solving it.	Making Sense: Asking Questions
3	Asked and Answered	Students learn to think carefully about a question by grappling with questions that can, and cannot, be answered.	Questions: Understanding the Question
4	What's the Question?	Students practice problem solving by creating questions and problems that yield a given solution.	Questions: Identifying Questions
5	Same Data, Different Question	Students practice thinking and reasoning as questions change from day to day.	Questions: Identifying Questions
6	How Do You . . .?	Students are presented with situations and then a question. Students determine how they would find the solution.	Reasoning: Solution Pathways
7	Same and Different	Students compare and contrast two problems to analyze the changing nature of contexts, numbers, and questions.	Making Sense: Problem Elements
8	What's the Sitch?	Students develop a process for analyzing different problem-solving situations (structures).	Making Sense: Analyzing Problems
9	They Did What?	Students examine strategies and solutions of worked examples.	Reasoning: Reasonable Solutions/ Pathways
10	This Number, That Number	Students practice the strategy of solving a simpler problem by working with identical problems that have different number complexities.	Reasoning: Simpler Problems
11	Imagine That	Students practice visualizing problems and generating useful representations to solve them.	Making Sense: Representing
12	Match the Equation	Students practice representing problems with equations.	Making Sense: Representing

	TITLE	BRIEF	TARGETED PROBLEM–SOLVING SKILL
13	And Then	Students experience two-step problems in an engaging way through a narrative that they control.	Making Sense: Two-Step Problems
14	Another Question	Students simply ask "another question" that generates another step resulting in more two-step problem practice.	Making Sense: Two-Step Problems
15	TMI	Students practice identifying important information as well as extra or irrelevant information in problems.	Making Sense: Relevant Information
16	It Can't Be	Students confront possible solutions to a problem and make arguments about why some of those possibilities can't be the solution.	Reasoning: Reasonable Solutions/ Pathways
17	Is It Reasonable?	A problem is posed. Students estimate the solution and discuss how they arrived at their estimates.	Reasoning: Reasonable Solutions/ Pathways
18	Sticky Patterns	Students build skill with looking for and using patterns to solve problems.	Reasoning: Using Patterns
19	Lots and Lots	Students practice finding more than one right answer as they solve open-ended problems.	Reasoning
20	The Swap	Students examine a set of numbers and determine why they think a certain number doesn't belong. Then, they create a new example that would fit the relationship.	Reasoning

NOTES

PART 2

THE JUMP-START ROUTINES FOR PROBLEM SOLVING

I WOULD SAY

About the Routine

Solving problems is hard because there isn't a formula or procedure that one can apply to each and every problem they encounter. Instead, the problem solver must think and reason. The act of solving a problem is within the individual. It cannot be delivered by a teacher to a student, but instead a student develops this skill through practice, experience, discussion, observation, and error. You might think of it as teaching reading comprehension to students. That is, you cannot understand a passage *for* your students. You must arm them with tools and experiences so that they can comprehend what they read on their own.

Problem solving starts with making sense of the problem in one's own mind. That means students must understand what is happening in the problem, identify what is being asked, determine what could be done to satisfy the question, and so on. Retelling stirs strategy selection and is useful for getting unstuck after a problem is started. Retelling is a "go to" strategy that every student can use and is one that potentially always works.

Brie's old phone could hold 2,500 minutes of music. Her new phone could hold 3,250 minutes of music. How many more minutes of music could her new phone hold?

Credit: alexey_boldin/istockphoto.com

Some students take to retelling problems (and stories) naturally while others need a lot of practice. In this routine, you provide that practice. You pose a problem and give students opportunities to retell what it is about in their own words. They share with partners and then the whole class discusses. The routine exposes students to others' thinking and perspective. The graphic organizers shared in the variations help you find ways to support students' retelling.

 All routines can be downloaded for your use at
https://qrs.ly/3cemjnt

How This Routine Helps With Problem Solving

This routine builds problem-solving skill by providing opportunities for students to

- process information in a problem without pursuing an answer,
- retell a problem in their own words (identity),
- organize their thinking to formulate a strategy for solving a problem (agency),
- identify the action in a problem to select an operation that could be used for solving it,

- distill a problem into manageable chunks of information in order to solve it,
- listen to how others interpret and describe a problem in their own words,
- give feedback to others about their ideas,
- make sense of a problem by thinking about it in diverse ways (agency), and
- determine questions to ask oneself when reading and working through a problem (agency).

What to Do

1. Pose a problem.

2. Give students time to process the problem and think about how they would restate it in their own words. Optional: Use questions or sentence starters to guide student thinking. Recording these on an anchor chart would be a good idea. Some questions you might use are below. See Routine 2: 3Qs (page 33) for additional questions to use.

   » What is the problem talking about?
   » What is happening in the problem?
   » What am I trying to figure out?
   » What will my answer tell me?

3. Have partners describe the problem to each other.

4. Bring the class together to share ideas. Have students listen carefully to how others retell the problem. Have all students signal that they agree (thumbs up) or have questions (thumbs down) about the retelling.

5. Optional: Share your own retelling of the problem. Note that you should share last so that you don't influence student thinking or suggest there is a correct retelling.

Each time a student shares, reinforce the big ideas that their retelling has in common with a classmate's retelling. If conversation is stalled, refer to the questions or sentence starters you used to prompt independent thinking. Be sure to avoid going over the answer during this discussion. You want the sole focus of this routine to be about retelling and nothing more.

SOMETHING TO THINK ABOUT: AVOID PROCEDURALIZING STUDENT THINKING AND REASONING

When thinking gets hard, a teacher can be tempted to stop the conversation and show students how to solve the problem. In an effort to make problem solving clean and successful, teachers sometimes find themselves teaching the problem-solving process in a procedural way. That is, the teacher presents steps to solving a problem and has students practice those steps to mimic them with new problems. It creates new challenges. Students who blindly follow steps without understanding find answers that don't make sense. Students forget the steps and are unable to carry them out. They are unable to explain what they're doing or why. Frustration abounds.

Unfortunately, the nature of problems and thinking for that matter is not algorithmic. Elementary teachers can be lured into procedural approaches due to the somewhat basic architecture of word problems in these grades. But as problem types change and problems with more than one step are introduced, problem-solving methods grounded in procedure lose efficacy. It is essential to make problem solving about sense making. It can be messy, and it will take time. But once realized, sense making and thinking do not fade away like poorly understood procedures. This routine focuses on the initial act of making sense—retelling. The upcoming variations give ideas about how you can help students structure and organize their thinking.

I WOULD SAY (VARIATIONS): GRAPHIC ORGANIZERS

Graphic organizers help thinking by providing organization and structure. To be effective, they must be simple and clear (Egan, 1999; William & Mary School of Education, n.d.). The graphic organizers highlighted in these variations can develop the act of summarizing and retelling a problem. There are different organizers because there are different ways to think about problems. Again, these should not be used procedurally. Use them to temporarily scaffold student entry points into retelling, until eventually students can retell without these tools. Each graphic organizer is available as downloadable content you can print out for students to use. Creating anchor charts or just sketching them freehand on the board would be also good supports for whole-class discussion.

Variation A: K–W–S Organizer for Retelling

A Know-What-Solve (K-W-S) organizer is a take on the traditional Know-Want-Learn (K-W-L) chart used in elementary schools. It is a useful tool for supporting student thinking, strategy formation, getting unstuck, and retelling what a problem is about (SanGiovanni et al., 2020). The first step is to identify what students know about the problem. In the example, they might say that they know (K) there are rows of apps, that there are screens of apps, that apps are on the phone, and so on. They might even share things about the context that isn't in the problem, such as their favorite app. This is OK! It helps them build on schema for better understanding and increased likelihood of solving the problem. They should identify that they are trying to figure out how many apps Deryn has (W). In the last phase, they think about how they might solve the problem. Here, they might use a picture of each screen, repeated addition, or multiplication. For the purposes of retelling, you can choose to only do the K and W portion of the organizer or do those two parts first, discuss, and then move into the third stage.

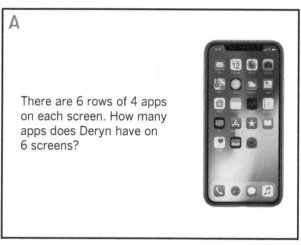

There are 6 rows of 4 apps on each screen. How many apps does Deryn have on 6 screens?

Credit: alexey_boldin/istockphoto.com

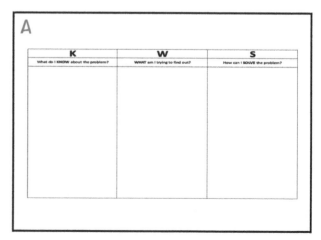

K	W	S
What do I KNOW about the problem?	WHAT am I trying to find out?	How can I SOLVE the problem?

Variation B: Three-Read Organizer for Retelling

Three Reads is a good strategy for making sense of problems (Kelemanik et al., 2016). It can be leveraged to help students organize their thoughts for retelling about a problem. With it, students read a problem and tell what it is about. They read it a second time to identify the question. They read it a third time to identify important information. Over time, teachers have modified Three Reads in all sorts of ways. For example, some use the first read for important words, the second for identifying the question, and the third for finding important numbers. It is important to note that this routine, like others, can potentially become another layer of procedure if used in a narrow, inflexible way. Be careful with forcing students to reread two and three times when they can describe the story and identify the question after reading it once. Conversely, encourage students to reread the problem once or twice when they cannot describe it in their own words after just one read.

B

550 tacos were made for lunch. 236 were bought by second and third graders. How many tacos were there for other grades to buy?

Credit: fcafotodigital/istockphoto.com

B

First Read: Read and retell what the problem is about.

Second Read: Read and tell what the question is.

Third Read: Read and tell what the important information is.

NOTES

Variation C: Three Asks for Retelling

Asking oneself questions is an approach to making sense of problems that you can read more about in Routine 2: 3Qs (page 33). When your students' retelling stalls, you want them to ask themselves questions to restart it. Sometimes, their experiences with questions in class lead them to believe that there are only certain questions of value when solving problems. When they can't remember those questions, the process grinds to a halt. To practice questioning for retelling, record different questions on index cards. Pose a problem like the one shown and have students think about how they might restate it. Without sharing their retellings, randomly select a question card for them to consider, such as, "What am I trying to figure out?" Discuss that question. Then, use another like, "what information in the problem is important?" Discuss that question and ask a third. After the third question, have students reconsider their retelling of the problem. Talk about how the questions used can help someone retell a problem when they are stuck. Close the routine with a few students sharing their retellings of the problem.

550 tacos were made for lunch. 236 were bought by second and third graders. How many tacos were there for other grades to buy?

Credit: fcafotodigital/istockphoto.com

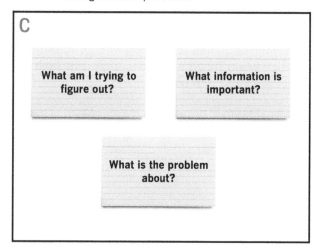

What am I trying to figure out?

What information is important?

What is the problem about?

Credit: Michael Burrell/istock.com

NOTES

Variation D: Big Idea and Important Details for Retelling

One reading comprehension strategy is to identify a big idea and then determine some details. This is a skill useful for retelling a problem. This variation takes that approach using a concept web to capture student thinking. In this example, the big idea is donuts, eating donuts, giving out donuts, or something similar. After summarizing a problem around a big idea, one begins to think about details. The details in the problem include the numbers, what happened (Maria bought donuts to share.), how many were eaten, how many were left, and so on. While this problem seems straightforward, you might find that a student notices a missing detail—it doesn't say that the people ate the donuts! As you know, sometimes problems require inference. Discussion about that detail should take place and students should be comfortable assuming those 23 people ate the donuts. Using this organizer can be especially helpful with multi-step problems.

23 people had one donut. Maria bought 48 to share. How many donuts were not eaten?

Credit: GaryAlvis/istockphoto.com

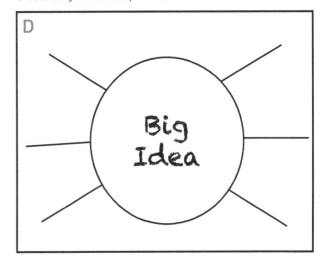

NOTES

_____

_____

_____

_____

_____

_____

_____

_____

_____

Variation E: Beginning, Middle, and End Organizer for Retelling

Thinking about a problem through the sequence of events is a way to retell it that works quite often. As shown in the organizer, you want students to think about the beginning, middle, and end of a problem. This connects with comprehensions strategies taught in reading class. This approach can be especially helpful with start unknown or change unknown problems like the one shown in the example. Notice that the context of the problem has a clear start (takeoff), middle (in flight), and end (landing). But this organizer doesn't work for certain problem types like comparison problems. For example, it wouldn't work if the problem said there were 38 people on the left side of the plane and 56 people on the right side of the plane and asked how many more people were on the right side of the plane.

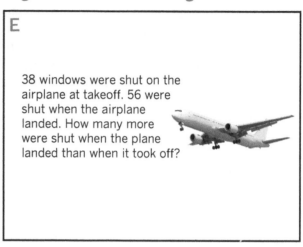

E

38 windows were shut on the airplane at takeoff. 56 were shut when the airplane landed. How many more were shut when the plane landed than when it took off?

Credit: sharply_done/istockphoto.com

E

Describe the BEGINNING	Describe the MIDDLE	Describe the END

NOTES

_____

_____

_____

_____

_____

_____

_____

_____

_____

Variation F: Teacher Retells and Students Agree or Disagree

Students can learn to retell a problem by listening to how others do it. In this variation of the routine, you want to pose a problem and have students think about how they would tell it in their own words. Then, you share how you might retell it or how someone else retold it. Have them listen to the example and decide if they agree or disagree with the retelling. Ask them to cite specifics in the retelling. Have them share their own to compare with the example. Be sure to occasionally leave out information or misrepresent the problem entirely. And when you use an accurate example, reinforce that it is just one example and not "the way" that they must think about how to retell the problem.

F

A plane flew 380 miles on its first trip and 495 miles on its second trip. How far did it fly on the two trips?

F

A plane makes 2 trips. The first trip is 380 miles, and the second trip is 495 miles. I'm trying to figure out how far it flew in total.

Credit: sharply_done/istockphoto.com

NOTES

Variation G: Extend to Two-Step Problems and Provide Choice

Putting a two-step problem into one's own words is both important and challenging. It is a good idea to circle back to this routine as your students begin to work with these types of problems. Try having them retell a one-step problem and then have them retell a related two-step problem. Doing this can help them transfer their retelling skills from one-step problems to two-step problems. It's possible that you have used some of the earlier organizers for retelling one-step problems. You can reintroduce them with two-step problems. You can even give students choice about the organizer they use if they choose to use one. Providing choice promotes student agency. Though choice is noted in this two-step problem, you would be wise to make use of it with one-step problems as well.

G

There 6 boxes of donuts for sale. Each box had 12 donuts. There were 30 sprinkled, 12 powdered, and the rest were glazed. How many were glazed?

Credit: GaryAlvis/istockphoto.com

Variation H: Solving Linear Equations

Solving equations with variables on each side can be just as challenging for eighth graders as solving two-step problems is for elementary students. In this problem, students must understand that they are not being asked to compare the prices but rather to determine at what point the cost for parking would be equal. They must make sense of the hourly rate and the additional fee at the West Garage. In this example, a K-W-S (Variation A) or a Three-Read tool (Variation B) can help them organize their thoughts and make a plan for finding a solution. You could also consider making other tools available, like a Beginning-Middle-End organizer (Variation F), asking students to think about the viability of the different options. In this problem, the Beginning-Middle-End organizer doesn't connect with the context and likely isn't very useful.

H

The West Garage charges a $7 fee plus $2 per hour of parking. The East Garage charges $4 per hour of parking. When will the cost to park be the same?

Credit: CHUYN/istockphoto.com

3QS (QUESTION, QUESTION, QUESTION)

About the Routine

How do you know what question to ask yourself when you are solving a problem? After all, there are so, so many questions you could ask. Is it your experience solving problems that has helped you know what to look for? Do you monitor your own progress through the problem, thinking about what you know and don't know? Do you always ask yourself questions, or are there situations in which you simply move through the problem with little to no thought because you just "know what to do?" Do you ask questions to help you get unstuck? 3Qs (Question, Question, Question) is a routine that aims to provide students with experience asking all sorts of questions. The goal is to help students develop metacognition about the questions they ask themselves to be productive problem solvers. To do this, you pose a problem and present different questions for students to talk about.

Before you get into how the routine works, take a moment to think about the variety of questions one might ask while solving a problem and the purpose those questions serve.

Problem solvers metacognitively monitor their progress with questions in the three phases of problem solving (before, during, and after) as shown in the chart on page 34. Within those phases, there are essential questions like "What is the problem about?" and "What do I need to do?" These essential questions are the essence of problem solving, and each serves a specific purpose along the way.

37 cookies were given out at a restaurant. 26 were eaten. How many were left?

Credit: PicturePartners/istockphoto.com

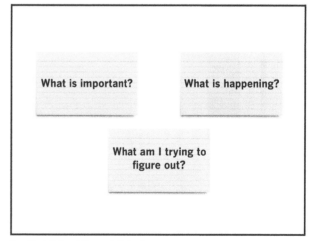

Credit: Michael Burrell/istock.com

 All routines can be downloaded for your use at
https://qrs.ly/3cemjnt

BEFORE Doing a Problem

WHILE Doing a Problem

AFTER Doing a Problem

Essential Question: **What is the problem about?**	Essential Question: **What is the important information?**	Essential Question: **What do I need to do?**	Essential Question: **Am I stuck?**	Essential Question: **Does my answer make sense?**
• What are we talking about in this problem?	• What information is helpful in solving the problem?	• What is the answer going to tell me?	• Did I answer the question yet?	• Did I answer the question?
• What is happening in the beginning, middle, and end of the story problem?	• Is there any information that I don't need?	• What is the problem asking me to do?	• What doesn't seem to be working?	• What was the answer going to tell me? Does it?
• What is happening in the problem?	• Is any information unnecessary?	• What am I trying to figure out?	• What am I confused about?	• How did I show my thinking?
• What does the problem look like in my head (or on paper)?	• What important information is given to me?	• What type of answer am I looking for?	• What questions do I have now that I'm working on the problem?	• Does my representation make sense?
• What is happening in the story?	• What information am I confused about?	• What's a good starting point?	• What tools can I use to solve the problem if I am stuck?	• Will someone else understand my thinking?
• Is there anything about the problem I don't understand?		• What operation(s) do I think I need to use?	• What am I confused about?	• Was my strategy best? Could I have done something else?
• What is the problem asking me to do?		• How can I show the problem (pictures, model, equation)?	• How is my answer/model similar or different from someone else's?	• Why did I add (subtract)?
• What am I trying to figure out?		• Do I only need to do one thing?	• What does this problem remind me of?	• How do I know my answer is reasonable?
		• What is being asked to find?	• Is there another strategy I could use instead of this one?	• Does my answer make sense in context with the problem?
		• What is the question asking me?		• Did I need more than one step? Did I do them?
		• What strategy makes sense?		• Does my plan have multiple steps? Did I answer the question yet?

Teaching students to ask questions is challenging for two reasons. First, problem solving isn't procedural. There is back and forth between those essential questions. To begin a problem, you might ask yourself, "What do I need to do?" And then, as you work through the problem, you might pause and ask yourself again, "What do I need to do?" That single question comes into play in the different phases of problem solving. It can be hard to realize that questions aren't "checked off" before moving to the next and the next until ultimately arriving at the solution to the problem.

The second simple, yet greater challenge, is that students don't know what questions to ask! This happens for all sorts of reasons including

- a lack of experience solving problems on their own,
- problem-solving and/or questioning experiences were primarily mimicry,
- limited exposure to asking questions and talking about them during problem-solving experiences,
- a feeling of being overwhelmed by the number and variety of questions to ask (bulleted list in the chart),
- a misunderstanding that many questions serve the same purpose (bulleted list),
- a misunderstanding about when to ask themselves a question and why to ask it, or
- an assumption that there is a single-best question to ask (and they don't know what that question is).

How This Routine Helps With Problem Solving

This routine builds problem-solving skill by providing opportunities for students to

- practice asking a variety questions;
- determine which questions to ask themselves, when to ask them, and why (agency);
- recognize that there are different ways to ask a question that serves the same purpose;
- monitor progress as they work through a problem;
- identify which questions are most helpful to them when they are solving problems (identity);
- listen to the questions that others ask themselves;
- recognize that it is OK for them to ask questions that are different from others (identity); and
- think about different ways to ask about the meaning, information, and prompt within a problem .

What to Do

1. Before doing the routine, prepare questions on index cards or sentence strips. Write one question per index card or strip. The questions in the table are a good place to start. Note that you can also use questions you create or the "getting unstuck" questions.

2. Pose a problem for the students to read.

3. Present a prepared question card to the students. Ask them to think about the problem through that question.

4. Have students signal (e.g., thumbs up) when they are ready to discuss the question.

Encourage those that aren't ready to reread the problem.

5. Discuss student ideas about the problem and the presented question.

6. Repeat the process with a second question and then again with a third question.

7. Optional: Create a chart or table with sections associated with the essential questions. At the end of the routine, have students look back at the three questions presented and decide which essential question the examples represent. In the fortune cookie example, the

upper left question, "What is important?" is an example of the essential question, "What is the problem about?" The upper right question is another example. The middle question, "What am I trying to figure out?" is an example of the essential question, "What is the problem asking?"

Something to Think About: Three Reads Versus Rereading

As noted in Routine 1, a Three-Read protocol is an excellent tool for building problem-solving capacity. It helps frame student thinking by having them reread a problem three times so that they can answer three of the big, categorical questions in the table. However, using Three Reads can create different problems. It can frustrate students who are able to answer those three big questions after just one read. It can also frustrate those who are able to focus in on a part of the problem to answer a big question without reading the entire problem. For example, typically, a student can identify the question in a problem by simply going to the last sentence in the word problem or looking for a question mark.

A bigger challenge with the Three-Read protocol and others like it is that many students need more than three reads! They might be led to believe that they *should* be able to answer a big question about a problem after each read. Yet, they might need to read the problem twice just to tell what it is about. Being unable to do it after just one pass can lead to feelings of inadequacy and anxiety. The underlying point of that protocol, among others, is to structure and organize student thinking, which is a good idea. It also helps slow the rush to calculate and find an answer. The act of problem solving is about metacognitive self-talk and self-questioning. And the number or reads it takes to do so varies from individual to individual.

3QS VARIATIONS: VARY A ROUTINE TO FOCUS ON A NEED

Create and use variations of this routine to focus on specific skills that you notice your students need more practice with. The original offering of this routine uses three questions at random. You might get a question from each category but you could also get two or three questions from the same category. If you notice that a certain skill, such as determining a strategy (representative of "What do I need to do?"), is particularly challenging to your students, modify the routine so that three questions related to that idea appear in the routine for a few days. The following variations give you some other ideas about the changes you might make to target different needs.

Variation A: Use Questions That Fit the What Is the Problem About Category

Retelling a problem shows understanding of it. Students can practice retelling with Routine 1: I Would Say (page 24). But when away from the routine, you might find that your students struggle with retelling. To retell, students must pause and ask themselves questions to process and organize their thinking. That's where this variation of 3Qs could be used to focus on questions related to the categorical question, "What is the problem about?" To do this, follow the directions within the routine but don't pull questions at random. Instead, use questions that focus on telling what the problem is about as shown in the example. As the routine unfolds, listen for student comments about the similarity of the questions. They might even say, "that's the same question!" Acknowledge their observations to make it clear that these different questions are all establishing the same big idea. And if your students don't notice, draw their attention to it by closing the routine for the day asking them how the questions were similar.

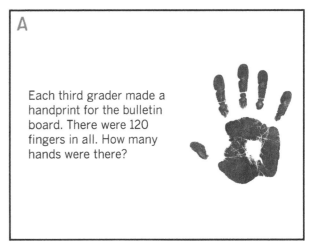

A

Each third grader made a handprint for the bulletin board. There were 120 fingers in all. How many hands were there?

Credit: malerapaso/istockphoto.com

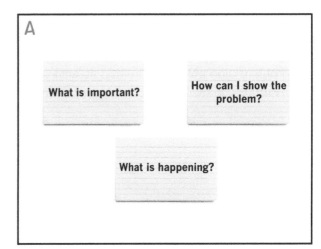

A

What is important?

How can I show the problem?

What is happening?

Credit: Michael Burrell/istock.com

NOTES

Variation B: Choose a Question That Fits Best

This routine helps students learn and practice the questions they can ask themselves to solve problems. You might find that some students fall into a trap of thinking that there are many questions to ask themselves before they can begin solving a problem. In this variation of the routine, you pose a problem and four or five questions as shown. You tell them that you don't understand the problem. Then, ask students to determine which of the questions you could ask yourself to help. Partners talk about their choices and then the class discusses. In the example, there isn't a beginning, middle, and end so you wouldn't want your students to select that question. Instead, the two questions on the right and possibly the lower left would be helpful. In other instances, you could say that you aren't sure what to do with a problem, that you are unsure what to expect about your answer, or that you aren't sure how to show the problem. Each of these are challenges students face. Regardless of the "problem" you pose, be sure that at least one of the questions can be used to address the challenge.

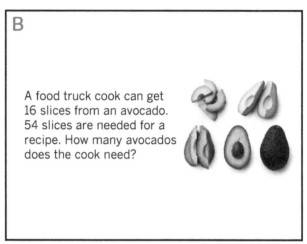

B

A food truck cook can get 16 slices from an avocado. 54 slices are needed for a recipe. How many avocados does the cook need?

Credit: baibaz/istockphoto.com

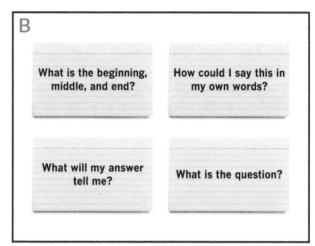

B

What is the beginning, middle, and end?

How could I say this in my own words?

What will my answer tell me?

What is the question?

Credit: Michael Burrell/istock.com

NOTES

_____

_____

_____

_____

_____

_____

_____

_____

_____

Variation C: Choose a Question, Where to Start?

Some students know what they want to ask first but aren't sure if it is the *right* question to get started with. In this variation, you present a collection of questions on an anchor chart that looks something the table on page 34. Pose a problem and ask each student to read it and identify one question from the chart that they would ask themselves to begin solving the problem. Many will lean toward questions that focus on summarizing the problem. But you may be surprised to find that some students look to begin by isolating the question or ask themselves what the problem looks like visually so they can start a retelling. This variation provides an important, possibly overlooked, aspect of problem solving. That is, individuals solve problems differently. And though there is logic to different problem-solving structures and process charts, you must remember that restating the problem isn't always the *first* move. In fact, it might not even be *your* first move. When using this variation, be sure to

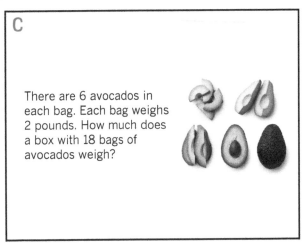

C

There are 6 avocados in each bag. Each bag weighs 2 pounds. How much does a box with 18 bags of avocados weigh?

Credit: baibaz/istockphoto.com

have students tell why they used a certain question first. It will provide insight into how they think and attack problems. You can then remind them of their preferred starting points when they get stuck with a problem.

Variation D: 3Qs With Different Number Types or Measurement Units

Certain mathematical features of a problem, such as number type, number magnitude, operation, number of numbers, or units of measure, can overwhelm a student as they read the problem. For example, a student who shows prowess solving a problem that calls for subtracting two-digit whole numbers can find themselves downright confused when a four-digit number or simple fractions appear instead. Skill with self-questioning is even more critical when this happens. This variation simply shows what the routine might look like with mixed numbers and units of measure. And remember, even students who have deployed self-questioning skills in the past may not necessarily transfer that skill to these new problems or number types. You want to help them see that even though the numbers may be different, the underlying principles of questioning remain the same. You can even add questions like, "What if I change the numbers to . . . " or "What would happen if the numbers were ___ and ___?"

D

The art teacher had $3\frac{1}{4}$ liters of paint but estimated that she needed $5\frac{1}{2}$ liters so that each student in the school could make a handprint. How much more paint does she need?

Credit: malerapaso/istockphoto.com

Variation E: 3Qs With Two-Step Problems

A whole new set of questions enter when working with two-step problems. The "big" questions remain in play and many of the questions within those categorical big questions are still useful. But now, your students need to ask themselves additional questions. Here are some to consider. You and your students should add to this list as needed.

- Is there something I must do before I can begin to work on the question?

- Do I have all of the information I need, or do I need to find something first?

- Do I need to do more than one thing?

- How do I know that I have (or don't have) to do more than one thing?

- How do I know what operations I need to do?

- What seems different or unusual about this problem?

- What information is/isn't useful or relevant?

E

There were 3 full boxes of 50 cookies and another that had 31 cookies in it. How many cookies were there?

Credit: PicturePartners/istockphoto.com

As you move to using two-step problems with this routine, don't forget to mix in one-step problems from time to time. Doing this should help galvanize students' questioning skills for both types of problems.

NOTES

ASKED AND ANSWERED

About the Routine

As a fourth-grade teacher, I witnessed my students attempting to solve a problem that couldn't be solved because of an error in the textbook. It is a reminder that students don't always read the problem. Some simply go straight to the question and ignore the "stuff" before it. They use that question to determine what to do with the numbers. Worse yet, some don't even take the time to read the question. They simply associate the word problem with the operation they have been learning about recently.

This routine takes aim at this challenge. In it, you provide context and data. You give students time to look closely at that information. Then, you pose a few questions. Students must determine if the questions you pose can be asked *and answered* based on the information you present. Class discussion afterward exposes student reasoning and interpretation. Using the routine over time should help students begin to think more carefully about information and questions in the word problems they encounter.

Also note that this routine is much more than a novel way to practice solving problems. At its core, this routine nurtures 21st century skills, including information literacy (Stauffer, 2022). It develops the thinking and reasoning students need to live in their world. It helps them learn to look at information critically. It provides opportunity to analyze viability and reliability of the questions and answers about quantity, data, and statistics.

Park Recycling

Month	Glass Bottles (in pounds)
May	1,898
June	2,163
July	2,988
August	2,754
September	1,765

Credit: AlexLMX/istockphoto.com

A How many more bottles were collected in July than in August?

B How many bottles were collected during the year?

C How many more pounds of bottles were collected than paper in July?

D How many more pounds of bottles were needed to make a goal of 3,000 in May?

online resources ➤ All routines can be downloaded for your use at
https://qrs.ly/3cemjnt

How This Routine Helps With Problem Solving

This routine builds problem-solving skill by providing opportunities for students to

- take time to read questions,
- determine whether a question can be answered with information presented,
- shift their approaches from grabbing numbers and doing something with them to focusing on the information and the question,
- recognize that questions can't always be answered from the given information,
- identify important information presented in problems or data charts,
- practice ignoring unnecessary information,
- experience problems with quantities presented in tables (i.e., not standard story or word problems),
- justify their thinking, and
- take ownership of the problem-solving process.

What to Do

1. Pose data for students to observe for a few moments. Optional: Have students turn and talk about the information by having them describe what it is about in their own words.

2. Pose three or four questions related to the data.

3. Have students think about which questions can be asked and answered with the data.

4. Have partners discuss their ideas about the questions.

5. Bring the class together to discuss their selections. During discussion, any question that probes their thinking is a good question. For this example, some questions you could ask include:

   » How could a question with a number that isn't in the table be asked and answered? (question D)

   » How did you know that question B couldn't be asked and answered?

   » Questions A and C both compare things. How did you know that question A could be answered but question C couldn't be answered?

   » What more information would you need to answer question B?

   » How would the equations for question A and D be similar?

6. Optional: After discussion, have students create new questions that can or can't be answered by the data. You can have each student generate one of each. Or you can have students pair with a classmate with one partner creating a question that could be asked and answered and the other partner creating something that can't be answered. If time permits, some student creations could be shared. Alternatively, they can be written down and saved for the next day.

Something to Think About: Where Do You Get the Data?

You might find yourself creating easy, contrived, trivial examples like survey results about favorite ice cream flavors. Instead, you want to use contexts that are interesting and meaningful to your students. But finding data appropriate for elementary students for lessons, let alone a routine like this one or Routine 5: Same Data, Different Question (page 57) can be quite the challenge. Your curriculum resources likely are a good place to start your search, but be sure to enlist your students and your colleagues.

One way to do this is to make it a homework assignment. Give an example or two of the types of data tables and graphs you want your students to create. Have students work with caregivers to create a table or graph relative to a source in their home like a newspaper, nutrition label on a food package, or something similar. Accept all that come in regardless of how well they fit into your instruction. At the least, they serve as great source material for you to modify. And remember to give this type of assignment some time. That is, give them a week or maybe more to return their product. Keep in mind that this approach spotlights student and family identity!

Collaborating with colleagues is another great way to create a warehouse of useful data. You can work together to create examples. Or each of you can create some examples independently and then share or pass around the team. Instead of creating, you could use the option above (student-created data) and share that with other teachers too. Don't forget that teachers in other grades can get in on this creating and sharing as well.

ASKED AND ANSWERED (VARIATIONS): STUDENT CREATIVITY

Variations of routines throughout this book present ideas about how you can tap student creativity for new, engaging twists. Creating examples and problems gives students voice and agency. It promotes higher-order thinking. It can be hard! But be sure that you don't avoid giving them opportunities to create because of this. Instead, scaffold the creation process. Introduce examples first and be sure they understand how the activity works. Have them create examples with groups or partners before doing it independently. Share how you go about creating an example through a think aloud.

NOTES

_____

_____

_____

_____

_____

_____

_____

_____

_____

_____

_____

_____

_____

Variation A: Asked and Answered Without Data Tables

This routine is presented with data tables, but it works quite well with traditional word problems too. In this variation, you share a problem stem like the one on the left, "A goose flew 31 miles in a day." Students then think about a question that could, or could not, be asked and answered based on that information. They might say, "How far did it fly in 3 days?" However, "How far does the goose have to fly?" couldn't be answered. On the right, you see a problem stem with a bit more information. Know that any approach is fine and that more information in the problem stem might be more helpful when students first work with this variation of the routine.

A
A goose flew 31 miles in a day.

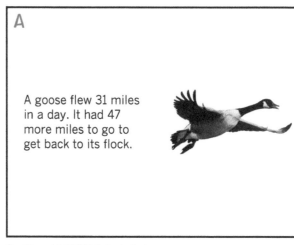

A
A goose flew 31 miles in a day. It had 47 more miles to go to get back to its flock.

Credit: nehls16321/istockphoto.com

NOTES

Variation B: Picking Between Two Questions

Ideally, you would have students deal with four or more questions when working with this routine. But at first, you might begin simply with two questions to limit distractions and potential confusion. This variation intentionally uses two questions that can be asked and answered. The idea is to use this simplified variation to practice choosing whether questions can be asked and answered. Notice that the two problems make use of different operations. In later grades, a multiplication or division problem might be included instead. This will help students learn that the routine is focused on the possibility of answering a question with no regard to the operation or method used for finding that answer.

Credit: 101cats/istockphoto.com

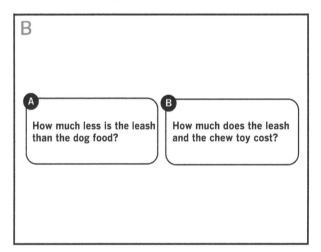

NOTES

Variation C: Use Questions That Can't Be Asked and Answered

Most, if not all, of your students' experience with problem solving, and math in general, has *only* been with questions that can be asked and answered. The notion that a question could be asked but not answered might be bizarre to them. This variation is another way to introduce the routine focusing solely on questions that can't be answered. You might use it just after Variation B where students grapple with more than one possible question. The conversation about these problems could get lively as students attempt to make arguments based on preference or interpretation. Throughout the discussion, you want details to be the focal point of the conversation. For example, question B is a question that students might argue can be answered. But it can't! The table shows boxes of donuts rather than number of donuts. Some might argue that there are 12 in a box but we don't know that for sure. Others will rely on the picture but again, we don't know exactly how many are in that box necessarily.

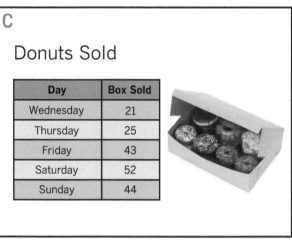

C

Donuts Sold

Day	Box Sold
Wednesday	21
Thursday	25
Friday	43
Saturday	52
Sunday	44

Credit: GaryAlvis/istockphoto.com

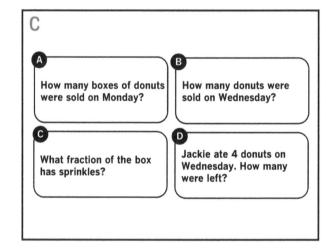

C

A How many boxes of donuts were sold on Monday?

B How many donuts were sold on Wednesday?

C What fraction of the box has sprinkles?

D Jackie ate 4 donuts on Wednesday. How many were left?

NOTES

Variation D: Students Generate Questions

As mentioned earlier, charging students with creating questions that can and can't be answered calls on higher-order thinking skills while offering other benefits. In this version, you simply provide context and data. Students then work to create a question that can or can't be answered based on that information. During class discussion, you can record questions in two columns—those that can be answered and those that can't. You are also free to have them create one of each question type or assign groups of students to a question type. Remember, this variation is not the starting point for this routine. It is an extension after students have had plenty of experience dealing with a question's possibilities.

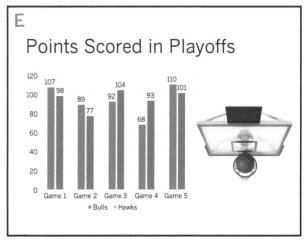

Dog Weights

Age	Weights (in pounds)
3 months	13
6 months	27
1 Year	38
2 Year	55
3 Year	71

Credit: 101cats/istockphoto.com

Variation E: Using Charts

A simple adjustment to this routine enables you to reinforce other skills and concepts naturally. Here, you see that the data table has been replaced with a bar graph. Students have to read and interpret the data from the graph to determine the viability of each question. When including data alternatives, be sure to talk about the differences in the data appearance and how that had no effect on the question or the mathematics. In this example, the data labels for each game are included. You should vary their appearance based on your students' readiness. Pictographs, line graphs, and line plots are also good choices for presenting data. It's even OK to use less traditional graphics like those you might find in a newspaper or magazine even if they aren't data types that are in your curriculum. Doing so promotes information literacy while adding an element of novelty to the routine.

Points Scored in Playoffs

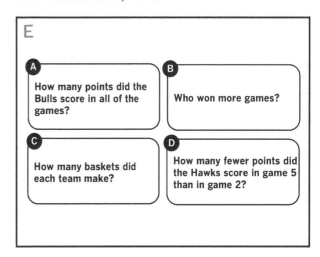

Credit: adventtr/istockphoto.com

E

A How many points did the Bulls score in all of the games?

B Who won more games?

C How many baskets did each team make?

D How many fewer points did the Hawks score in game 5 than in game 2?

Variation F: Is It Even a Question?

Much of this book is focused on how you can help students make sense of problems, represent them, select operations to solve problems, and justify their thinking. It's much about problems with operations. But there are questions that can be asked and answered that don't require operations, such as question B and even question C as they both deal with the concept of comparing fractions. There are questions that students are interested in, like question A, that aren't necessarily mathematics questions. So, in this variation, you mingle a variety of questions, some that call for operations to solve like question D and others like those already mentioned. It will be interesting to listen to student perspective about which questions can be asked and answered and which cannot. You may be surprised to find that some students have overly generalized what *is* a "problem."

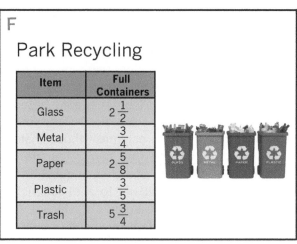

Credit: AlexLMX/istockphoto.com

F

Park Recycling

Item	Full Containers
Glass	$2\frac{1}{2}$
Metal	$\frac{3}{4}$
Paper	$2\frac{5}{8}$
Plastic	$\frac{3}{5}$
Trash	$5\frac{3}{4}$

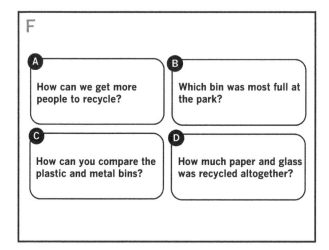

A How can we get more people to recycle?

B Which bin was most full at the park?

C How can you compare the plastic and metal bins?

D How much paper and glass was recycled altogether?

NOTES

Variation G: Asked and Answered With Rates

Asked and Answered works well with any content. The chart in the problem shows the rate of rotations for a spinning amusement park ride based on the number of riders. C and D are rate questions that can be asked and answered whereas A and B cannot. Additionally, B is a problem that has nothing to do with rates. It shows that you could modify this routine for students to consider whether questions can be asked and answered and to practice discriminating between ratio and nonratio situations. The problem below is an example of a nonratio problem that could be asked and answered, whereas question B in the sample is a nonratio problem that couldn't be answered.

There are 326 people in line for the ride. How many times would the ride have to run holding 24 people each time?

G

Rotations on the Spinner

Riders	Rotations per Minute
4	20
8	18
12	16
20	12
24	10

Credit: bmcent1/istockphoto.com

G

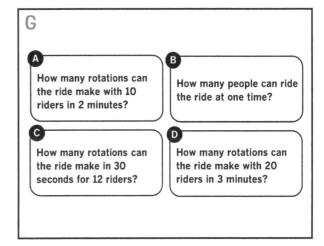

A How many rotations can the ride make with 10 riders in 2 minutes?

B How many people can ride the ride at one time?

C How many rotations can the ride make in 30 seconds for 12 riders?

D How many rotations can the ride make with 20 riders in 3 minutes?

NOTES

_____

_____

_____

_____

_____

_____

_____

_____

_____

WHAT'S THE QUESTION?

About the Routine

Most elementary students can point to a question mark and know that a question is being asked. Understanding what the question is asking is a different story. You can challenge students to make sense of the context of a question or how it is worded. Others have misconceptions about questions. They might think only certain questions can be asked because of the size or type of numbers in the problem. They might believe that the keyword within a question is what triggers an operation. As challenges and misconceptions mingle, productive problem solving can grind to a halt.

This routine takes a completely different approach to building skill with problem solving. With it, you give students the answer and ask them to generate the question or problem that would yield that answer. You might think of it as "reverse engineering" for problem solving. That is, the act of generating problems and questions helps students learn to be better problem solvers. Having students create a problem is a worthwhile task in any grade level because it engages students and develops confidence with problem solving (Barlow & Cates, 2007). Over time, doing this routinely helps students begin to get comfortable with the many ways questions can be asked. They learn to think about how contexts and actions influence the outcome of a situation or problem. Students practice

The answer is
16 buttons.

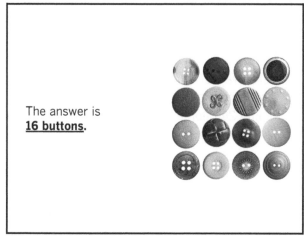

Credit: Paperkites/istockphoto.com

thinking about how numbers work together. They recognize that there are myriad questions (and answers) in the math they do.

In the example of 16 buttons, a first grader might create a problem about adding buttons (e.g., $10 + 6 = 16$), comparing how many more buttons someone has (e.g., $21 - 5 = 16$), or about how many buttons are left after some are lost (e.g., $18 - 2 = 16$). Whereas a fifth grader might create a problem about one-fourth of 64 buttons in a box ($\frac{1}{4} \times 64 = 16$) or how many buttons are in a group when there are 192 buttons and 12 groups ($192 \div 12 = 16$).

All routines can be downloaded for your use at
https://qrs.ly/3cemjnt

How This Routine Helps With Problem Solving

This routine builds problem-solving skill by providing opportunities for students to

- think about how questions are asked in a problem,
- identify the question and its meaning in a problem,
- recognize that different questions can yield the same answer,
- consider how numbers interact with one another due to the question or problem posed,
- observe that the solution is the result of the question,
- challenge assumptions about skill or concept associations,
- think critically,
- show their brilliance and creativity (identity),
- generate interest and increased motivation, and
- build confidence (agency).

What to Do

1. Display an answer to students (e.g., 16 buttons).

2. Give students time to independently think about a problem or question that would yield an answer that matches what you display.

3. Have partners share their ideas.

4. Bring the class together to share a few examples.

5. Listen to student examples and record the question that is asked. Write the equation that goes with their example.

6. Ask the group about the problem being shared. Use questions like:

   » What do you notice about ___'s question?

   » Do you agree that ____'s problem would have this answer?

   » What do you think about the equation I wrote that shows ___'s problem?

   » How is ____'s problem the same as or different from your problem?

7. Optional: After a few student examples are discussed, share your own problem with the class for them to compare to the problems from the group discussion or their own problem.

Note: It can be hard to remember one's problem when listening to others share. To minimize this challenge, you could remove the partner sharing step of the routine. Or you can have students record some notes about their problem without writing the entire problem. For the 16 buttons example, a third-grade student might write "Lexie 8 buttons, 2 boxes, how many buttons" to help them remember "Lexie had 2 boxes of buttons and each box had 8 buttons. How many buttons did Lexie have?"

Something to Think About: What to Listen For

Creating a question is an example of higher-order thinking, which comes with natural difficulty. If your students are having a tough time creating problems or questions, you can provide question starters or slotted sentences to help them. Before they begin, you might even discuss what students know about the context of the answer you present (e.g., How are buttons used? How are they packaged? What could happen to a button?). Or you can briefly discuss the words they might use in their question.

But know that students who are quick to create a problem may not be doing as well as you think. As you repeat the routine, listen for the types of problems or questions that students are creating. Think about individual students and your whole class. Ask yourself if they are using the same operation in every problem (e.g., Are their problems always about addition?). Consider the wording they use for certain operations (e.g., Do they always include "altogether" in their addition or multiplication question?). You might also find that students create problems based on the picture you use to help them understand the context (e.g., Sam put 4 buttons in 4 rows. How many buttons were there?).

WHAT'S THE QUESTION (VARIATIONS): SIMPLE ROUTINES AND RICH VARIATIONS

A routine like What's the Question is simple, straightforward, and easy to use. It might seem like such simplicity doesn't lend to rich variations. Yet as you use it with your students, you'll notice that patterns within the questions and numbers they create emerge. To counter, you can add restrictions about the type of questions or problems you want them to create. Or you might feel the need to swap out whole numbers for fractions or contexts (e.g., buttons) with measurement units (e.g., inches, ft^2). As with any routine, even simple ones such as What's the Question, you can adjust and modify them in countless ways. Here are a few to consider.

Variation A: Require a Certain Operation or Condition

Imagine that your students frequently, if not always, use addition in their problems. What would you do? You would likely change the directions to force them to start to think about other operations. This variation shows just that as it directs students to create a question with the answer 24 pencils but they have to use subtraction. You can easily change the operation, but there are other aspects about the problem you might change as well. If you notice in the picture, there are pens and pencils. You might direct students to create a problem that compares pens and pencils with an answer of 24 pencils. Or you might ask them to create a problem that has three numbers in it and an answer of 24 pencils. For example, an addition question with that answer might be, "There are 10 red pencils, 6 blue pencils, and 8 green pencils. How many pencils are there?" Two-step problems could be an option with a problem like, "There are 6 pencils missing from 3 packs of 10 pencils. How many pencils are there?" As mentioned in Part 1, pictures used in these routines help students understand the context of a problem. You might have to remind them that the

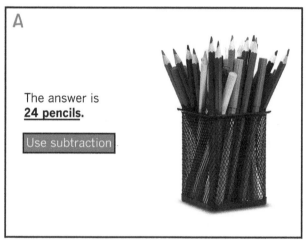

The answer is
24 pencils.

Use subtraction

Credit: Ilya_Starikov/istockphoto.com

image itself does not always reflect the answer. In this example, there aren't 24 colored pencils. The image helps students think about how pencils are stored or activate another idea about pencils like the different colors they come in or how they are different from thin markers.

Variation B: Create Two Questions

In time, you will find that your students are creating problems and questions with ease. When you do, change the routine to ask them to create two different questions that have the same answer. The intent here is not simply to provide more work for students. Instead, it can give you insight into their creativity and flexibility. It might also help you better recognize patterns within an individual's questions (e.g., Do they use the same problem structure each time?). You can add restrictions as noted in Variation A. For example, you can have them create two different multiplication problems that ask the question in a different way. Or, you can have students create two different questions that feature different operations. Keep in mind that this variation might especially call for students to write notes about their problem, if not the entire problem.

The answer to two different questions is **12 oranges.**

Credit: dcdr/istockphoto.com

Variation C: What Can't Be the Question?

There is value in having students not only think about a question for a given result but also a question that cannot yield that result. In this variation, you pose the answer and students create a problem that couldn't be the question. Here, a student example might be, "There were 50 balloons and 20 of them popped. How many were left?" There are endless possibilities, and your students might get a tad silly. But that's OK! Have fun and laugh. But be sure they know why a question doesn't work or why it's ridiculous. And as noted earlier, listen for students who tie their question to the picture. A student who says, "How many balloons are there?" satisfied a question that doesn't work but misses the mark for the intent of the routine. Also note that as students share their examples, this can be a great time to help them think about why an answer doesn't work. For example, 32 balloons doesn't work for "There were 28 balloons and 6 popped. How many balloons were there?" because the problem creates fewer balloons and there were never more than 30.

The answer is **32 balloons.**

Credit: ncognet0/istockphoto.com

Highlighting this type of reasoning helps students experience what they should think about as they solve problems.

Variation D: Students Create the Answer

Once students are comfortable with the routine, you can try this twist in which students create the number and the context for the answer. From there, you can choose to create a problem that would or wouldn't match. Students must then determine whether your question works and why. Alternatively, you can have them generate the number and the solution and then carry out the routine as directed. Either way, having students identify a context gives you an opportunity to see who they are, what interests they have, what foods they like, place they go, and so on. You might even have each student record their number and their context on an index card and then use those as the prompt for later offerings of the routine. Doing this positions them as meaningful contributors to math class and it also means that there is one less thing for you to do!

D

The answer is
___ _____.

Variation E: Answers Without Images, Labels, or Both

As you have noticed, each problem in this book is presented with a picture. Using pictures or images offers entry points and supports student comprehension and sense making. But obviously, students will encounter word problems without pictures. In this variation of the routine, you simply provide the answer without an image, as shown on the top. Without an image, students will create problems about all sorts of balls. On the bottom, you see how you could choose to remove the label instead. Now, students might interpret the answer to be about soccer balls, goals scored, or the number of players on a team. Or you can remove both the image and the label leaving nothing but a number. This is likely the most challenging for your students because they have to generate a context, operation, and question.

E

The answer is
35 balls.

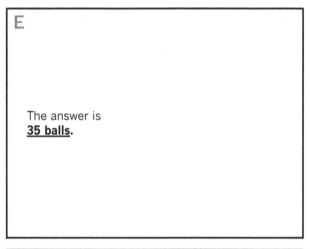

E

The answer is
40_____.

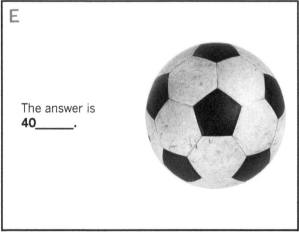

Credit: Udomsook/istockphoto.com

Variation F: Fractions and Decimals

Changing the answer to a fraction or decimal is obviously a good idea. But this variation is a bit more complex than that. Here, you give two different answers: one with a whole number and one with a fraction, mixed number, or decimal. Then, you have students create two similar problems for each answer. A problem for the top answer might be, "There were 20 pieces and 12 were eaten. How many were left?" and a problem for the bottom answer might be, "There were 3 pizzas with 8 slices in each. 5 slices were eaten. How much pizza was left?" Subtraction is used in both problems. But how the slices and the pizzas are referred to in the problem helps students think about how numbers work within a problem. It helps them see relationships and can help reduce confusion or anxiety when fractions or decimals appear in problems. Note that this is an advanced version of the routine, and it is a good idea to have partners create questions together for this version. Also note that you could have half of your class create a problem for one answer and half create a problem for the other answer before talking about the similarities and differences between the problems.

The answer is **8**.

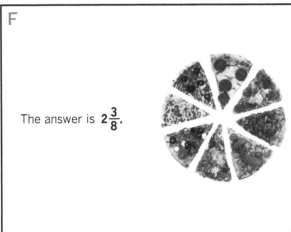

The answer is $2\frac{3}{8}$.

Credit: aluxum/istockphoto.com

NOTES

_____

_____

_____

_____

_____

_____

_____

_____

_____

_____

Variation G: Student Choice

This variation is about giving students choice. You give students two different answers to create a problem for. You can do this with any problem type and any grade-level content. In third grade, one answer could have a two-digit whole number while the other has three digits. Or, in fifth grade, one answer could be a whole number and the other could be a decimal. The example shows how it might play out in seventh grade with an answer about a percentage problem and an answer with a negative number. A problem for the first answer might be, "The Wildcats won 9 of 20 games. What percent of their games did they win?" For the second answer, a student could create, "The Wildcats lost by 16 points in game 1, won by 4 points in game 2, and won by 9 points in game 3. What was their point differential for the three games?"

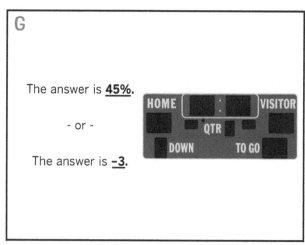

Credit: alptraum/istockphoto.com

NOTES

SAME DATA, DIFFERENT QUESTION

About the Routine

When helping students work with problem solving, in school or at home, adults often finding themselves ready to scream, "Did you even read the question?" At that moment, the answer to that question is (likely) no! Some students blindly solve problems without much thought. They assume they know what to do, grabbing the numbers from the problem and doing something with them. They might use the operation that they have been learning about most recently. They might default to an operation that they are most comfortable with when the problem seems to make sense and an operation they aren't comfortable with when a problem is confusing.

Perceptions about math and what it means to do math can compound the issue. Students might rush to solve a problem, making assumptions without reading the question, because they believe that faster is better or that good students do math quickly. These students might rely on the order of the numbers to signal what to do (e.g., larger number before smaller number in the problem means to subtract). Or they might use the context alone to determine what to do (e.g., dogs eating bones, eating is take away or subtraction).

This routine intends to slow the problem-solving process down for students. They will take a little time to examine the data before you reveal the question. The catch is that you will end up using the same data for three or four offerings of the routine, changing the question asked each new time. By using the same data over the course of three or four days, you can disrupt their assumptions about how to solve the problem.

Amusement Park Ticket Sales

Day	Attendance
Monday	2,345
Tuesday	1,708
Wednesday	1,413
Thursday	2,660
Friday	3,117

Credit: bmcent1/istockphoto.com

In time, the experience should cause them to read, pause, and think about a problem before rushing in. When you begin using this routine, don't be surprised if your students give you an answer on day two that is the exact same as the day before even though the question has changed.

Amusement Park Ticket Sales

Day	Attendance
Monday	2,345
Tuesday	1,708
Wednesday	1,413
Thursday	2,660
Friday	3,117

How many tickets were sold on Monday and Wednesday?

Amusement Park Ticket Sales

Day	Attendance
Monday	2,345
Tuesday	1,708
Wednesday	1,413
Thursday	2,660
Friday	3,117

How many more tickets were sold on Monday than Wednesday?

Amusement Park Ticket Sales

Day	Attendance
Monday	2,345
Tuesday	1,708
Wednesday	1,413
Thursday	2,660
Friday	3,117

What is the difference in tickets sold between the day with the most and the day with the least tickets sold?

Credit: bmcent1/istockphoto.com

All routines can be downloaded for your use at
https://qrs.ly/3cemjnt

How This Routine Helps With Problem Solving

This routine builds problem-solving skill by providing opportunities for students to

- slow down as they move through the problem-solving process,
- observe the changing nature of questions,
- determine necessary and unnecessary information,
- compare and contrast solution paths relative to the problem or question posed, and
- experience the variety of ways questions can be asked so that they move away from misinformed shortcuts like keyword strategies.

What to Do

1. Pose information for students to observe without a prompt or question.

2. Have students discuss their observations about the data. The sentence starters below can be used to support their discussions.

- » I noticed that …
- » One thing I can say about …
- » One thing I can't say about …
- » I think that …

3. Optional: Share highlights from the partner discussion with the whole class.

4. Reveal a problem or question for the students to solve (as shown in the upper right-hand side image).

5. Discuss strategies and solutions as a group.

6. Close the routine.

7. The next day, use the routine again with the same information or data but swap out the question for a new one (as shown in the different images). During this day's debriefing discussion, be sure to compare the new question, solution, strategies, and representations to the previous day's work.

8. Repeat the routine for a third day using the same information and process with a new problem (as shown in the different images).

Something to Think About: Use Routines for Centers and Homework

Same Data, Different Question is a routine that could be complemented with independent work. You could provide the information from the routine on paper with additional questions for the students to answer. You might have them do this during seatwork or possibly for homework. In the provided example about amusement park tickets, new questions might be:

1. How many tickets were sold on Monday and Tuesday together?

2. How many tickets were sold on Friday and Thursday?

3. How many more tickets were sold on Friday and Monday than on Tuesday?

4. Tickets were buy-one-get-one on Wednesday. How many people were in the park?

5. All people get to the park by buses from the parking lot. Each bus holds 50 people. How many buses would be needed to get everyone to the park on Thursday if they all showed up at the same time?

This routine would make a good center in your classroom. To do this, print the data and information component on a half-sheet of paper. Then, write different prompts and questions on index cards or something similar. Write one per card and create maybe six to 10 cards. When students work at the center, they pull the information half-sheet and a pick a question card. They solve the problem for that question, record their thinking in their journals, and then pick a new question card. You might have them solve three or four problems per experience.

SAME DATA, DIFFERENT QUESTION (VARIATIONS): CONSIDERING CONTEXT

Contextual information in a story problem helps students make sense of the situation and the problem. But when there is too much going on in a problem or when the context is unfamiliar it can become distracting and confusing. The vagueness of a pronoun can create challenges (Rowland, 1999). Proper nouns create a special challenge because they can be hard to read or because young readers miss context clues about what they refer

to (Edwards et al., 2009). This routine puts forth information in data tables with little to no context or background information. It intends to get right after the question. You can choose to give a little information if you deem it necessary. In Variation C, you might say that scientists are catching fish to measure their growth, or in Variation D you might say that five friends went bowling. Take a look at some other ways to vary this routine.

Variation A: Use Traditional Word Problems

This routine works well with traditional word problems like the one shown. Again, you provide information and context. Then, over the course of three days you pose different problems. Data doesn't pop as much in written form. Students might need to reread it a few times. Students will benefit from observing and discussing the information before working with a question in this variation more than others because of the text. And though you might not introduce the routine with this version, it's important that you include it somewhere along the way. In fact, a clever way to do this might be to provide data and context through a table for a few days and then present the same information through text in the next offering. That means in this example, you would show the types of cards in a table for the first three times you use it. Then with the text (as is) the next three times you use it.

A

Game Cards

Jake and three friends counted their cards. They had 16 rare cards, 48 uncommon cards, 112 common cards, and 12 cards that were torn.

A

Game Cards

Jake and three friends counted their cards. They had 16 rare cards, 48 uncommon cards, 112 common cards, and 12 cards that were torn.

They split the common cards between each of them. How many common cards did each person get?

A

Game Cards

Jake and three friends counted their cards. They had 16 rare cards, 48 uncommon cards, 112 common cards, and 12 cards that were torn.

They removed the torn cards. How many were left to play with?

A

Game Cards

Jake and three friends counted their cards. They had 16 rare cards, 48 uncommon cards, 112 common cards, and 12 cards that were torn.

They figured each rare card was worth 75¢. How much were their rare cards worth altogether?

Credit: NoDerog/istockphoto.com

Variation B: Different Questions, Same Problem Type

This variation of Same Data, Different Question promotes practice with the same type of problem over the course of three days with the routine. Each example in this variation are comparison problems with group size unknown. Though an elementary student doesn't need to identify the problem type, they do need to experience them repeatedly to find skill in solving them comfortably. Providing the same type of problem again and again in this routine provides repetition spurring capability and confidence. With each new day, it would be wise to connect the new problem to that of the day before, helping students see how the question is slightly different (e.g., different numbers) but the structure of the problem (multiplicative comparison) and the operation needed to solve it is consistent.

B

Bowling Scores

Player	Score
Ebony	285
Aimee	207
John	144
Steph	168
Gina	219

B

Bowling Scores

Player	Score
Ebony	285
Aimee	207
John	144
Steph	168
Gina	219

Ebony scored three times more than Dax. What did Dax score?

B

Bowling Scores

Player	Score
Ebony	285
Aimee	207
John	144
Steph	168
Gina	219

John scored twice as much as Kristen. What did Kristen score?

B

Bowling Scores

Player	Score
Ebony	285
Aimee	207
John	144
Steph	168
Gina	220

Gina scored four times more than Kim. What was Kim's score?

Variation C: Different Number Types

This routine is ripe for use with fractions and decimals. Variation C shows what they might look like. There are different fish measuring different lengths. Each problem is a comparison problem using addition or subtraction. This variation also highlights another way that you can create many more problems with a set of data. Notice that it adds a seventh fish that isn't part of the table. Doing so opens the door to limitless problem possibilities.

Keep this in mind as you create your own problems. Also remember that you can mingle questions and prompts that don't call for operations. In this example, you might ask which fish is the longest or you can ask the students to put them in order of shortest to longest. You might be surprised in doing so that some students still jump quickly to doing something with the numbers even though no operation is necessary.

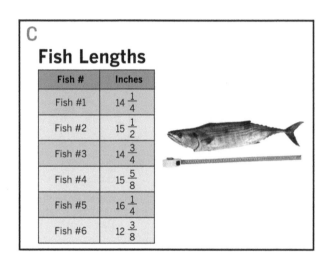

C

Fish Lengths

Fish #	Inches
Fish #1	$14\frac{1}{4}$
Fish #2	$15\frac{1}{2}$
Fish #3	$14\frac{3}{4}$
Fish #4	$15\frac{5}{8}$
Fish #5	$16\frac{1}{4}$
Fish #6	$12\frac{3}{8}$

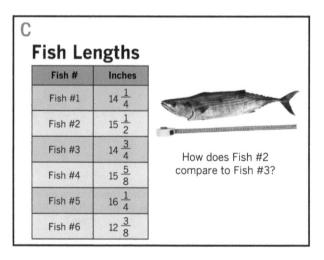

C

Fish Lengths

Fish #	Inches
Fish #1	$14\frac{1}{4}$
Fish #2	$15\frac{1}{2}$
Fish #3	$14\frac{3}{4}$
Fish #4	$15\frac{5}{8}$
Fish #5	$16\frac{1}{4}$
Fish #6	$12\frac{3}{8}$

What is the difference in length between Fish #2 and Fish #3?

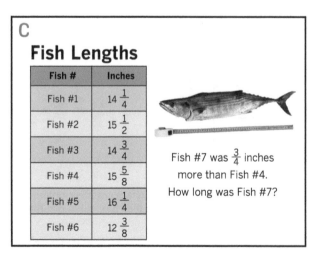

C

Fish Lengths

Fish #	Inches
Fish #1	$14\frac{1}{4}$
Fish #2	$15\frac{1}{2}$
Fish #3	$14\frac{3}{4}$
Fish #4	$15\frac{5}{8}$
Fish #5	$16\frac{1}{4}$
Fish #6	$12\frac{3}{8}$

Fish #7 was $\frac{3}{4}$ inches more than Fish #4. How long was Fish #7?

C

Fish Lengths

Fish #	Inches
Fish #1	$14\frac{1}{4}$
Fish #2	$15\frac{1}{2}$
Fish #3	$14\frac{3}{4}$
Fish #4	$15\frac{5}{8}$
Fish #5	$16\frac{1}{4}$
Fish #6	$12\frac{3}{8}$

How does Fish #2 compare to Fish #3?

Variation D: Primary Examples

As you may have figured, this routine is perfect for primary students. Changing whole numbers to fractions is perfect for fourth and fifth graders while changing the data to numbers less than 20 is perfect for younger students. But also notice how the questions have changed. There are options for simple comparisons (upper-right example), unique word problems (lower-left example), and possibilities to connect with basic facts (lower-right example). Using this and other routines early helps students forge foundational problem-solving skills and productive dispositions toward problems.

D

Playing Cards

Player	Score
Alex	13
Marissa	8
Meg	7
Zeke	18
Antonio	23

D

Playing Cards

Player	Score
Alex	13
Marissa	8
Meg	7
Zeke	18
Antonio	23

Who has 10 more than Alex?

D

Playing Cards

Player	Score
Alex	13
Marissa	8
Meg	7
Zeke	18
Antonio	23

How many more does Meg need to get 20 cards?

D

Playing Cards

Player	Score
Alex	13
Marissa	8
Meg	7
Zeke	18
Antonio	23

Who could have made their cards into a stack of 5 and a stack of 3?

Credit: NoDerog/istockphoto.com

Variation E: Two-Step Problems

There are different ways to incorporate two-step problems into this routine. One way is to simply use a different two-step problem each day instead of a different question. And while this will work fine, you can also use problems in consecutive days to build from one step to two. Offer a one-step problem on the first day. Then, build off that problem for the second step on the following day. You can see how this plays out in the examples. The first day asks a one-step problem about combining rider totals (upper left-hand example). The next day, you would ask something that uses the information from the first day. In the example (upper right-hand example), you are asking about an amount less than the combined total from the previous day. You see a similar pairing in the bottom example. This approach enables students to see how a two-step problem can branch off from a first or one-step problem while building on their success from solving the first problem.

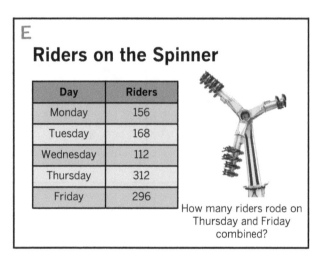

E

Riders on the Spinner

Day	Riders
Monday	156
Tuesday	168
Wednesday	112
Thursday	312
Friday	296

How many riders rode on Thursday and Friday combined?

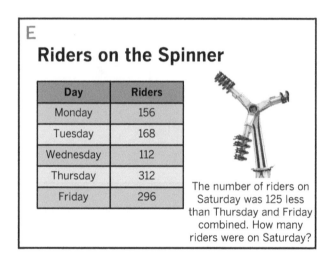

E

Riders on the Spinner

Day	Riders
Monday	156
Tuesday	168
Wednesday	112
Thursday	312
Friday	296

The number of riders on Saturday was 125 less than Thursday and Friday combined. How many riders were on Saturday?

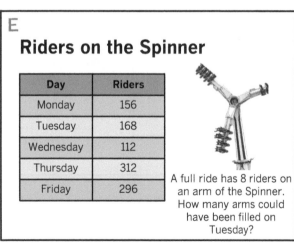

E

Riders on the Spinner

Day	Riders
Monday	156
Tuesday	168
Wednesday	112
Thursday	312
Friday	296

A full ride has 8 riders on an arm of the Spinner. How many arms could have been filled on Tuesday?

E

Riders on the Spinner

Day	Riders
Monday	156
Tuesday	168
Wednesday	112
Thursday	312
Friday	296

A full ride has 8 riders on an arm of the Spinner. How many more arms could have been filled on Friday than on Tuesday?

Variation E: Questions That Can't Be Answered

Routine 3: Asked and Answered (page 41) charged students with determining whether certain questions could be asked and answered based on given information. This variation of Same Data, Different Question shows how you could use questions within the routine over the course of a few days so that students can practice determining why multiple questions can't be asked and answered. After agreeing that a question can't be answered, ask students to identify what other information they would need so that the given question could

be answered. For example, students might say they don't know how many people are on team 4 for the bottom left example. Have them describe why that information is important. Then, if you like, give them more information so that they could answer the question. If you are wondering about the sequence of these routines (Routines 3 and 5), know that you can reverse them if you think that it makes more sense to think about different possible questions first before playing with the idea of a question that can't be answered.

E

Bowling Scores

Player	Score
Team 1	719
Team 2	856
Team 3	1,125
Team 4	798
Team 5	993
Team 6	905

E

Bowling Scores

Player	Score
Team 1	719
Team 2	856
Team 3	1,125
Team 4	798
Team 5	993
Team 6	905

Who scored the most on Team 5?

E

Bowling Scores

Player	Score
Team 1	719
Team 2	856
Team 3	1,125
Team 4	798
Team 5	993
Team 6	905

How much did each player on Team 4 score?

E

Bowling Scores

Player	Score
Team 1	719
Team 2	856
Team 3	1,125
Team 4	798
Team 5	993
Team 6	905

There were 5 players on Team 6. Each scored more than the players on Team 2. How many points did the players on Team 2 score?

Credit: Talaj/istockphoto.com

Variation F: Students Write the Questions

Variation F asks students to write a question (that can be answered) from the data you present. However, instead of having them write new questions each day, have each student write one question in their journal or on an index card on the first day you use a certain data set. Have them share their questions with partners. Then, for the next two or three days, use the data set and highlight a different student's question. You could choose to do two student questions each day if time permits. When doing so, make sure that there is some discussion about how the questions, strategies for solving them, operations, and representations are different.

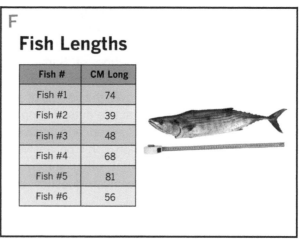

F

Fish Lengths

Fish #	CM Long
Fish #1	74
Fish #2	39
Fish #3	48
Fish #4	68
Fish #5	81
Fish #6	56

Credit: gece33/istockphoto.com

NOTES

Variation G: Revisiting and Reviewing

This variation shows how the routine might be used in a middle school classroom. You can see that it would work well with concepts of ratio, percent, and statistics. It highlights that any routine can be used to revisit topics taught earlier in the year. This is a clever way to review for improved retention. Also keep in mind that a routine can mix content from different units of study. In other words, if you are teaching a unit on number systems, your routine doesn't have to use problems connected to number systems. Instead, you could use numbers and concepts.

Screen Time

	Games	Social Media	Videos
Monday	36 min	92 min	15 min
Tuesday	5 min	66 min	43 min
Wednesday	102 min	54 min	116 min
Thursday	34 min	22 min	15 min
Friday	25 min	73 min	155 min

Which day had the highest ratio of game to video time?

Screen Time

	Games	Social Media	Videos
Monday	36 min	92 min	15 min
Tuesday	5 min	66 min	43 min
Wednesday	102 min	54 min	116 min
Thursday	34 min	22 min	15 min
Friday	25 min	73 min	155 min

If these were the only screen time activities, what percent of the day was spent on the device?

Screen Time

	Games	Social Media	Videos
Monday	36 min	92 min	15 min
Tuesday	5 min	66 min	43 min
Wednesday	102 min	54 min	116 min
Thursday	34 min	22 min	15 min
Friday	25 min	73 min	155 min

If these were the only screen time activities, what percent of Wednesday's time was spent on social media?

Screen Time

	Games	Social Media	Videos
Monday	36 min	92 min	15 min
Tuesday	5 min	66 min	43 min
Wednesday	102 min	54 min	116 min
Thursday	34 min	22 min	15 min
Friday	25 min	73 min	155 min

What is the mean number of minutes spent on social media this week?

Credit: alexey_boldin/istockphoto.com

HOW DO YOU . . . ?

About the Routine

Not surprisingly, students don't always fully read a problem. They don't always pause to think about how and why their approach will solve the problem. They will just rush into a problem to be quick. Or they just want to get the problem over with because they aren't often successful with word problems. Some generalize that certain contexts trigger certain operations (e.g., boxes of things must be multiplication) causing little need for thought. Some use the order of numbers to determine the operation (e.g., larger number first indicates subtraction). Some choose operations based on how clear (i.e., must be an operation I'm good at) or confusing (i.e., must be a "hard" operation) a problem is. And, most likely, you can add to this list!

None of the "approaches" mentioned are good for consistent, successful problem solving. That comes from helping your students learn to pause, take in a problem, and ask themselves, "How do I . . . ?" This routine is based on that very question. The routine is an opportunity for students to examine situations and think about how they would put things together, take them apart, find groups of them, and so on. The routine is for discussing what the question is asking and for thinking about how a solution can be found.

The routine is special because it isn't about just one problem. It has two different problems with a similar context. But the two problems, usually, require different operations to solve. As you can see in the example, both problems are about packs of hot dogs, deliveries, food trucks, and hot dogs sold. One problem calls for division and the other calls for subtraction. You want your students to talk

Many packs of hot dogs were delivered to different food trucks. Each food truck got the same number. Some were sold.

How do you find out the number of hot dogs each truck got?

Many packs of hot dogs were delivered to different food trucks. Each food truck got the same number. Some were sold.

How do you find out how many hot dogs were not sold?

Credit: kcline/istockphoto.com

about what's happening, what is being asked, and how they can find an answer to that question. And don't be surprised if some of your students use the same operation for both problems.

How This Routine Helps With Problem Solving

This routine builds problem-solving skill by providing opportunities for students to

- take time to process and make meaning of contexts and questions,
- explore solution paths for different problems,
- deepen their conceptual understanding of operations,

- select and use operations to solve problems, and
- recognize misconceptions about problems and shortcomings of faulty strategies like keywords (when included in the debriefing discussion).

What to Do

1. Pose a context and confirm that students understand it.
2. Reveal two different questions as shown in the example.
3. Have students talk about how they would answer the two different questions.
4. Bring the group together to discuss their ideas about how they would solve each problem. As you discuss, ask questions like:
   » How are the problems the same? How are they different?
   » How does the operation you selected solve the problem?
   » Why can't you use the same operation for both problems?

   » Why isn't (operation) a good choice for this question when it was for the other question?

5. Optional: After your class has discussed how they would solve each problem, introduce numbers into the context. Have them represent the two problems with drawings and equations. Connect their representations to the respective problems and highlight how the drawings and equations are different. For example, the hot dog problem might become:

   84 packs of hot dogs were delivered to 4 food trucks. Each food truck got the same number. 27 packs of hot dogs were sold.

Something to Think About: Problem Solving Can't Be Rote

Literature discrediting a keyword approach to problem solving points out that keywords can be misleading. It notes that keywords add a layer of procedure and call for students to rely on something other than sense making. The same is true for approaches like "C-U-B-E-S" (page 4) because they focus problem solving on procedure and answer. These can create hollow, rote problem-solving experiences. To "help" students, teachers might model how they solve problems and then work to get their students to replicate their approaches in a form of gradual release. This act undermines both their thinking and their agency. And it often proves unsuccessful as students are unable to transfer a given approach to new situations or settings.

Problem solving isn't rote! Students need opportunities to try it on their own first before discussing what worked and what didn't. As a teacher, you want to ask questions to poke their reasoning. Charge them with explaining why. Help them call on past experiences. Have them compare and contrast problems and situations. And remember that you can (and should) show how you think about a problem. You simply want them to try it first, find their own strategies, determine what doesn't work for them, and consider other approaches (like yours) that are possibly more efficient or more effective.

HOW DO YOU . . . ? (VARIATIONS): CHANGING THE PROCESS

There is no wrong way to go about any routine. This one centers on the question, "How do I solve this?" It is shown with two problems, but you might find that you need to focus on just one with your students first as shown in the first variation. Your students might need numbers to help them think about the problem. You might find that posing three problems is a good challenge for your students. You could even use three problems of the same operation in which two have a common situation and the third doesn't (e.g., two take away subtraction problems and a subtraction comparison problem). Look at some of the following ideas. Use them and improve on them to yield the best results for your students.

Variation A: Single Problem (Focused Example)

Using one problem is a good place to begin with students, especially primary students. Here, they can focus on this context and a single question. In this example, discussion is about the group of rubber ducks floating down the river and the comparison between ducks who finished and didn't finish the race. Students might ask about why they didn't finish the race—which is fine. It shows they're trying to understand the problem. After discussing the single problem, you can end the routine or introduce a new question with the same context.

A

Rubber ducks were raced down a river. How do you find out how many didn't finish the race?

Credit: Heike Faber/istockphoto.com

NOTES

Variation B: Compare Different Structures of the Same Operation (+/−)

Subtraction can be overemphasized as taking away. Subtraction is also used for taking something apart or comparing. You can use this routine to practice problems that use the same context and the same operation though they represent different structures or situations. In the running example, subtraction can be used to compare the number of laps that Jackie ran as compared to Oscar. On the right, subtraction is not a comparison but instead finding out how many laps are left after some have been completed (taken away). The squirrel examples are provided as addition problems. They also highlight why thinking carefully about what is happening and how a problem would be solved matters so much. On the left side, the notion of gathering nuts lends well to addition. However, students are likely to think about eating as taking away, overlooking the fact that they need to add the new amount eaten to the first amount eaten.

B

A race has many laps. Jackie ran some laps. Oscar ran some laps.

How do you find out how many more laps Jackie ran than Oscar?

B

A race has many laps. Jackie ran some laps. Oscar ran some laps.

How do you find out how many more laps Jackie needs to finish?

B

A squirrel had some acorns and gathered walnuts. She ate some nuts and then ate some more.

How would you find how many nuts she gathered?

B

A squirrel had some acorns and gathered walnuts. She ate some nuts and then ate some more.

How would you find how many nuts she ate altogether?

Runner Credit: XiXinXing/istockphoto.com, Squirrel Credit: Credit: legna69/istockphoto.com

Variation C: Compare Different Structures of the Same Operation (×/÷)

This variation is provided for two different reasons. First, it shows different structures for multiplication and division. Like addition and subtraction, these operations can take on one meaning more often than others. For example, equal groups might be the predominant example of multiplication in a classroom while array and comparison situations are used less often. For division, problem types might most often be about how many are in a group (left example) instead of how many groups (right example). The variation is also the first that shows numbers in the problems. You can do this routine with or without numbers. Your students might need the numbers to help them process how they would solve it. If so, be sure to include them. In some classes, students might use a relationship they see within the numbers to solve the problem rather than the meaning of the problem. In those cases, it would be a good idea to omit numbers.

C

There are toy trucks on the shelf each with the same number of wheels.

How would you find the total number of wheels on the shelf?

C

There are 8 times more action figures than trucks on the shelf.

How would you find the number of action figures?

C

There 48 push pins to put in packs.

How would you find how many packs you need?

C

There 48 push pins to put in packs.

How would you find how many are in 6 packs?

Toys credit: Fascinadora/istockphoto.com, Pins credit: AlexeyVS/istockphoto.com

Variation D: Use Tables

Tables can be quite useful for this routine because you can switch up your questions easily.

You can ask about the difference between plain and mustard hot dogs sold and then ask about how many plain and cheese sauce were sold together. You can add a new category to a table or new information. For example, you might add that 500 of each hot dog were made asking how many of each were left as shown. Because there are multiple categories, you can have students generate a new prompt that would be solved in a similar way. If you did so, students could discuss the problem on the left and then create something like how many cheese sauce and ketchup and mustard hot dogs were sold. This new problem is an add-to problem like the original. Throughout the book, you'll find examples with data tables like this. Some routines rely on them. Keep in mind that tables are just one display you use. Other displays, such as bar graphs or line graphs, would also be great options. And as you incorporate these, you're providing practice with other skills (reading charts) within your curriculum.

D

Toppings	Sold
Plain	384
Mustard	117
Ketchup and Mustard	261
Cheese Sauce	425
Ketchup, Mustard, and Onions	403

How do you find how many plain and mustard were sold?

D

Toppings	Sold
Plain	384
Mustard	117
Ketchup and Mustard	261
Cheese Sauce	425
Ketchup, Mustard, and Onions	403

500 hot dogs with cheese sauce were made.

How do you find how many were left?

Credit: kcline/istockphoto.com

Variation E: Find a Partner

In this variation, you give a context and some options as shown. Students then create a problem based on the information. When signaled, students walk around and talk with classmates, trying to find a problem that would be solved in the same way as the problem they created. You can choose to have them sit down when they find a partner or continue looking for others who have matches. After some time, bring the class together to discuss matching examples. Consider discussing examples that don't use the same operation and discuss why. Note in the example that some possible conditions (toys on a shelf, toys sold, types of toys, broken toys) are given to students as suggestions. They don't have to use these ideas, but offering them can help expedite their problem writing.

E

Toys on a shelf

Toys sold

Types of toys

Broken toys

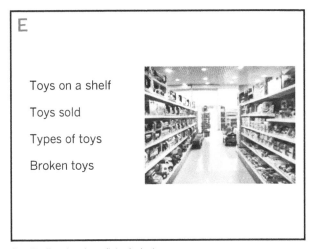

Credit: Fascinadora/istockphoto.com

Variation F: Mixed List

This variation is a simple list of different situations relative to the same context. It can be a good assessment of their conceptual understanding of different operations. There are examples with numbers and without. As noted earlier, use the version that works best for your students. The left examples show addition and subtraction situations and would be good for primary students. Right examples would be good options in third, fourth, or fifth grade because it mingles operations. It may be challenging to fit in a discussion about each bullet during a quick, five- to 10-minute routine. To avoid the challenge, choose two bullets to discuss during your whole-group debriefing.

F

How do you find ___ if . . .

- 18 ducks floated, 4 ducks sank
- 4 ducks launched, then 18 ducks launched
- Jared had 18 ducks, Kristen had 4 ducks
- 18 ducks finished the race, then 4 ducks finished

F

How do you find ___ if . . .

- 18 packs of 4 ducks
- 18 ducks floated, 4 ducks sank
- 4 rows of 18 ducks
- 4 ducks put in the water, then 18 ducks put in the water
- 18 ducks put into 4 streams

F

How do you find ___ if . . .

- Some ducks floated, some ducks sank
- Some ducks launched, then some more ducks launched
- Jared had some ducks, Kristen had some ducks
- Some ducks finished the race, then some ducks finished

F

How do you find ___ if . . .

- Some packs of some ducks
- Some ducks floated, some ducks sank
- Some rows of some ducks
- Some ducks put in the water, then some more ducks put in the water
- Some ducks put into 4 streams

Credit: Heike Faber/istockphoto.com

Variation G: Percent Change

Talking about percent change problems is essential for developing an understanding of them. Sometimes, a problem is introduced and discussion proceeds straight to setting up the problem, the calculations, and so on. This routine is perfect for the vital first step—sense making! Here, different situations involving percent (A) mingle with percent increases and decreases. You can give students choice about which one or two prompts that they want to discuss with their partners. Or, borrowing from Routine 5 (page 57), you could focus on a different prompt each day discussing how students can think about it and then how it compares to prompts from previous days. Keep in mind this routine isn't about finding the solution but how to reason about and represent a problem.

G

A. Falcons' percent of shots made

B. 10% increase in Bears' shots made

C. About a 25% increase in shots taken by the Gators in the next game

D. Number of shots Hawks needed to make for 75%

E. A team who made 50% fewer shots on the same number of attempts as . . .

Team	Shots Attempted	Shots Made
Bears	36	24
Falcons	42	37
Gators	22	15
Hawks	29	16
Tigers	18	15

Credit: adventtr/istockphoto.com

NOTES

SAME AND DIFFERENT

About the Routine

Comparing and contrasting is an effective way for learning about concepts. It is also a powerful thinking and reasoning strategy. When students are challenged with a problem, teachers often ask students to think of a similar problem, a familiar problem, or something that is the exact opposite of the current challenge. But you know that this can be quite hard for elementary students. This routine, Same and Different, is an opportunity for students to analyze two similar but different problems. It helps them see that the same operation can be applied to two problems with similar contexts and actions as shown in the dog treat example. In this second-grade example, you want students to talk about how both problems are about dog treats, how the dog ate treats in both problems, how the toy had 32 treats in it each time, and that both are asking about the number of treats remaining. You would also want them to focus on the key difference—the number of treats the dog ate. Bringing this to students' attention can then help them think about how the equation and solution will be similar (subtraction, fewer treats remaining) and different (different subtrahend, different difference).

With clever variations, your students can compare important aspects of problems. You can help them see how the same equation can be used for problems that have a similar action but completely different numbers and contexts. You can prompt students to notice that changing numbers changes the result even when everything else about a problem is identical. Using this routine consistently builds an essential

Sam added 32 treats to her dog's toy. The puppy ate 24 of the treats. How many treats were left in the toy?

Sam added 32 treats to her dog's toy. The puppy ate 18 of the treats. How many treats were left in the toy?

Credit: clubfoto/istockphoto.com

"problem-attack" skill. But as you use it, be sure to close each time asking students why looking at how problems are the same and different can help them with a new, challenging, or confusing problem.

All routines can be downloaded for your use at
https://qrs.ly/3cemjnt

How This Routine Helps With Problem Solving

This routine builds problem-solving skill by providing opportunities for students to

- develop critical-thinking skills about the architecture of word problems;
- shift focus from unreliable strategies to proven methods of thinking and reasoning;
- grow their confidence with word problems by developing an approach to analyzing problems (identity);
- help them generate an entry point with challenging, confusing, or complex problems (agency);
- build skill with decontextualizing problems by focusing on the actions within them;
- foster perseverance by teaching a strategy for helping one get unstuck (agency); and
- reinforce an essential reasoning skill that can be transferred to other learning situations.

What to Do

1. Pose a problem to students.
2. Give students time to individually think about the problem. Ask them to ask themselves questions like:
   - » What do I know about the problem? What is it about?
   - » What's happening in the problem? What is it about?
   - » What could I do to solve the problem? What equation could I use?
3. Have partners share their ideas about the problem.
4. Bring the class together to discuss the problem. During discussion, be sure to highlight context, action, numbers, and other important features about the problems.
5. Then, unveil a similar, but different problem.
6. Have students independently identify how the second problem is similar to and different from the first.
7. Have partners discuss their ideas and encourage them to think about the context and actions of the problem.
8. Bring the class together again to talk about their ideas.
9. After the class discussion, ask students how comparing and contrasting two problems can help them solve new problems.

Something to Think About: Scaffolding the Routine

Scaffolding routines increases access to these important experiences. Remember that scaffolds should be temporary. However, there isn't a set number of experiences before you should take them away. The decision is based solely on your students' needs. It is likely a good idea to remove them when you notice that students are using them mindlessly, when the scaffold is becoming another procedure to complete, or when students go back to the scaffold after they have already made sense of the problem or even solved it.

Charting student thinking is a good way to scaffold these routines because it documents ideas without causing students to keep too many thoughts in their working memory. With this routine, a traditional Venn diagram is an excellent tool to record and organize ideas. Other ways to scaffold this routine might be to first have students compare very familiar things like a basketball and a soccer ball, a dog and a cat, or snow and rain. This helps students understand the process for examining two different word problems. Recording ideas on sticky notes or lapboards is a good move too. Having students do this first will help them remember it and focus their thoughts when they share.

SAME AND DIFFERENT (VARIATIONS): DIFFERENT POSSIBILITIES FOR MODIFYING

This routine is possibly the most important for you to modify. Simply, there are many different things you want students to consider when comparing two different problems. The dog treat example shows how two problems can be identical except for the numbers used. But you can change the contexts, actions, numbers, number types, and much more to provide rich, diverse experiences. As you modify, think about what you've noticed as students solve problems. If you see that they are grabbing numbers and adding, provide two problems with different questions or actions. If you see that they struggle when numbers become larger, pose two problems that are identical except for the numbers used. The following are just some of the ways that you can modify to harness the power of this routine.

Variation A: Changing the Operation

Variation A is one of the best ways to modify this routine. The first problem is a subtraction problem with a known start and change. The second is a multiplication problem with an unknown product. Mentioning the pack, the number of bottles, and including the same name are intentional similarities. In this example, you want fourth-grade students to articulate how and why the operations are different. In a primary example, you might change the second problem to read "Dax put 17 bottles on a table. There were 24 bottles in a pack already on the table. How many bottles were on the table now?" While the two problems aren't quite as similar, they do provoke students to think about how 17 is subtracted in one problem and multiplied in another.

A

Dax gave out 17 bottles of water. There were 24 bottles in the pack. How many more water bottles could Dax give out?

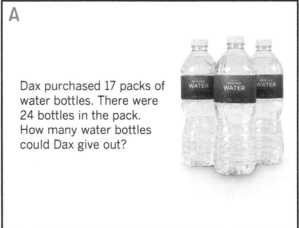

A

Dax purchased 17 packs of water bottles. There were 24 bottles in the pack. How many water bottles could Dax give out?

Credit: Xacto/istockphoto.com

Variation B: Same Problem, Different Contexts

Sometimes the context of a problem is a barrier to student solutions. Contexts can be challenging due to each students' unique culture and experience. You can modify this routine to offer problems with different contexts. In this example, the two problems are essentially identical comparison problems. The context in one compares cola and diet cola and the other compares two different candy bars. The "store" context is shared here for simplistic vocabulary and familiarity. You could change the context to a school fundraiser, sales at a soccer game, or something else for greater relevance. Listen for students who note that they are the same problems because they give the same numbers in the same order. This is accurate but you also want to be sure that students recognize that the two quantities are being compared. When using this version of the routine, work to establish the equation that would be used for solving both problems and help students see how the numbers and operation connect explicitly to both.

B

A store sold 98 cases of cola and 53 cases of diet cola. What is the difference in the number of cases sold?

B

A store sold 98 cases of candy bars with nuts and 53 cases candy bars without nuts. What is the difference in the number of candy bars?

Soda can credit: scanrail/istockphoto.com, Candy bar credit: mbbirdy/istockphoto.com

NOTES

Variation C: Compare Language

The way a problem is phrased can distract or confuse any of us. Perception and inference mingle with prior knowledge and experience to generate comprehension. A subtle turn of phrase, change in number, or change in the order of action can be enough to completely stall the problem-solving process. This example shows how you can use two problems to help students broaden their word problem experience. In both examples, bottles are being put on a table, creating an addition problem. But how each problem is phrased creates a slightly different order of addends. Also note that the way the question is phrased is different.

C

Kai put 37 bottles of water on a table that already had 39 bottles of water on it. How many bottles were on the table when Kai was finished?

C

There were 28 bottles of water on the table. Kai put 57 bottles on the table. How many were on the table when Kai was done?

Credit: Xacto/istockphoto.com

NOTES

Variation D: Changing Number Types

That first example seems ridiculous unless you are thinking about batches made at a factory! The real point of this variation and example is to show how the routine can be used to help students make sense of context and operation when different number types, namely fractions, are introduced in fourth and fifth grade. In this example, you want students to talk about group size (6 pounds) and the number of groups (4 batches). Help them think about what the problem looks like and the equation that they would attach to it. Then, introduce the second problem that is almost the exact same. The only difference now is that the group size has changed from 6 to $\frac{1}{5}$. And as you suspect, this same approach can be used with different operations, decimals, or problems where both numbers are fractions.

D

A batch of yogurt calls for 6 pounds of berries. How many pounds are in 4 batches of yogurt?

D

A batch of yogurt calls for $\frac{1}{5}$ pounds of berries. How many pounds are in 4 batches of yogurt?

Credit: Yasonya/istockphoto.com

NOTES

Variation E: Three Problems

It makes sense to modify this routine to have students compare more than two problems. When doing so, you can choose to have students focus on two of the three to compare. Or, you can have them think about all three at the same time. In this example, the contexts are similar, and all three begin with the same number of students. Discussion about these three problems can become quite rich as students talk about what is happening, the resulting operations, the related equations, and, ultimately, the different solutions. Keep in mind that this is just one example of different problems. You could swap out the last problem with, "64 students are on the bus. 37 get on the bus at the next stop. How many are on the bus?" This problem is very similar to the first with a different number of students getting on the bus. With this change, you could focus on the difference in situation when students get off the bus.

E

64 students are on the bus. 27 get on the bus at the next stop. How many are on the bus?

E

64 students are on the bus. 27 get off the bus at the first stop. How many are left on the bus?

E

64 students are on the bus. There are 4 buses with the same number of students. How many students are there altogether?

Credit: suprun/istockphoto.com

Variation F: One-Step and Two-Step Problems

Same and Different is excellent for introducing two-step problems to primary students or strengthening older students' skill with them. Simply pose a one-step problem and have students discuss it. Then, present a second problem that triggers another action or step. In the example, you notice that the number of treats and the number eaten remain the same. You want your students to speak to that during discussion. You also want them to note that the question is the exact same and that the idea of the problem is to find how many treats remain. Your students should be able to home in on the notion that the second will have fewer because another puppy ate more. Discussion about the equations used to solve each problem could be very interesting. It's likely that most students will argue that you subtract the number eaten each time. But it's possible that a student might speak to combining the number eaten before subtracting, offering yet another way that differences might bubble up in the routine.

F

Sam added 50 treats to her dog's toy. One puppy ate 13 of the treats. How many treats were left in the toy?

F

Sam added 50 treats to her dog's toy. One puppy ate 13 of the treats. Another puppy ate 22 of the treats. How many treats were left in the toy?

Credit: clubfoto/istockphoto.com

NOTES

Variation G: Students Create Their Own Comparisons

It can be challenging for students to create a problem when only given numbers or an equation. There is a lot for them to think about that can muddy the process. In this variation of Same and Different, you pose a problem for students to work with and discuss. Then, you have them craft a new question, creating a new problem to compare to the original. In other words, you take away the question and have them write a new one. Have students share their different problems and choose one student-generated example to compare with your original problem. Instead of having them create a new question to compare, you could give the exact same problem without the numbers. In this example, the second problem wouldn't include the number of pages for each book and students would be charged with creating them instead.

G

Kirby's favorite book is 395 pages. Nick's favorite book is 413 pages. Gina's favorite book is 525 pages. How much shorter is Kirby's book than Gina's?

G

Kirby's favorite book is 395 pages. Nick's favorite book is 413 pages. Gina's favorite book is 525 pages.

Credit: Fototocam/istockphoto.com

NOTES

Variation H: Comparing Inequalities and Equations

Same and Different is the perfect routine for comparing inequalities and equations. To do this, you can use a problem like the one on the top or in the center and compare them with the problem on the bottom. The routine is also a good tool for seeing how inequalities can change as well. Take a look at the inequalities on the top and in the center. They will have a common feature of adding 25 and a comparison of greater than or equal to 300. Of course, there is a clear difference as well. Seeing these situations side by side helps students make better sense of problems and the symbolic representations of them. And remember, you're surrounded with good examples. You can use any equation or inequality word problem from your mathematics series. Simply write a new one to compare by changing some feature of the original.

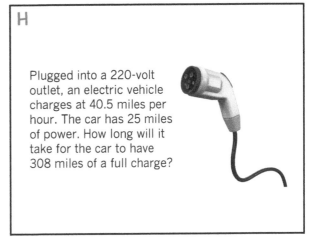

H

Plugged into a 110-volt outlet, an electric vehicle charges at 4 miles per hour. The car has 25 miles of power. How long will it take for the car to have at least 300 miles of charge?

H

Plugged into a 220-volt outlet, an electric vehicle charges at 45.5 miles per hour. The car has 25 miles of power. How long will it take for the car to have at least 300 miles of charge?

H

Plugged into a 220-volt outlet, an electric vehicle charges at 40.5 miles per hour. The car has 25 miles of power. How long will it take for the car to have 308 miles of a full charge?

Credit: Nerthuz/istockphoto.com

WHAT'S THE SITCH?

About the Routine

A good math friend and colleague often playfully says, "What's the sitch?" when she encounters a problem or situation at work that she needs to think deeply about. She's really asking, "What's the situation?" in a poor attempt to be clever, hip, or cool. Though it might not be any of those, "What's the sitch?" does have a charm to it, causing it to stick with me through the years. In fact, colleagues latch on to it and even find themselves saying it. It turns out to be the perfect question for students to ask when they solve problems. Problem solving is about analyzing a situation, taking into account all that is involved, including contexts, numbers, situations, extra information, and so on. As your students come across problems, you want them to pause and ask themselves certain questions that help them analyze the problem leading to possible solution paths. You might even imagine this analytical approach as a flowchart highlighted in Figure 8.1.

This routine frames much of the analytical conversation you want your students to have metacognitively. It begins by asking students to think about the action between the things in the problem before thinking about the details of those things in the problem and ultimately the operation they might use to solve it. Note that there are steps to the process, but the approach itself is not algorithmic. The individual acts based on the questions and answers that they ask themselves. There are no artificial steps like highlighting the keyword or circling the numbers.

There are 176 cars in the parking lot and 114 empty spaces. How many cars can park in the lot at one time?

Credit: pigphoto/istockphoto.com

The Thinking Chart (that follows the directions) shows the process for addition and subtraction problems, and the variations show a process for multiplication and division as well as a version for all four operations.

This routine comes with the added benefit of helping students develop analytical skills. It also provides experience with different problem situations (or structures) that you read about in Part 1 (pages 12 and 13). You want students to work with all sorts of problems and have strategy and skill to solve them. Making sense of the structure is one of those skills! But remember, elementary students shouldn't be required to identify and name problem structures.

online resources

All routines can be downloaded for your use at
https://qrs.ly/3cemjnt

How This Routine Helps With Problem Solving

This routine builds problem-solving skill by providing opportunities for students to

- learn how to analyze problems,
- practice analytical questions in a group setting so that they can eventually use them independently and metacognitively,
- develop their own process for analyzing problems (identity, agency),
- experience a variety of problem-solving structures,
- reinforce conceptual understanding of operations, and
- acquire a strategy for getting unstuck when solving a problem.

What to Do

1. Create an anchor chart of the routine's Thinking Chart (Figure 8.1).

2. Pose a problem and give students a few moments to examine it.

3. Ask about what is happening in the problem (phase 1 in Figure 8.1). Have students discuss and come to agreement. In the parking lot example, students should say that they are putting together the spaces with cars and the empty spaces to find out how many spaces there are in the parking lot altogether. Note that you can cover the anchor chart so that only one phase is showing, or show the entire chart at once.

4. Have students reread the problem to themselves (optional). Ask students the questions in phase

2 that are triggered by the answer in phase 1. In the parking lot example, students should say they are putting together the spaces with cars and the empty spaces to find the total spaces.

5. Have students reread the problem to themselves (optional). Ask students the questions in phase 3 that are triggered by the answers in phase 2. In the parking lot example, students should say that they would add because they are putting two things together.

6. Reveal a correct equation for the problem. Connect the numbers and operation in the equation back to the problem as well as the questions (and answers) in each of the three phases.

FIGURE 8.1 WHAT'S THE SITCH THINKING CHART

1

Is the problem . . .

- Adding To -or- Putting Together
- Taking From -or- Taking Apart
- Comparing Things

2

- What is being added? Whate is being put together? / What is the total?
- What is the start? What is taken? What is left? / What was the whole? What is a part? What is a part?
- Which is bigger? Which is smaller? / How much bigger or how much smaller?

3

To solve, I will

- Add or Subtract? Why?
- Add or Subtract? Why?
- Add or Subtract? Why?

Something to Think About: Whole-School Agreements

Whole-school agreements are decisions that an entire school takes on for a cohesive, coherent mathematics experience that benefits each and every student (Karp et al., 2021). Schools need agreements about the language used, the "tricks" they won't teach, the shortcuts they'll avoid because they don't always work, the strategies for computation that students will learn, and what common notations and generalizations will be used and encouraged. Whole-school agreements about problem solving and problem-solving routines have great value as well.

Agreements about not using keywords or certain acronyms for procedural approaches are necessary. Agreements about using routines consistently, even talking about which routines might be used in different grades, is also helpful. Think about it. Students who learn how to engage with a routine one year are prepared to use it the following years. They have opportunity to deepen their understanding of the experience and are positioned to transfer their skills to new content. Imagine a second grader who works with this routine over the course of the year. Then, when they get to third grade, their teacher continues to use it with addition and subtraction before working in multiplication and division. In fourth grade, they use it for all four operations and then eventually with fractions, decimals, and so on. Repeatedly analyzing problems in the same way undoubtedly yields much more capable problem solvers.

WHAT'S THE SITCH? (VARIATIONS): STRENGTHENING THE PROCESS

Figure 8.1 shows the core process for analyzing a problem. It's a start. There are questions you might add to the process asking students to think about how they might represent the problem or how they'll know if their answer will make sense. As you introduce new problem types, you might have them practice only a certain sequence of questions as shown in the first variation. And, if your students need to work with two-step problems, you might add questions to the sequence. These ideas are captured in the following variations, but they are just a few of the possibilities. Pay attention to your students' problem-solving missteps and try to include questions they can use to better analyze problems and avoid those errors.

NOTES

_____

_____

_____

_____

_____

_____

_____

_____

_____

Variation A: Focus on One Structure

You can modify the routine to focus on one problem type or structure like simply putting things together, taking them apart, or comparing. This is a good idea for isolating a structure so that students can better understand its architecture (e.g., parts and the whole or how one thing is compared to another). And though routines are intended for practicing skills and concepts that students have already learned about, you could use this version to introduce and practice a specific structure. For example, you would pose a comparison problem like the one shown, and your anchor chart would only show a flow for comparison problems. As students show skill with comparison problems, you can use different problem types (e.g., put together) with the comparison questions to see if students argue that the problem isn't a comparison.

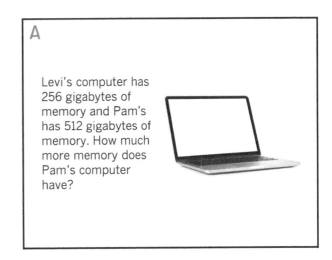

A

Levi's computer has 256 gigabytes of memory and Pam's has 512 gigabytes of memory. How much more memory does Pam's computer have?

Credit: karandaev/istockphoto.com

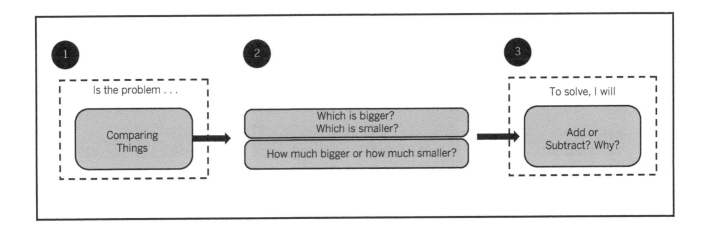

1 — Is the problem . . . Comparing Things →

2 — Which is bigger? Which is smaller? / How much bigger or how much smaller? →

3 — To solve, I will Add or Subtract? Why?

NOTES

Variation B: Multiplication and Division Structures

The same approach used for addition and subtraction can be applied to multiplication and division. To analyze these problems, students can first ask if there are equal groups, arrays, an area, or if things are being compared (note that multiplicative comparison is not introduced until fourth grade in many curricula). Once that is determined, they go on to ask themselves about the groups, group size, and so on. In the flower shop example, students should describe the vases as groups of flowers. They should go on to say that they know how big the groups are (4 red flowers) and the total (56 red flowers), but they don't know how big or how many groups there will be. From there, they could divide 56 by 4 but it would also be fine for students to think multiplication, making groups of 4 and building up to 56.

B

The flower shop puts 4 red flowers in every vase. How many vases will they need if they have 56 red flowers?

Credit: esolla/istockphoto.com

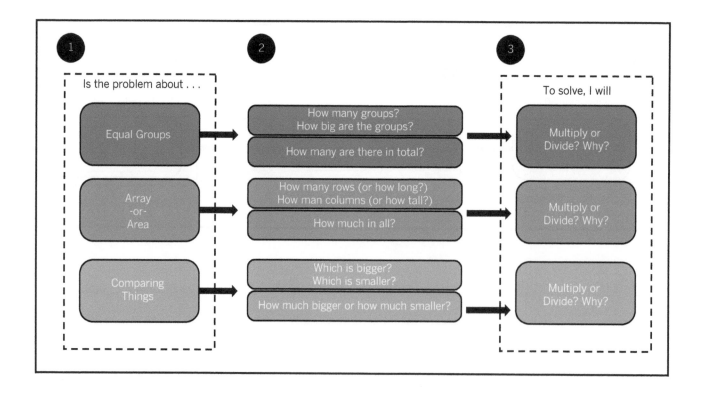

1 Is the problem about . . .

- Equal Groups
- Array -or- Area
- Comparing Things

2
- How many groups? How big are the groups?
- How many are there in total?
- How many rows (or how long?) How man columns (or how tall?)
- How much in all?
- Which is bigger? Which is smaller?
- How much bigger or how much smaller?

3 To solve, I will
- Multiply or Divide? Why?
- Multiply or Divide? Why?
- Multiply or Divide? Why?

Variation C: All Four Operations

A challenge that many teachers face with problem solving is skill association. Skill association is using a skill or operation that has been the focus of instruction most recently to solve any problem a student encounters. Unfortunately, skill association is propped up when word problems are saved for the bottom of a textbook page after students have been practicing a given skill. For example, a second grader might solve a word problem with subtraction because they have been working with subtraction for the past few days. In second grade, the likelihood of success is better because students only know of two operations. This variation of the routine is for students in later grades. As you can see, it begins by having students assess which of the four operations the problem is about before continuing to questions about how the numbers are related, the total, and so on. It is probably a good idea for students to focus on both sets of operations separately before mixing all four within the routine.

C

Asha is working on a 1,000-piece puzzle. By her count, she has 412 pieces left. How many pieces has she placed?

Credit: unstock/istockphoto.com

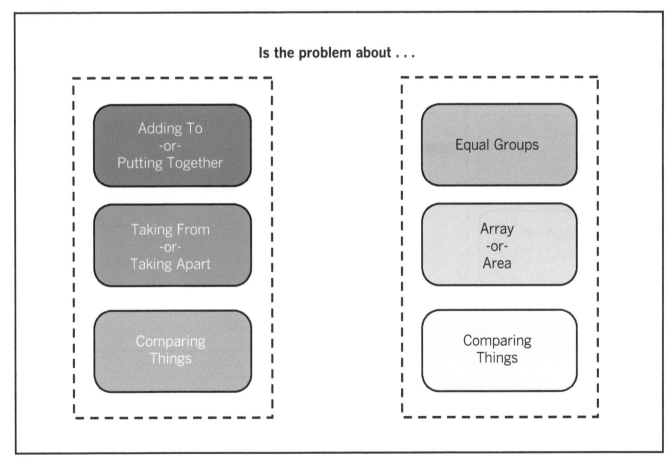

Is the problem about . . .

Adding To
-or-
Putting Together

Taking From
-or-
Taking Apart

Comparing
Things

Equal Groups

Array
-or-
Area

Comparing
Things

Variation D: Adding New Layers

You want your students to practice analyzing problems with this routine. As you notice them comfortably asking and answering the core series of questions, you can begin to add new layers that play important roles in problem solving. The image on the right gives you a sense of some other questions you might ask. Feel free to use "new" questions however you like. For novice problem solvers, you might start with "Do I need a drawing?" and "What is the equation?" Students who do those things well might not need those questions. Instead, you might ask them to estimate a solution, which is certainly helpful with multidigit whole numbers and decimals, as shown in the example.

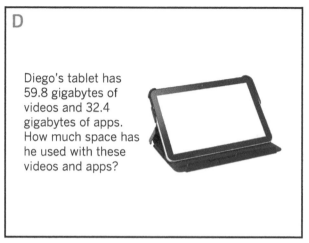

D

Diego's tablet has 59.8 gigabytes of videos and 32.4 gigabytes of apps. How much space has he used with these videos and apps?

Credit: s-cphoto/istockphoto.com

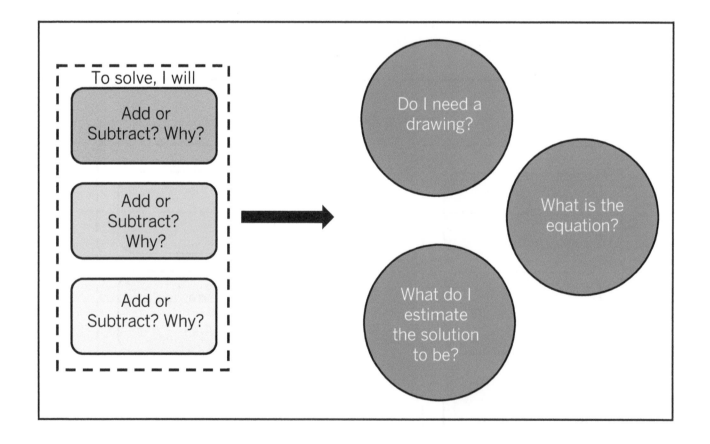

Variation E: Applying the Routine to Different Number Types

Whole-school, even whole-district, agreements to use a routine like this pays dividends over time. A good example of this is when upper elementary and middle school students begin to work with rational numbers. Problems with these numbers can prove challenging, even to students who have shown skill with solving whole number problems. Those students may overlook the basic, familiar structure of a problem because of these seemingly more complicated numbers. They may believe proven strategies no longer work. But students who have had practice analyzing problems in routine ways, year after year, throughout elementary school and into middle school are better positioned for success. They may pause when fractions appear in problems, but they know how to move forward because they know how to analyze a problem. These two problems are good examples. The cargo ship problem poses two mixed numbers with unlike denominators. Identifying that the problem is taking from (unloading cargo from loaded ships) helps them then think about the start, the change, and what's left leading them to determine an operation and a solution path. The reservoir problem mixes a negative decimal and a positive fraction, causing even more experienced students to pause. Before they do anything with the numbers, you want them to think about what is happening. They should talk about how the water level is changing (it's dropping), how they know (negative number), and how long it has been dropping. This can help them imagine or draw the picture of what's occurring. They can then connect the values and determine an equation they might use to solve the problem.

E

$5\frac{1}{2}$ cargo ships docked to be unloaded. $3\frac{3}{4}$ of the ships were unloaded in a day. How much was left to unload?

E

Workers at a reservoir measured a −2.4 meter change in water level per month over a $4\frac{1}{2}$ month drought. How much did the water level change?

Cargo ship credit: bfk92/istockphoto.com; beach image credit: NNehring/istockphoto.com

THEY DID WHAT?

About the Routine

Using worked examples is an effective instructional strategy to help students understand and solve problems (Renkl, 2014; Star & Verschaffel, 2016; Woodward et al., 2018). They help students notice missteps in others' work that they themselves also make (McGinn et al., 2015). You might use several worked examples as part of a full lesson, center, or independent practice. In this routine, one worked example is used for a brief class discussion about what someone did to solve a problem.

Try not to feel overwhelmed by finding worked examples for this routine. There are some easy ways to alleviate the burden. First, don't feel pressure to find the perfect example; any example works! Think carefully about using your students' work during the routine because feedback and criticism can be taken hard. Examples don't have to be authentic student work. You can create them yourself. However, if you prefer that the work is authentic, have a colleague do a problem with their class and make copies of it to discuss with your students. You can reuse examples from year to year. But you also don't have to feature a different problem and a different worked example each day you do the routine. Instead, you could use the dinosaur problem with different worked examples over the course of two or three days.

Worked examples are a way to expose students to ideas without teaching them directly. This worked example shows how a number line could be used to compare the lengths of the two dinosaurs. It even plots those dinosaurs on the number line. Keep in mind that discussion about the worked example should focus on its viability

A T.rex was about 39 feet long A Brachiosaurus was about 71 feet long. How much longer was the Brachiosaurus?

Credit: Kitti Kahotong/istockphoto.com

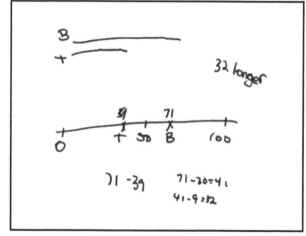

not its correctness. In other words, a student might show their thinking in another way. That doesn't mean the given example is wrong. Also remember, this experience is not about solving the problem, it is about critiquing the reasoning and the solution of someone else.

online resources ▶ All routines can be downloaded for your use at **https://qrs.ly/3cemjnt**

How This Routine Helps With Problem Solving

This routine builds problem-solving skill by providing opportunities for students to

- consider the reasoning of others,
- compare different approaches to solving a problem,
- determine viable alternatives to reasoning and representing,
- develop their approaches by examining the thinking of others,
- monitor their progress while working through a problem, and
- think about the clarity of their own explanations.

What to Do

1. Pose a problem and give students a few moments to examine it.

2. Ask if they have ideas about what they might do to solve it and have them share their thoughts with a partner. Optional: Share these early thoughts about the problem as a class before the next step.

3. Display a worked example for the problem, giving time for students to examine it as well.

4. Discuss the worked example with your class using questions like:

   » What do you notice about this person's work?

   » How is the problem represented in the person's work?

   » What do you like about the person's work?

   » What would you do differently than this person?

   » How is this work like your own thinking?

   » What's missing from this work?

   » Why do you think the student did _____?

   » What advice would you give this person?

   » What can this work help you remember when solving a problem on your own?

You can choose to facilitate the discussion in the way that best suits you. For example, you could pose one question, have students discuss with a partner and then as a whole group, and then move on to a new question. Or you could discuss many of the questions as a whole group without having each individual question discussed with partners first. A helpful tip for efficient, effective conversations is to create an anchor chart with the questions you use for this routine. Then, highlight the two or three you plan to ask in a given experience. That way, students can prepare for the whole-group conversation before it happens, possibly meaning less wait time when you ask those questions to the group.

Something to Think About: More Than Just the Right Answer

The right answer matters, but when you're learning to solve problems it's not the only thing that matters. Looking at others' thinking is a way to emphasize this. Yet the right answer infiltrates other aspects of teaching and learning math, including assessment and grading. When grading problem solving, examine the reasoning and justification as well as the answer. Calculation errors happen often, and you must be careful that they don't tarnish the good, meaningful work that your students have accomplished. These rubrics are adapted from *Answers to Your Biggest Questions About Teaching Elementary Math* (SanGiovanni et al., 2021). The first one is a good tool for you to assess your students' problem-solving development. The bottom one is for student self-assessment.

Got It	Getting There		Not Yet
Advance Extend Enrich	Reinforce Practice	Reteach	Reteach
Student demonstrates full understanding of the problem. • The solution is correct. • Reasoning is provided through pictures, words, or numbers/equations. • Justification is complete. • Minor errors may be present but do not impact the response.	Student demonstrates understanding of the problem. • The solution may be incorrect but can be attributed to a computational error rather than flawed logic. • Reasoning is provided but may not be complete.	Student demonstrates some understanding of the problem. • The solution may be correct but it is situational or coincidental. • Reasoning is based on flawed logic or misconception of the concept yielding a correct answer.	Student demonstrates no understanding of the problem. • The solution is incorrect. • There is no justification or reasoning. • Numbers or terms are disconnected from the prompt or the prompt is restated.

Source: SanGiovanni, 2021

I Get It	I'm Starting to Get it	I Don't Get It Yet
❑ I explained my thinking clearly. ❑ I used pictures, numbers, or words to explain my thinking. ❑ My strategy works.	❑ I think I explained my thinking clearly. ❑ I used pictures, numbers, and words to explain my thinking. ❑ I am pretty sure my strategy works but there might be a better one.	❑ I am not sure how to explain my thinking yet. ❑ I am not sure how to use pictures, numbers, or words for this yet. ❑ I think my strategy works or ❑ I'm not sure of a strategy for this yet.

Source: SanGiovanni, 2021

THEY DID WHAT? (VARIATIONS): DIFFERENT WORKED EXAMPLES

Worked examples can be adapted in all sorts of ways to target specific areas of need or to create new enthusiasm for the activity. Worked examples typically fall into three categories. There are correct worked examples, which show accurate reasoning with full explanations. There are incorrect worked examples that have flawed logic and incorrect solutions. Then there are partially worked examples, which can be anything from a correct process that hasn't been completed to a complete process with a hollow or unclear explanation. The following variations show how these different types can be worked into the routine. Don't settle for just these. Feel free to mix-and-match, create, and adjust worked examples to generate a customized experience for your students.

Variation A: Samples With Multiplication

This multiplication variation would work well in third or fourth grade. It provides much to think and talk about. First, the problem doesn't seem to have enough information because there is only one number (Routine 15: TMI, page 143). The drawing shows chairs without the same detail in the picture or of chairs in general. This is fine and important for students to notice because some are compelled to draw highly detailed, inefficient diagrams of problems. A good discussion could be had about the "32 legs," asking students where they think that number comes from and how they could make the explanation clearer for the reader. Questions about labels on the drawing or accompanying equations would also be good to include. This example also is a moment to remind you that multiplication problems are often posed as equal group situations like the one shown here. Be sure that you include arrays, area, and comparison problems.

There are 8 chairs at a table. How many legs are there?

Credit: davidnay/istockphoto.com

Variation B: Wrong Answer, Right Process

This variation encourages you to use work samples that have the wrong answer but the correct process. Doing so reinforces that process and thinking are as important as the right answer in mathematics class. These variations could spark lively debates. In this example, the work uses partial products so some students will question why the work multiplied twice. Others will wonder where the numbers come from because there is no obvious 0.5 in the problem. And some might be confused by two operations when surely one is all that is needed for this problem. Their debate opens the door for talk about how to clearly represent their thinking—especially when they make a calculation error. The calculation error in this problem results in a house cat weighing 61.6 pounds! That is a big cat, and it's entirely unreasonable. Experiences with the right process and wildly wrong answers is another way to incorporate discussions about anticipating answers and considering reasonableness discussed in other routines like Routine 17, Is It Reasonable? (page 158).

B

Jinx the cat weighs 8.8 pounds.

Chubs weighs $2\frac{1}{2}$ times more.

How much does Chubs weigh?

Credit: CHUYN/istockphoto.com

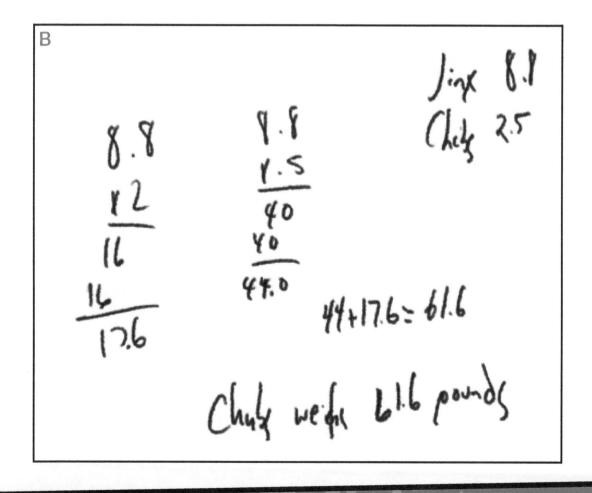

Variation C: Incorrect Examples

Incorrect examples offer opportunity for students to critically examine the work of others. That practice can help them recognize aspects of their own work that can be unclear or inaccurate. In fact, you can be clever by creating incorrect examples that mimic reasoning, representational, or calculation flaws that you notice in your students' work. This is helpful because it can be hard for students (and adults) to see flaws in their thinking as they work a problem. Through this routine, they can see similar, flawed thinking through a completely different lens. You can use this routine to review situations that students need to practice more, like multiplication with fractions. In this example, the work finds the difference of the two cats, but the problem calls for finding the amount one cat eats in a week or seven days. These examples allow for students to think about how and why errors come about. In this example, they might say that the person probably subtracted because they saw two cats and two fractions and figured you were comparing the two.

C

Tia the cat eats $\frac{2}{3}$ of a cup of food each day and Frisky eats $\frac{1}{4}$ of a cup. How much does Tia eat in week?

Credit: CHUYN/istockphoto.com

C

Tia   Frisky

$\frac{2}{3}$ − $\frac{1}{4}$?

$\frac{8}{12} - \frac{3}{12} = \frac{5}{12}$ Tia eats $\frac{5}{12}$ more in a day.

Variation D: Partially Completed Samples

A partially worked example is one in which the problem has been started but isn't complete. At first glance, it might appear incorrect to students. In the example, it looks like a representation for 6 × 4 or 24 ÷ 4. To avoid this challenge, be clear. Tell students that the problem has been started and isn't finished. Ask them to make sense of what has been done so far, where they think the individual was going with their work, and what is left to do. As you can imagine, this can lead to very rich discussions. It can also train students to monitor their own thinking as they work through a problem.

D

There are 4 dumplings sold in an order. 48 dumplings were sold at lunchtime. How many orders were sold?

Credit: JackF/istockphoto.com

D

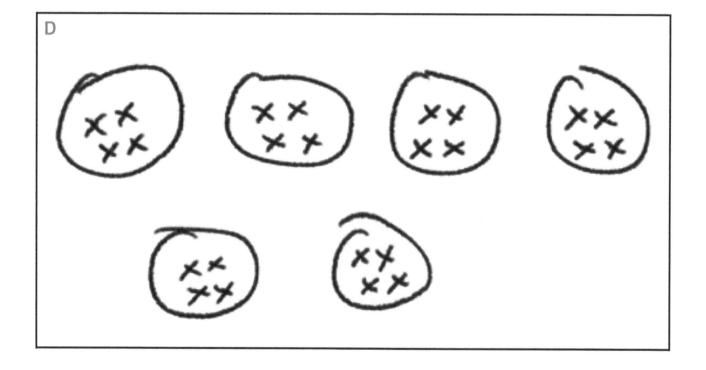

Variation E: Two-Step Problems

Like variations of other routines in this book, They Did What? works well with two-step problems. You can use correct, incorrect, or partially completed examples with these problems. With an example like this, consider beginning the discussion by asking students what they notice about the worked example. Listen for thoughts about the labels, operations, and other details of interest. Ask them how the work connects directly to the problem. And because this problem calls for two steps, be sure that discussion highlights what those two steps are and why they're necessary. Sometimes when solving a two-step problem, the steps can be reversed without affecting the solution (see the next variation). But that isn't always the case. So, during discussion of these, ask if the steps could be reversed. Here, the student multiplies to find the amount of wood needed for thin pieces and legs, then adds those amounts together. After discussing the work, you could ask students if it is possible to add the pieces of wood per chair and then multiply by eight. Be careful; reversing the process doesn't always work. That doesn't mean you should avoid the conversation. Instead, you want them to work with diverse problems so that through experience and discussion they recognize the differences independently.

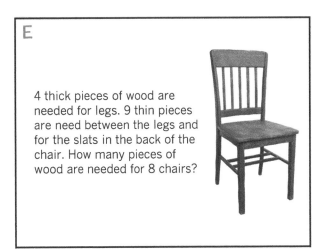

E

4 thick pieces of wood are needed for legs. 9 thin pieces are need between the legs and for the slats in the back of the chair. How many pieces of wood are needed for 8 chairs?

Credit: davidnay/istockphoto.com

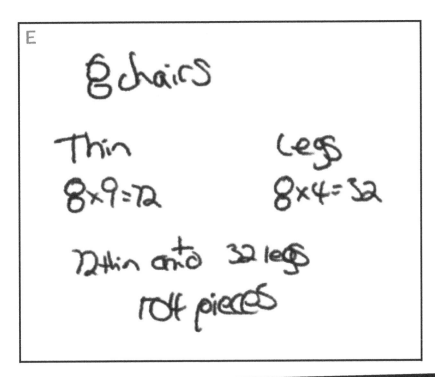

E

8 chairs

Thin
8×9=72

Legs
8×4=32

72 thin and 32 legs
104 pieces

Variation F: Comparing Two Different Samples

Two work samples call for a different discussion to unfold during the routine. With two, your students can compare and contrast different approaches. They can discuss which makes more sense to them, which is clearer, and possibly which is more efficient. The left example shows a student who found the difference of the two dinosaurs (54) and then used partial products to find the number of pounds. The right example finds the weight in pounds in each dinosaur then subtracts. Both are correct of course, but the one on the left may not be a natural approach for your students. Exposing it to them increases the likelihood of them using it or something similar in the future. And though these two examples are correct, you could use any combination of examples, such as a correct and an incorrect, a correct and a partially correct, two incorrect examples, and so on.

F

Dionsaur	Length (feet)	Weight (tons)
Brachiosaurus	69	58
Brontosaurus	72	15
Apatosaurus	75	22
Titanosaur	121	69

There are 2,000 pounds in a ton. How many more pounds was a Titanosaur than a Brontosaurus?

Credit: Kitti Kahotong/istockphoto.com

F

$69 - 15 = 54$

$54 \times 2 = 108$

$108 \times 1,000 = 108,000$

It was 108,000 more pounds.

F

$$\begin{array}{r} 2,000 \\ \times\ 69 \\ \hline 18,000 \\ 12,000 \\ \hline 138,000 \end{array}$$

$$\begin{array}{r} 2,000 \\ \times\ 15 \\ \hline 10,000 \\ +20,00 \\ \hline 30,000 \end{array}$$

$$\begin{array}{r} 138,000 \\ -\ 30,000 \\ \hline 108,000 \text{ more pounds} \end{array}$$

THIS NUMBER, THAT NUMBER

About the Routine

Solving a simpler problem is a traditional problem-solving strategy taught to students. As you know, the goal of this strategy is to rethink a problem in a more simplistic way. It isn't about making the solving easier, but it makes the comprehension of the context and what it's asking more accessible. It could be that the problem is restated in fewer words with less distractions. Most often, solving a simpler problem is about changing the numbers in it so that it is easier to think about. It can be a powerful approach when problems have more complicated numbers like fractions in elementary school and rational numbers in middle school. It is also an asset to students whose computational skills are still developing and who are likely to get overwhelmed when they think about computing multidigit numbers.

Though solving a simpler problem is a useful strategy, it isn't necessarily a strategy that students take hold of and use. Your students' understanding and skill with this strategy is evident in its appearance (or not) in their work. Do you see them use it? Are you the only one who mentions it from time to time? Do they use it as a tool for getting unstuck? Why not?

You likely have taught or at least talked about solving a simpler problem, making a problem less wordy, or swapping out the numbers. But often that discussion happens after struggle with a problem has occurred and mental fatigue has set in. It's possible that any discussion about the strategy wasn't heard or understood. This routine provides a practice opportunity for rethinking problems with simpler numbers. Students discuss a simple

Weight of Different Bears

Black Bear	3 pounds
Grizzly Bear	7 pounds
Kodiak Bear	12 pounds
Polar Bear	11 pounds

How much less does the black bear weigh compared to the Kodiak bear?

Weight of Different Bears

Black Bear	346 pounds
Grizzly Bear	751 pounds
Kodiak Bear	1,203 pounds
Polar Bear	1,188 pounds

How much less does the black bear weigh compared to the Kodiak bear?

Credit: geyzer/istockphoto.com

problem before seeing the same problem with more complicated numbers. Then, afterward, they reflect about how the process could be reversed if they were first trying to solve the more complicated problem. The intent is that discussion, along with practice, will help students assimilate this strategy into their problem-solving toolbox.

 All routines can be downloaded for your use at
https://qrs.ly/3cemjnt

How This Routine Helps With Problem Solving

This routine builds problem-solving skill by providing opportunities for students to

- experience the problem-solving strategy of using simpler numbers or solving a simpler problem,
- reframe problems so that they can focus on the meaning and question,
- gain confidence working with problems that have unfriendly numbers (identity),
- add a new strategy for them to use to get themselves unstuck when solving a problem (agency), and
- determine when to use the strategy of simpler numbers for solving a problem (agency).

What to Do

1. Pose an initial problem with simplistic numbers (top problem in the example).

2. Have students think independently about the problem, making sense of it, determining the question, identifying a solution path, and so on.

3. Have partners discuss their ideas about the problem.

4. Reveal the second problem with more complicated numbers (bottom problem in the example).

5. Give students time to independently examine the two problems.

6. Bring the whole group together to discuss the two problems. Use questions like:

   » How are the problems the same and different?

   » How did your work with the first problem help you think about the second problem?

   » How did the simple numbers help you think about the problem?

   » How could thinking about easier numbers help if you were stuck with a problem that had harder numbers?

   » What if you saw the problem with the harder numbers first and you weren't sure what to do? How could changing the numbers help?

Something to Think About: Why So Many Routines?

As you have read about the different routines in this book, you may have asked yourself, "Why are there so many routines?" It's a good question with a few different right answers. First and foremost, you want problem solving and discussion about it to be dynamic and vibrant. You want (and need) your students to be enthusiastic and engaged. The same routine done every day loses its luster. When overdone, even the best routine becomes boring and played out. Having a large collection to choose from alleviates this challenge.

Because problem solving is about thinking and sense making, it's important to practice different skills through a variety of routines. Using the same protocol repeatedly could inadvertently insinuate an expected process for working with problems. It's also important to note that everyone thinks differently. A routine might work well to develop a certain skill while others need a different routine to realize the goal. Teachers are different too. You might prefer certain routines while colleagues prefer others. The intent is to give you many options to meet the needs of your students through the approaches that are most comfortable and engaging.

THIS NUMBER, THAT NUMBER (VARIATIONS): GRADE LEVEL CONTEXT

These problem-solving routines work across grades. You might have to tinker a bit to get the best match for your grade level and your students. Variations give you some ideas about how you might do that. Some variations show how a routine would work with second or third graders working with multidigit whole numbers (Variation C). Other variations show how a routine can work with fractions or decimals (Variation E). In other instances, variations reverse a routine, challenging students to create contexts, numbers, or questions, increasing the level of cognitive demand and rigor. And yet, the variations presented for each routine are just starting points. You can, and should, explore other ways to modify routines that work best for your students.

Variation A: Reverse the Order of Number Complexity

This variation is the opposite of the first offering, which began with simplistic numbers so that students can really grapple with making sense of the problem. Then, they see the same problem with more complicated numbers. Here, you would begin with the more complicated numbers (four-digit numbers in this example) and move to the simpler problem. Don't have students solve the initial problem. Instead, have them only think about what is happening. Avoid a group discussion. Hold that after the simpler problem is presented and they have time to think about how it compares to the one with more complex numbers. Have students share their observations, and then guide the conversation to conclude that both problems are essentially the same. They ask the same question only the second problem uses numbers that are more comfortable. Close with a discussion about how "easier" numbers can help students attack problems that might seem harder. In fact, this version might do better to drive home the point of simplifying numbers as a means for entering a problem or getting unstuck.

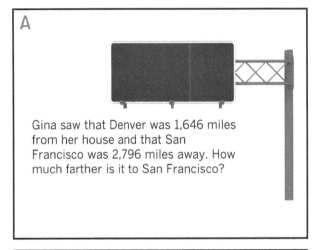

Gina saw that Denver was 1,646 miles from her house and that San Francisco was 2,796 miles away. How much farther is it to San Francisco?

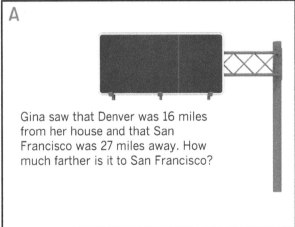

Gina saw that Denver was 16 miles from her house and that San Francisco was 27 miles away. How much farther is it to San Francisco?

Credit: alexsl/istockphoto.com

Variation B: Problems Without Numbers

An alternative to using simpler numbers is to think about the problem without numbers. Numberless Word Problems are a great way to do this (Bushart, n.d.). With this approach, you present a problem without its numbers. Students make sense of the problem. Consider having them retell it or create a representation of it. Then, introduce the "real" problem with numbers. Have students work to transfer their understanding from the problem without numbers to the problem with numbers. At the end, you want them to reflect on how removing numbers can help them understand the problem. Once they understand what a problem is about, they can go back into the problem with the numbers having ideas about how to solve it. Be sure to recognize that with many problems you can't simply remove the numbers because it won't read well. This could create an artificial barrier to student sense making. In the example, the numberless problem on the left adds the word *some* in both instances.

B

A race was some laps long. A kart raced some laps before it needed more gas. How many laps were left after it got more gas?

B

A race was 125 laps long. A kart raced 71 laps before it needed more gas. How many laps were left after it got more gas?

B

A building is some meters tall with a foundation of some meters deep. What is the total length of the building?

B

A building is 43.7 meters tall with a foundation of −38.5 meters deep. What is the total length of the building?

Car image credit: Fotonen/istockphoto.com; building image credit: Maxiphoto/istockphoto.com

Variation C: Single Digit to Two Digit

It might seem that solving a simpler problem works best with complicated numbers that appear in later grades. But for young students, two- and three-digit numbers are just as challenging to process as a signed fraction (e.g., $-\frac{3}{4}$). For them, problems with two- and three-digit numbers can feel daunting. This variation shows how the routine might work in earlier grades. Here, the problems show how you would begin with a simple problem (top example) and move to the more complicated problem (bottom example). You could reverse the order of the problems as described in Variation A. In this example, the single-digit numbers in the top problem are the same as their tens place counterparts in the other problem. Though any simpler number can be used, lopping off trailing digits might be a good way for students to make simpler numbers on their own. Another benefit to using this routine in early grades is that it builds skill and comfort with a reliable problem-solving strategy that students can call on in later grades.

C
Juice Sold by Day

Day	Jugs Sold
Monday	5
Tuesday	4
Wednesday	6
Thursday	1

How many jugs were sold between Tuesday and Wednesday?

C
Juice Sold by Day

Day	Jugs Sold
Monday	50
Tuesday	47
Wednesday	61
Thursday	16

How many jugs were sold between Tuesday and Wednesday?

Credit: Jamesmcq24/istockphoto.com

NOTES

Variation D: Symbols Instead of Numbers

Using symbols to represent unknowns is fundamental in mathematics. Work with this idea begins in elementary school. This variation works similarly to the numberless problem version (Variation B). The obvious difference is that letters are used. This variation is likely not the best place to begin work with this routine, but it is a good extension for students who need more challenge. After students learn about unknowns in your curriculum, you can use this variation to strengthen their understanding of them. To maximize the effect, after students discuss their interpretation and solution paths for the problem, have them write equations to represent it. For example, the problem on the top could be recorded as $t + c = ?$ and the one on the right could be $34 + 61 = ?$. As mentioned, you could reverse the presentation of the two problems, moving from a problem with numbers to one with unknowns.

D

Tre finished t laps and Chris finished c laps. How many laps did they finish together?

D

Tre finished 34 laps and Chris finished 61 laps. How many laps did they finish together?

Credit: Fotonen/istockphoto.com

NOTES

_____

_____

_____

_____

_____

_____

_____

_____

_____

_____

_____

Variation E: Fractions to Decimals

Some people find that decimals are much easier to work with than fractions. This variation is for students who have that viewpoint. It is a practice opportunity for replacing fractions with "simpler" decimals. This is clearly not a variation for young grades. When using this variation, use common fractions, such as halves, quarters, tenths, and so on. Use these so that the focus of the work is not on mechanically converting fractions to decimals but instead moving between them swiftly to create more simple problems. You might even consider providing an anchor chart along with the routine that captures those common fractions and their decimal equivalents. This variation also serves as an example of how these routines can be used cleverly to practice a range of skills and concepts in addition to the problem-solving strategy that you are focused on.

E

$5\frac{1}{2}$ gallons of apple juice were bought for a class party. $3\frac{1}{4}$ gallons were left. How much apple juice was drank during the party?

E

5.5 gallons of apple juice were bought for a class party. 3.25 gallons were left. How much apple juice was drank during the party?

Credit: Jamesmcq24/istockphoto.com

NOTES

Variation F: Students Change the Numbers

The goal of this routine is to shape student comfort and competency with changing challenging problems into something simpler. The other variations present two problems that illustrate this idea. This variation is subtly different. Here, you pose a problem and have students pick the simpler numbers they would use in it. This creates student agency and autonomy through their own number selection. After students make their modifications, have them share out to hear the different approaches to changing the numbers. Listen carefully to ensure that they are in fact using simpler numbers. Question how the new numbers could help when you aren't sure about their changes. In this example, students might change the problem to 6 in a box and 6 boxes in a crate though there are many different viable options. This example also shows what the routine might look like with a multiplication problem.

F

There are 64 fortune cookies in a box and 60 boxes in a crate. How many cookies are in the crate?

Credit: PicturePartners/istockphoto.com

Variation G: Choosing Numbers

One last variation for This Number, That Number uses different options for the numbers within the problem. Students choose the set of numbers (e.g., first number 8 with first number 5) they want to work with to solve the problem. It does well to provide insight into the numbers they are most comfortable working with (Land et al., 2014). The twist here is that you want students to discuss what the problem is about and how it is solved regardless of the numbers they picked. During discussion, you want students to really understand that the answer is the result of what the problem is asking and that a solution will change based on the numbers used but the general architecture of a problem as well as that solution path are unchanged. Also note that the fourth option in each set is a symbol. That is an option you may include or omit relative to your students mathematical maturity and readiness.

G

There were {8, 81, 816, m} male bears and {5, 67, 719, f} female bears in a national park. How many bears were there?

Credit: geyzer/istockphoto.com

IMAGINE THAT

About the Routine

You have likely been taken aback when asking a struggling student to draw a picture and you heard them say, "I don't know how to." You have asked, "What do you think it looks like?" and been met with puzzled looks. You have probably tried to start a picture for students asking them to connect it to the problem or to finish drawing it for you only to find that they don't know what to do next. It's possible, if not likely, that you have had these experiences with every one of your students at some point or another. That is, you have tried to help them make sense of a problem by having them model or draw it only to find they have no idea how to do exactly that. And to make matters worse, many of your students are naturally creative artists who like to draw and doodle!

Drawing pictures helps students understand a problem and make sense of what is happening in it. It is seemingly intuitive. But that isn't so for all students. Some can't begin to draw a picture because they simply can't visualize the problem. Some are challenged because they perceive there is a "right and wrong" way to draw a problem, and they don't know the "correct" way to do it. There are students who believe drawing a picture is for "babies" or people who can't do math. Some students are shy about their drawings or don't think they draw very well. And there are those who can draw a picture but create such

There were 48 sticky notes left after Ms. Perez passed some out. She started with 120 sticky notes. How many sticky notes did she pass out?

Credit: archives/istockphoto.com

intricate, complicated drawings that the act itself is inefficient or overwhelming.

This routine is an opportunity for students to practice drawing or diagramming problems. Number routines (SanGiovanni, 2020) and the problem-solving routines in this book are mostly opportunities for thinking and doing math mentally. This routine is different. In it, you want students to use whiteboards or journals to sketch their images. You want them to consider, create, and discuss the many ways to show a problem. In time, using variations of this routine, you want them to focus on certain models or diagrams, efficiencies, and accuracies.

All routines can be downloaded for your use at
https://qrs.ly/3cemjnt

How This Routine Helps With Problem Solving

This routine builds problem-solving skill by providing opportunities for students to

- interpret and represent problems (identity),
- make decisions about how they can represent a problem (agency),
- observe others' drawings and give feedback about them,
- compare and contrast their representations of problems with other examples,
- describe what their drawings represent,
- explain how their drawings connect to the problem, and
- reflect on the representations they create so that they can improve their efficiencies and accuracies.

What to Do

1. Present a problem.

2. Have students independently draw a picture of the problem on individual whiteboards or in their math journals.

3. Give partners time to discuss their pictures.

4. While partners are talking, look for a few examples to spotlight during the whole-group discussion. Consider selecting correct images that show the problem differently, and various images that show the problem in a similar way but with accuracy differences (e.g., incorrect addend).

5. Bring the class together to highlight the examples you select, then have a class discussion.

   » What was hard about drawing the problem?

   » What did you think about drawing first?

   » What do the ___ (feature of a drawing, e.g., squares) represent in the problem?

   » How else might have you shown the ___ (feature of the problem, e.g., sticky notes)?

   » How did ___'s drawing show ____ (the operation, e.g., addition—combining the sticky notes)?

   » How is ___'s and ____'s drawing similar/different?

   » How does your drawing compare to ___'s?

6. Write an equation that could be used to solve the problem. Have students connect the equation to the picture and the problem noting how the numbers and operation are captured in each representation.

7. Honor student work and effort. Note: Students can feel vulnerable when solving problems and drawing pictures of them. They may think about how well they can draw rather than how well they can represent the problem. It is essential that you honor all efforts after the routine. Be sure that students hear that this routine is about how well problems are represented. Praise those who had their work discussed by the class. Thank them for letting the class learn through their thinking.

Something to Think About: Representations That Match Situations

Representations are windows into student thinking. Use this routine as an opportunity to better understand how they interpret problems and make sense of problems. Allow it to help you understand how and why they choose the pictures and operations they do. Be vigilant of your own abstract thinking and how you use it to make connections between contexts, pictorial, and abstract representations that students don't really have. For example, when a dog eats treats, an amount is being taken away. Students might add up to find the difference, but that is how one does subtraction; it doesn't really represent what is happening in the problem. You make sense of their work because you move between the situations abstractly. They might too. But it's also possible that they add up because of the order of the numbers in the problem or because subtraction is a strategy that they learned the week before and now they are using it simply because it's recent.

Your fourth- or fifth-grade students might use an area model for partial products in a multiplicative comparison problem type. You recognize that the problem is multiplying and know that you can move between interpretations (comparisons and areas) to find more efficient ways to calculate. However, they are using an area model because they have been multiplying for the past week and assume that this problem is another multiplication problem. They use an area model because that's how they multiply multidigit numbers. In actuality, they haven't made sense of anything. They've simply pulled numbers, assumed an operation, and used a model that doesn't fit the context (multiplicative comparison) but does work for the computation.

IMAGINE THAT (VARIATIONS): BUILDING AGENCY

Drawing and diagramming problems are foundational ways to think about and solve problems. There is no one way to do it correctly. When you think about it, representing a problem is mathematical identity and agency at its purest (Aguirre et al., 2013). How a student chooses to show a problem is deeply rooted in who they are and how they interpret their world. It is part of their mathematical identity. The act of selecting what to draw, where to position items, how things are labeled (or not), among many other acts of representing are great examples of choice and doing or agency. Help students see that there is great diversity in how problems can be represented. And be sure that students understand that the way you show a problem is intended to help them think about how they might show it rather than how they *must* show it. Variations of this routine can unlock new ways of thinking about and representing problems for students.

Variation A: Provide a Picture for Discussion

A good way to introduce this routine is to provide a problem and an image that you create for students to determine if it is an accurate representation of the problem. You might even provide more than one image for students to debate. If you do so, consider giving two correct images or two incorrect images to enliven the math debate your students have. Try to capture things you have noticed during instruction so that students can see them through another lens. The image in the example doesn't represent the problem but there are elements that students might gravitate toward. This includes 3 candy bars that all look the same, the number 48, cutting the bars into pieces, and even the addition symbol (because the word *altogether* appears in the problem).

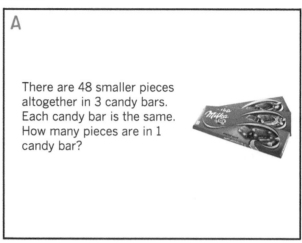

There are 48 smaller pieces altogether in 3 candy bars. Each candy bar is the same. How many pieces are in 1 candy bar?

Credit: mbbirdy/istockphoto.com

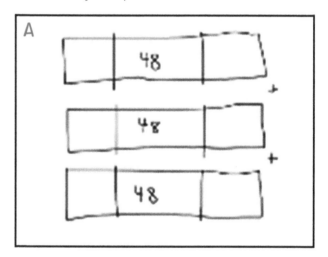

Variation B: Do I Even Need a Picture?

You want your students to have the agency to make choices about how they draw or diagram a problem. That includes having them choose if they even need to draw the problem. This variation of the routine is intended to grow that agency because it's possible that over time students naturally default to drawing when they really don't need to. Choosing to draw the problem should be up to them. You want them to consider if the problem makes sense, can they say it in their own words, do they understand what is happening, do they have a sense of what operation to use to solve the problem, and so on. In this variation, those questions could make a good anchor chart (SanGiovanni et al., 2021). Pose a problem like the example and have students discuss the questions on the anchor chart with partners before discussing as a class. Know that some students will determine they needed a picture, and some won't. That is OK. You want your students to grapple with the *why*.

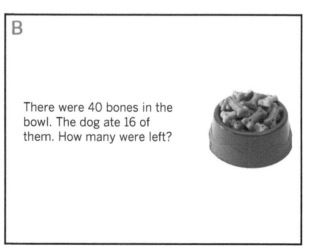

There were 40 bones in the bowl. The dog ate 16 of them. How many were left?

Credit: Teamarbeit/istockphoto.com

Variation C: Use Graphic Organizers to Scaffold

Certain organizers, like part-part-whole (p-p-w) mats, work especially well to help students make sense of addition and subtraction problems. Incorporating them in this routine for some time can sharpen their sense making and skills with representations. To do this, pose problems and have students represent those problems on their own p-p-w mat. Have them share and bring the class together to discuss the different results. Be sure to lift up the idea that the parts can be recorded in either cell and that students can use pictures or numbers. Record equations that connect to the work and talk about how the equations are shown in the mat. Over time, you can begin to remove the mat. Keep in mind that this routine is not a lesson for introducing p-p-w mats. It is intended for practice.

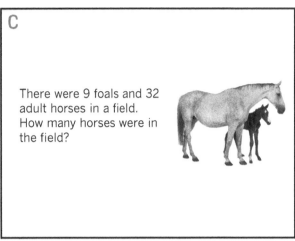

C

There were 9 foals and 32 adult horses in a field. How many horses were in the field?

Credit: GlobalP/istockphoto.com

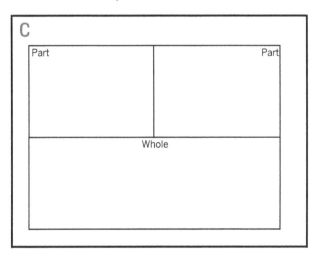

C

Part		Part
	Whole	

Variation D: Showing Large Numbers Efficiently

Large numbers create problems for students when they think about drawing each item in a problem. You can show them more efficient ways, but it may be best learned through experience and exposure to peer thinking. For example, with this problem there are students who will try to draw 25 small squares for each sticky note in a pack and then 12 packs on top of that. "More efficient" students will use tally marks. But the efficiency you want to expose is a drawing of the number 25 (the sticky notes) inside 12 rectangles (the boxes). Students can then draw conclusions about which is efficient and why. Be on the lookout for efficient models and be sure to hold discussions about them. Be careful not to insinuate that they are the only correct examples, but be sure that students have to think about efficiency.

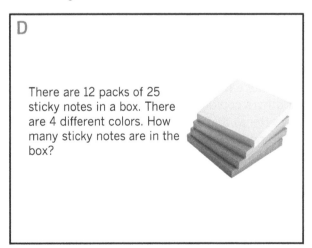

D

There are 12 packs of 25 sticky notes in a box. There are 4 different colors. How many sticky notes are in the box?

Credit: archives/istockphoto.com

Variation E: Requiring a Specific Representation

Representations can actually be obstacles to sense making and problem solving. This happens when a representation doesn't match the problem type. Think about it. The horse example is a comparison problem. Using a part-part-whole mat to represent the amount of hay these two horses ate is a confliction. A better representation might be a bar diagram or a number line so that students can show how the two horses compare. The sticky notes in boxes problem (Variation D) is another example. It is an equal groups problem but because there are two, two-digit factors we might see (or encourage) an area model, which doesn't represent the problem. So, in this variation, you pose a problem and require students to show it in one or two certain ways. As your students progress, you might even present "bad representations" and have them talk about why they don't work well for the problem.

E

A foal ate 15 pounds of hay. The mother ate 57 pounds of hay. How much more did the mother eat than the foal?

Credit: GlobalP/istockphoto.com

Variation F: Focus on Efficiency

Students are imaginative. Unfortunately, their creativity can gum up the problem-solving works. For instance, a problem about boys and girls on a bus becomes a whole other problem when a student tries to draw each person wearing different clothes, some with pigtails, some with glasses, and so on. The people on the bus can be shown simply with circles or something similar. In the example, students might try to draw each exact dog bone which could be inefficient when a quick rectangle would work. But even that is a problem when you think about drawing 29 and 33 bones. So, during this routine you want to charge students with thinking about the most efficient way they can show the problem. For some, each single bone might still be needed. But others could choose to translate the image into sticks (tens) and dots (ones). Others might shift to p-p-w models and so on. As with other variations, be careful to avoid "correctness" of a drawing and instead celebrate efficiency. Reinforce how drawings are related and have students, rather than you, make arguments for which is easier.

F

The dog ate 29 bones in the morning and 33 in the afternoon. How many bones did she eat that day?

Credit: Teamarbeit/istockphoto.com

Variation G: Comparing Problems: Operating With Integers

This variation is provided for a few different reasons. First, it shows that imagining or visualizing a problem or situation is a powerful way of making sense that doesn't expire in elementary school. After all, if you have ever taught operations with integers, you know how important it is to contextualize a naked computation to make sense of your answer. This variation borrows from Routine 7: Same and Different (page 76). It has students visualize two similar, yet different problems leading to a discussion about their differences, how they were visualized differently, and ultimately how they are solved differently. The variation is also a good reminder of the importance of relevant contexts. Yes, football can be a good context for gains and losses or positives and negatives. Yet, it isn't something that every student is passionate about or familiar with. Remember, to imagine a problem students have to understand the context and relate to it.

G

A football team lost 5 yards on a penalty then gained 22 yards. What was the team's net yardage on the two plays?

G

A football team lost 5 yards on a penalty and then lost 22 yards on a bad play. What was the team's net yardage on the two plays?

Credit: GeorgePeters/istockphoto.com

NOTES

_____

_____

_____

_____

_____

_____

_____

_____

_____

_____

MATCH THE EQUATION

About the Routine

It is critically important that students use manipulatives and draw pictures to represent problems to make sense of them and to solve them (NCTM, 2014; Moore et al., 2020; Morrow-Leong et al., 2020). These forms of representation are comfortable for students and help build bridges between word problems and equations. Unfortunately, those connections are hard for many students. They are challenged to write and use equations to model problems. Some continue to rely on pictures long after those representations lose their practicality and efficiency. This routine is an opportunity for students to practice representing word problems with equations.

One thing you'll notice about the equations is that a solution is offered in each. That is because this routine is about representing rather than solving. It intends to factor out the computation so that students can focus on the numbers and operation as related to the context and action or question of the problem. Also, seeing the answer can help them think about what makes sense in the problem. For example, how many bottles were sold should cause a student to think about joining the amounts, resulting in a number greater than each. Equations A and B can help students "see" that outcome. Note that there is a variation of this routine later that poses equations with unknowns.

As you begin working with this routine, don't hesitate to let your students draw the problem first if needed. Those drawings can serve as an entry point into the reasoning and discussion about

36 bottles of honey were sold in the morning. 28 bottles of honey were sold in the afternoon. How many bottles of honey were sold?

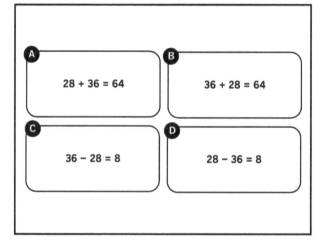

| **A** 28 + 36 = 64 | **B** 36 + 28 = 64 |
| **C** 36 − 28 = 8 | **D** 28 − 36 = 8 |

Credit: joebelanger/istockphoto.com

the equation that represents the problem. As students progress, begin to move away from the option to draw as appropriate. Most importantly, as you discuss the different equations with your students, be sure to explicitly connect the numbers and the operation back to the problem and their drawings (when used).

How This Routine Helps With Problem Solving

This routine builds problem-solving skill by providing opportunities for students to

- visualize a problem,
- think deeply about the action of the problem and the corresponding operation,
- write equations to solve problems,
- reason about problems abstractly,
- generate equations with symbols that represent the unknown in a problem,
- critique the accuracy of equations they write to solve problems, and
- recognize that there can be different equations that represent the same problem.

What to Do

1. Select a word problem and create three to four equations.

2. Present a problem and three to four equations to students.

3. Have students independently think about which equation can be used to model the problem. Optional: Allow students to draw a picture to represent the problem if needed.

4. Allow partners to briefly discuss the equation they selected and why.

5. Bring the class back together and ask which equation students think represents the problem.

6. Discuss how students know which equation is correct. Ask questions like:

   » How are the numbers in the problem the same in the equation?

   » What do the numbers in the equation represent in the problem?

   » How did you know that the equation needed addition?

   » Why does this order of numbers make sense in the equation? Could they be different?

   » How do the equation, your drawing, and the problem all connect?

7. Optional: After discussing the correct equation, have students think about how the equation would change if aspects of the problem were changed. In the honey bottle problem, you might ask how the equation would change if 49 bottles were sold in the afternoon.

SOMETHING TO THINK ABOUT: USE WHAT YOU KNOW ABOUT YOUR STUDENTS

Any routine is an opportunity to intentionally practice underdeveloped skills or strategies. Use what you observe during lessons, what you hear in student explanations, and what you see in student work to help you think about what those needs are. For example, subtraction and division word problems often prove more challenging for elementary students. During instruction, you might notice that it is a challenge for your students too. So, you would then feature those operations in the problems you use with this routine.

Before you begin to target specific needs, start with your students' comfort zone. That is, introduce the routine with problem types, operations, and numbers that students can be successful with. For example, before you get to subtraction problems or start unknown problems, use addition problems and result unknown situations in the routine. Working with comfortable situations helps students understand how this routine works. It builds their confidence with recognizing and writing equations. It will serve as an anchor experience for the new, more challenging problem situations you introduce later.

MATCH THE EQUATION (VARIATIONS): TARGET NEEDS

Using what you know about your students can really help you think about what you want to target with a routine. It can help you think about how you might modify a routine to go after certain skills or concepts. It can also help with nuances of problem solving, including how an equation is written, how one can capture an unknown, or how two equations are needed for two-step problems. No matter how you modify this routine, remember that you must directly connect the correct equations back to the problems and you must do this over and over again. These are some of your options for varying the routine.

Variation A: More Than One Equation

As you know, there is often more than one equation that can be used to represent a problem. This example shows how concepts of multiplication and repeated addition might be reinforced and connected to a word problem in third grade. But there are other ways to offer more than one equation. With this example, 6 × 8 = 48 is one of two multiplication equations that could be used (8 × 6 = 48 is the other). If the latter was posed, students might have trouble recognizing it as a correct option because the order of the factors can create uncertainty. They can also create inaccurate ideas about the problem. In situations like this, be sure students understand the problem as 6 crackers in 8 packs (6 × 8) or 8 packs of 6 crackers (8 × 6) or 6 crackers in 8 groups (6 × 8).

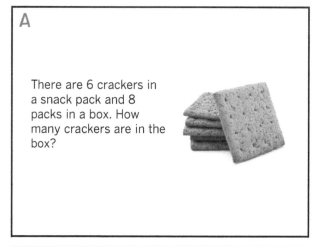

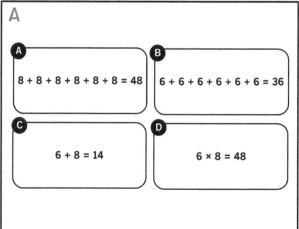

Credit: subjug/istockphoto.com

Variation B: Equations With Unknowns (Elementary and Middle School)

Writing an equation that includes an unknown is a natural variation for this routine. When transitioning to the unknown in elementary school, it is especially important to focus on the relationship between the problem and the numbers and symbols. In this problem, you would point out the weight of the two gorillas. You would want to focus on the idea that their weights are being compared. The word *difference* signals that subtraction is one way to do this. But be prepared for students to suggest that you could add the unknown to 298 to find the male's weight ($? + 298 = 446$). After discussion about the matching equation, you can choose to solve the problem but remember that the point of this routine, and many others in this book, is making sense of the problem rather than finding the solution to it.

The lower examples are problems and equations you would find in middle school mathematics. Again, students should look to make explicit connections between the problem and the equation. You want them to articulate what the unknown represents and how the two sides of the equation are related. This example also has a twist in that both C and D are equations that could be used for the problem. C subtracts the diagnostic fee to find the number of hours whereas D joins the fee and the hourly cost. Be on the lookout for students who are convinced there is always *one* equation that can be used for solving any problem.

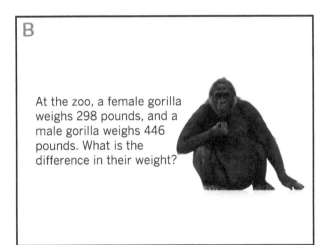

B

At the zoo, a female gorilla weighs 298 pounds, and a male gorilla weighs 446 pounds. What is the difference in their weight?

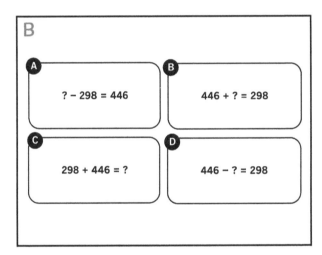

B

A — $? - 298 = 446$

B — $446 + ? = 298$

C — $298 + 446 = ?$

D — $446 - ? = 298$

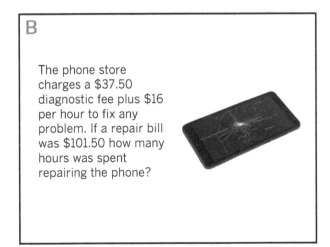

B

The phone store charges a $37.50 diagnostic fee plus $16 per hour to fix any problem. If a repair bill was $101.50 how many hours was spent repairing the phone?

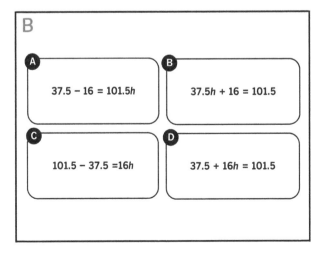

B

A — $37.5 - 16 = 101.5h$

B — $37.5h + 16 = 101.5$

C — $101.5 - 37.5 = 16h$

D — $37.5 + 16h = 101.5$

Gorilla image credit: GlobalP/istockphoto.com; phone image credit: Richard Villalon/istockphoto.com

Variation C: Students Write and Match

A different take on this routine is to provide a problem like the one shown and have students generate the equation they think goes with it. After they have time to write down their idea on a sticky note, or something similar, they share their thoughts with partners. Then, the whole class comes together to share and discuss the different possibilities. At this time, you want to help them focus on the numbers, their relationship, the operation needed to satisfy the question, and so on. This variation could also be a nice lesson to do with students before introducing the routine.

C

The art teacher counted 168 paint brushes. She can fit 8 in a jar to clean. How many jars does she need?

Credit: dalton00/istockphoto.com

Variation D: Changing Problem Types (Start Unknown)

Students must work with and practice diverse problem-solving structures or problem types. This is important to note because without monitoring the types of problems you use, it's likely that students will gain many experiences with certain types and possibly no experience with other types. Moreover, teachers sometimes shy away from the problems that they anticipate being more difficult for their students to solve. This variation is a reminder to change up your problem types and give special attention to start unknown problems like the one shown here. Start unknown problems can be especially hard for writing equations and, ultimately, solving. Clearly, equation B and C are not options. Equation A does well to connect directly to the problem because it captures exactly how many fish were added and the result or total. Equation D could be justified if students are able to identify 85 as the current amount and that they had to find the difference between it and the amount added to determine the starting amount.

D

16 clown fish were added to the aquarium; then there were 85 clown fish. How many clown fish were in the aquarium to start?

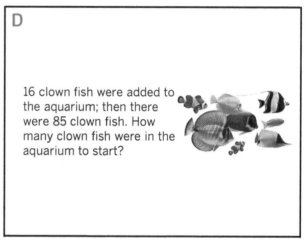

Credit: cynoclub/istockphoto.com

D

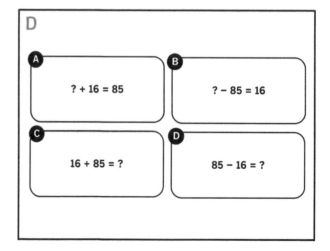

A $? + 16 = 85$

B $? - 85 = 16$

C $16 + 85 = ?$

D $85 - 16 = ?$

Variation E: Changing the "Side" of the Answer

Primary students have the misconception that the equal sign means "answer." This can undermine their ability to represent and solve problems because it compromises how they think about the relationship between the numbers in the problem. In addition and subtraction situations, they need to think about how one quantity relates to the combination or separation of two (or more) others. Here, they need to think about the whole (all paint brushes) and the two parts (dirty and clean brushes). Students might shy away from the correct equation in B because it has the "answer" on the left side. It's even possible that students who find the correct solution will gravitate toward C and justify the subtraction because the equation looks correct. Be careful here. C can be explained, but when one thinks carefully about the problem, there are two types of brushes being combined. C only plays into the conversation once the 23 is determined by adding the two types.

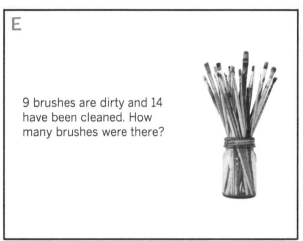

E

9 brushes are dirty and 14 have been cleaned. How many brushes were there?

Credit: dalton00/istockphoto.com

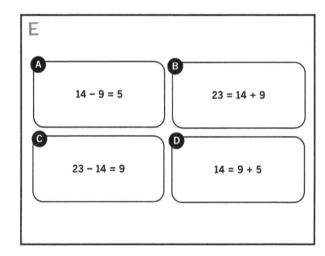

E

A $14 - 9 = 5$

B $23 = 14 + 9$

C $23 - 14 = 9$

D $14 = 9 + 5$

NOTES

_____

_____

_____

_____

_____

_____

_____

_____

_____

Variation F: Changing Numbers

This variation shows how fractions can be used with this routine. This is a good idea because making sense of problems and writing equations can become more difficult for students as they move from work with whole numbers to fractions or decimals. These numbers can overwhelm. Thinking about how to compute these numbers can distract students from making sense of the problem. Even when they understand the problem, they can have difficulty writing an equation. Practice with this routine alone can help. You can maximize the effect by helping students make connections between problems with whole numbers and fractions. To do this, pose a Match the Equation with whole numbers, discuss it, and then pose the exact same problem with fractions. In this example, the first problem might read, "A baker needs 2 bottles of honey and 4 cups of sugar for a cake recipe. She's making 8 cakes to sell. How many bottles of honey does she need?" Then, you would pose the problem in the example. This move also helps students practice recreating problems with easier or simpler numbers, which is a useful, effective problem-solving strategy.

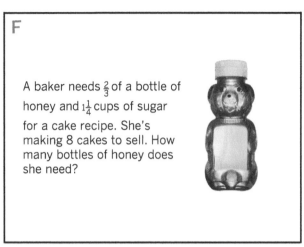

F

A baker needs $\frac{2}{3}$ of a bottle of honey and $1\frac{1}{4}$ cups of sugar for a cake recipe. She's making 8 cakes to sell. How many bottles of honey does she need?

Credit: joebelanger/istockphoto.com

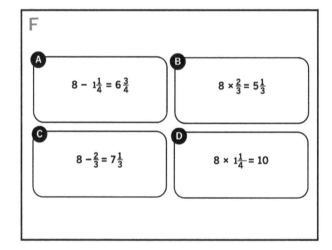

F

A $\quad 8 - 1\frac{1}{4} = 6\frac{3}{4}$

B $\quad 8 \times \frac{2}{3} = 5\frac{1}{3}$

C $\quad 8 - \frac{2}{3} = 7\frac{1}{3}$

D $\quad 8 \times 1\frac{1}{4} = 10$

NOTES

Variation G: Two Equations for Two-Step Problems

Elementary students can solve two-step problems with two equations rather than one equation that accounts for both steps. This variation of Match the Equation plays out more like Match the Equations. Implement this version in a similar fashion to the original directions. The difference here is that your students need to determine which equations should be used and the order in which they need to use them. Be prepared for students to create a first step equation that is slightly different than what you offer. Instead of correcting their thinking, help them see how their ideas and those in the examples are related. In this example, equation A could be used by determining that 71 is the total and that one could subtract one type of fish and then subtract the other type of fish. Note that equation A subtracts the second fish (22) first. This is intentional to see if students who think about subtracting the different fish recognize that order in this case doesn't matter. You also see that equation C is a correct approach as well. Students could join the two types of fish and then subtract that number from the total.

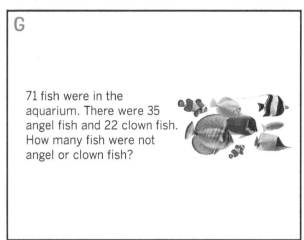

G

71 fish were in the aquarium. There were 35 angel fish and 22 clown fish. How many fish were not angel or clown fish?

Credit: cynoclub/istockphoto.com

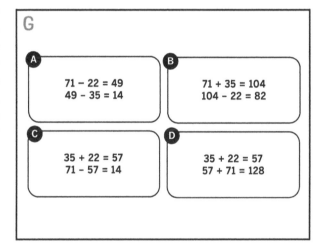

G

A
71 − 22 = 49
49 − 35 = 14

B
71 + 35 = 104
104 − 22 = 82

C
35 + 22 = 57
71 − 57 = 14

D
35 + 22 = 57
57 + 71 = 128

NOTES

AND THEN . . .

About the Routine

Two-step problems can be quite the challenge for elementary students. This routine helps them build skill with two-step problems by first making sense of a one-step problem before confronting a new problem. In this fourth- or fifth-grade example, students would chat about how they found the number of cupcakes the school bought. They should note the number of trays and the number of cupcakes per tray. They should connect this to how multiplication can be used to find the total amount. You should also elicit the equation they could use to find the solution. After discussion, you repeat the problem and exclaim, "And then . . ." This prompts them to think of what happened next. Students think about an "and then" situation and share their ideas with a partner and then the whole group shares. In this example, you might hear statements like:

- And then, $\frac{1}{2}$ of the cupcakes were eaten. How many cupcakes were left?

- And then, the school bought 8 more trays of cupcakes. How many cupcakes did they have for field day?

- And then, 3 trays were dropped. How many cupcakes were left for field day?

- And then, $\frac{1}{2}$ of the cupcakes were chocolate. How many were chocolate?

After students share some of their "and then" statements, you pose your own "and then." Students then focus on your prompt individually before the whole class discusses how they

16 cupcakes are in a party pack. The school bought 15 packs for field day. How many cupcakes did the school buy?

16 cupcakes are in a party pack. The school bought 15 packs for field day. How many cupcakes did the school buy?

AND THEN . . .

Credit: olivertoledo/istockphoto.com

thought about the new problem, the operation they used, how the information from the original problem was used, and so on.

online resources All routines can be downloaded for your use at
https://qrs.ly/3cemjnt

How This Routine Helps With Problem Solving

This routine builds problem-solving skill by providing opportunities for students to

- experience two-step problems in a fun and engaging way to reduce stress, anxiety, and misgivings about problem solving;
- recognize that two-step problems have multiple questions and that there is an order to the problems that need to be solved;
- create a reasonable second question that could be in a two-step problem;
- find their voice as they create questions and share observations; and
- discuss diverse approaches to solving two-step problems due to the questions being asked in them.

What to Do

1. Pose a one-step problem to students.
2. Give students time to think about how they would solve the problem.
3. Have students share their thinking with a partner.
4. Bring the class together to discuss the context and action of the problem. Focus discussion on the operation students might use to solve the problem. Help students think about how they might represent the problem and what the equation might look like to solve the problem.
5. After discussion, reread the problem and say, "and then . . ."
6. Give students time to think about what might happen next in the situation. This is the "and then" statement.
7. Have partners share their "and then" statements.
8. Solicit some "and then" statements from the class. Highlight how the student-generated statements are similar and different.
9. Pose your own "and then" statement/question for students to discuss and solve.

SOMETHING TO THINK ABOUT: INTRODUCING THE ROUTINE

And Then . . . is perfect to introduce through a whole-class math lesson. There are different ways to do this to fit with your students' strengths and your teaching preferences. One way to do this is through a station rotation. First, pose the original problem. Have small groups of students work to solve the problem, and then bring the group together to discuss their understanding of the problem, strategies, and representations. Then, confirm that all agree on the solution. After discussion, have students go to different stations where different And Then . . . prompts are given. At each station, students work to solve the unique prompt before rotating to a new station. After students have moved through each station, bring the class together to compare and contrast the questions at each station, the solutions, the actions or operations needed to solve the prompt, and the representations used to solve them. At this time, you want to highlight that there were distinctly different problems even though there was a common starting point.

Another way to introduce this routine is to provide a one-step problem for groups to solve and discuss as a class. Next, students go back to their groups and write the And Then . . . problem. Then, groups come together to share their created prompts. They discuss how their prompts are similar and different. To finish the lesson, you pose your own And Then . . . for them to solve and discuss. Regardless of how you introduce this routine, and others, take time to debrief with students about the process, what they noticed about the experience, and whether or not they would do or think differently if they were to do the activity again.

AND THEN . . . (VARIATIONS): BE CREATIVE

You can modify And Then . . . to help students in a variety of ways. The following variations are just some of your options. Be creative. Make your own variations of this routine and others to stretch student thinking, engage, and enjoy solving problems. The examples here can be changed to feature fractions or decimals by using an initial problem with whole numbers and then a fraction or decimal in the "and then." And though the routine intends to develop skill with two-step problems, you can create "and then" statements that don't rely on solving an initial problem. For example, look back at the original cupcake tray problem. An "and then" could be something as simple as "and then" 4 brownie trays were bought with 8 brownies on each tray, asking students to find the number of brownies.

Variation A: New Question With the Same Operation

Example A poses an equal groups, product unknown problem. Students should conclude that they can multiply to find the total number of pieces in a box. In this variation of the routine, you ask students to create an "and then" situation that uses the same operation. For example, students might say, "and then there are 8 packs of gum in a box. How many pieces are in the box?" Or, students might say, "and then Erin bought 6 packs of gum. How many pieces did she buy?" This variation of the routine changes the randomness of the second question to be more exact. It provides practice with two-step problems that use the same operation. As you discuss your students' "and then" statements, be sure to highlight the different ways multiplication might be posed in the second step (e.g., packs in a box, packs purchased).

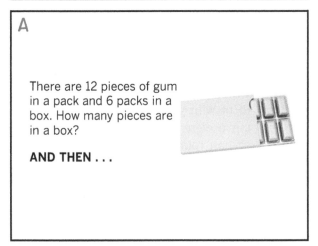

A

There are 12 pieces of gum in a pack and 6 packs in a box. How many pieces are in a box?

A

There are 12 pieces of gum in a pack and 6 packs in a box. How many pieces are in a box?

AND THEN . . .

Credit: Inhabitant/istockphoto.com

Variation B: New Question With a Different Operation

Sometimes, students use the same operation in both steps of a two-step problem with little thought. They might even use the numbers in the exact order that they appear in the problem. Here, you have students solve the initial problem. But in this variation, you charge them with creating an "and then" prompt that requires a different action or operation to solve. In this example, students would first find that the elephant eats 450 kilograms in 7 days. They might add, "and then she also eats 100 kilograms of fruit in a week. How much does she eat in all?" Or, a student might say, "and then she also eats 325 kilograms of grass at night in 7 days. How much does she eat altogether?" In both examples, the first step is to multiply but both of the "and then" prompts ask students to add. Students might even create multistep problems, adding something like, "and then, her baby eats 30 kilograms in the morning. How much do they both eat together in a week?"

B

An elephant eats 65 kilograms of grass during her morning feeding. How many kilograms does she eat in 7 days?

B

An elephant eats 65 kilograms of grass during her morning feeding. How many kilograms does she eat in 7 days?

AND THEN . . .

Credit: ixki/istockphoto.com

NOTES

Variation C: Numbers for Younger Grades

This routine naturally works with any number type or any operation. Here, this variation shows how it might be used with addition and subtraction in younger grades. The initial problem is a put together, total unknown. But student contributions in the second step offer endless possibilities. You might hear, "and then 5 more spilled out of the box. How many were left in the box now?" But a student might say, "and then 5 more spilled on the floor. How many are on the floor now?" Note that this second example doesn't lend itself to a two-step problem. And that is OK! This second example holds the potential for a conversation about necessary and unnecessary information in a problem.

C

There were 10 crayons on the floor and 23 crayons in the box. How many crayons were there?

C

There were 10 crayons on the floor and 23 crayons in the box. How many crayons were there?

AND THEN . . .

Credit: Photograpther/istockphoto.com

NOTES

Variation D: Introducing Problems and Questions

And Then . . . is a nice routine for simply introducing students to the idea of questions and problems. This variation can be used in primary grades where students generate questions that call for addition or subtraction. For example, pose that there are 16 cupcakes on a tray. Students might say, "and then mom bought 5 more. How many cupcakes are there now?" Or a primary student might say, "and then we ate 10 of them. How many cupcakes were left?" In later grades, students' questions can be introductions to multiplication saying, "and then there were 5 trays. How many cupcakes were there altogether?" Or they can ask division questions with an "and then" statement like, "and then the tray was shared with 4 friends. How many cupcakes did each friend get?"

D

There are 16 cupcakes on a tray.

D

There are 16 cupcakes on a tray.

AND THEN . . .

Credit: olivertoledo/istockphoto.com

NOTES

Variation E: And Then, And Then (Multistep Problems)

As your students become comfortable with two-step problems, you can modify this routine to practice multistep problems. Variation E shows what that might look like. This variant initially plays out like the original routine. Students solve the initial problem and then come up with an "and then" prompt. Discuss some of their "and then" creations, then settle on one and focus on its solution. After agreeing to a solution of the initial problem and the second step, introduce yet another "and then" creating a potential third step. In this example, the first solution is 36 pieces. A second statement might be, "and then he gave out 7 pieces. How many did he have left?" A third statement might then be, "and then he got a new pack of gum. How many pieces did he have now?" As mentioned in Variation D, it's possible that students offer a second "and then" that elicits a third step, and that is OK.

E

Javy had 3 packs of gum that each had 12 pieces. How many pieces of gum did Javy have?

E

Javy had 3 packs of gum that each had 12 pieces. How many pieces of gum did Javy have?

AND THEN . . .
AND THEN . . .

Credit: Inhabitant/istockphoto.com

NOTES

Variation F: Compare Student Questions (Elementary and Middle School)

In this example, students use addition or subtraction to compare the number of crayons that each person has. This variation is a twist on the original example of the routine that poses a teacher example for students to investigate. Instead, have students think about possible "and then" statements. Solicit and record two of their statements. Then, have the class compare and contrast how the new problems are similar and different. For example, one student might say, "and then Malik got 5 more crayons. How many does he have now?" Another might say, "and then they put their crayons together. How many do they have?" Neither idea prompts a second step, but instead causes different actions for students to consider. In the first, they ignore how many Jax had. In the second, they add the amount and ignore the original prompt that compares the two quantities.

F

Jax had 10 crayons. Malik has 12 more crayons. How many crayons does Malik have?

F

Jax had 10 crayons. Malik has 12 more crayons. How many crayons does Malik have?

AND THEN . . .

Credit: Photograpther/istockphoto.com

NOTES

This second offering shows how the routine could work with markups and discounts. The initial problem asks for the price of a game controller after a markup. After students talk about how they solved it, they then create their own question. Some might talk about additional markups on the new price whereas others might talk about the new price being discounted after new inventory was in stock. But don't assume students will stay within the content you're teaching. For example, a student might say, "and then I paid for the controller with four, $20 bills. How much change did I get back?" Or another student might say, "and then, I resold the controller for $125. How much money did I make?" You can put restrictions on the types of questions you want them to ask, but first you might surprise yourself with their creativity.

F

A game controller costs $48. With only a few left, a website marks up the price 50%. What's the new price of the game controller?

F

A game controller costs $48. With only a few left, a website marks up the price 50%. What's the new price of the game controller?

AND THEN . . .

NOTES

Variation G: Students Create a Similar Question

There is no limit to the ways you can modify this routine. In this variation, students again discuss and solve the first problem. Afterward, you pose an "and then" for them to discuss and solve. You want to focus their attention on the action, how the problem is changing, what information is needed, and what operation was needed to solve the "and then." Then, prompt students to create their own "and then" that is similar in context and action. For example, the given "and then" calls for students to add 7 to the first solution to find the distance of the second herd. They might generate a question that has a second herd roaming a different number per day but still asking how many more miles it roams per day.

G

A herd of elephants roamed 450 miles in 30 days. They roamed the same distance each day. How far did they travel per day?

G

A herd of elephants roamed 450 miles in 30 days. They roamed the same distance each day. How far did they travel per day?

AND THEN . . .

A different herd roamed 7 miles more per day. How far did it travel per day?

Credit: ixki/istockphoto.com

NOTES

ANOTHER QUESTION

About the Routine

Two-step problems are hard for many reasons. Students need to make sense of two actions or questions though only one question seems apparent. Some who recognize two steps simply use the same operation for both without thinking about what is happening in the problem. Others are still building skill and confidence with one-step problems. This routine is good for practicing two-step situations by starting with a one-step problem and building on it through student creativity and discussion. It addresses challenges with two-step problems by focusing on the sequence of two-step problems. Extra information and the second part of the problem is withheld until students make sense of an initial problem.

A full cooler at the supermarket can hold 18 rows of 8 bottles. How many bottles are in the full cooler?

Credit: non_Pichit/istockphoto.com

In the example, fourth graders should share that they are trying to find the number of bottles and thought of multiplying 18 × 8 (144) because they thought about an array of bottles. After group discussion, students think of another question that could be asked. Here, one student might share that "a family bought six of them so another question would be, how many are left in the cooler?" This student thinks about all of the bottles before taking some away. A second student says, "there were 5 coolers so another question would be, how many bottles are in all of the coolers?" This offering requires another step of multiplication or repeated addition. A third classmate might create a second step with division (or multiplying by a fraction) saying, "$\frac{1}{2}$ of the bottles were 1% milk so another question is how many bottles were 1%?"

The first few times you do this routine with your students you should provide the "another question." This will help students understand how the routine works and help you better understand their skill with two-step problems. Pivot to asking them to generate another question as described in the directions the third or fourth time you use the routine.

This routine is similar to Routine 13, And Then . . . (page 126) with one key difference. Routine 13: And Then . . . creates a specific sequence within a two-step problem. In this routine, "another question" is not always sequence-dependent, therefore opening doors to start unknown variations among others (see Variation G). As you use similar routines, be on the lookout for students who see the relationships between routines. Encourage others to think about how the problems, processes, wording, possibly the equations, and most importantly their thinking are also related between the activities.

How This Routine Helps With Problem Solving

This routine builds problem-solving skill by providing opportunities for students to

- identify a question being asked,
- analyze how a question affects the solution,
- connect questions with operations,
- recognize that a problem can have more than one question (even if it only has one question mark),
- talk with classmates about how they interpret a problem,
- experience two-step problems through two distinct questions so that they can transfer their understanding to traditional two-step problems with seemingly one question (or at least one question mark),
- be creative, and
- gain confidence with two-step problems in a low-stakes, collaborative setting.

What to Do

1. Pose a one-step problem for students to think about independently.

2. Have partners discuss their ideas about how to solve the problem.

3. As a class, discuss the problem. Be sure to ask students to retell the problem, identify what it is asking, and what operation they could use and why.

4. After agreement, record an equation that could be used to solve the problem. Note that you can ask students to write an equation, or you can do it for them.

5. Have partners talk about something to add to the problem to generate "another question."

6. Bring the class together to solicit and discuss a few. As the class discusses the new questions, ask questions like:

   » What does ____'s another question ask you to do in the problem?

   » Why do you still have to find the same first answer (e.g., 144 milk bottles) before you answer ____'s another question?

   » How does ____'s and ____'s another question compare? How would the operations you use be the same or different?

   » What other equation would be needed for ____'s another question?

7. Optional: After another question is asked, rewrite the problem so that the first question is no longer included. Talk with students about how the adjusted problem compares. Using the second student's another question about milk bottles from above, you would write, "A full cooler at the supermarket can hold 18 rows of 8 bottles and there are 5 coolers. How many bottles are there?" Notice that this is the original problem that no longer prompts for the number of bottles in the cooler. This option can be especially useful for students who have challenges with two-step problems because there is seemingly one question.

SOMETHING TO THINK ABOUT: BUNDLING ROUTINES

Bundling routines is a good way to practice. For example, you might use Routine 5: Same Data, Different Question (page 57) to practice understanding the question and thinking about how different questions elicit certain operations. Then, you could use this routine shortly after to help students think about how changing questions might (or might not) change the operation and how a problem might have more than one question.

You might use Routine 1: I Would Say (page 24) to help students practice putting problems into their own words. Then, shortly after, practice with this routine, first putting the problem into their own words, sharing "another question," and then putting the new problem into their own words. You might work with Routine 12: Match the Equation (page 118) where students practice writing equations for problems. Then, use this routine and include equations for students to choose from that represent both parts of the problem.

ANOTHER QUESTION (VARIATIONS): KEEP IT FRESH

Though different routines may have similar approaches, the variation of each routine opens a whole new world of possibilities. You should use different routines to keep your instruction fresh and engaging. Variations of a routine enable you to do that too. You can also use variations of a routine to build toward a specific goal. Use variations to scaffold, differentiate, or extend a routine. Variations help you think about how you might begin working with a routine (Variations A and B), how it might be used in a different grade (Variations A and B), or how it can be used to target very specific misconceptions or problem-solving challenges (Variations C and D).

NOTES

_____

_____

_____

_____

_____

_____

_____

_____

_____

_____

_____

Variation A: A Different Question for the Same Operation, One-Step Problems (Elementary and Middle School)

Before working with two-step problems, you can vary this routine to provide experiences for students to think about different ways a question can be asked. The intent here isn't to ask a question that changes the operation. Instead, you want them to think about different ways an operation, in this case addition, could be asked. To do this, have students think about what is happening in the problem and how they could go about solving it. During the whole-group discussion, come to agreement that the problem could be solved with addition. Then ask students to think of another question that could be asked that would also require addition. In this baseball problem, another question they could ask includes:

- How many hits did the team get altogether?
- How many hits did the team get in the two games?
- How many hits did the team get in the combined games?

Each of these are differently worded questions that are essentially asking the same thing.

This variation can also be thought of as a different question for the same concept. This works well with ratio and rate situations. In the example, students use the unit rate of the blinking light to determine how many blinks would occur in 5 minutes. Another question students might ask that uses the same idea might be about the number of blinks in 2 minutes, 3 minutes, or even 30 seconds.

A

A team got 17 hits in their first game and 39 hits in their second game. How many hits did the team get?

Credit: k_samurkas/istockphoto.com

A

The red light on a cell phone tower blinks 39 times per minute. How many times does it blink in 5 minutes?

Credit: rendear/istockphoto.com

NOTES

Variation B: A Different Question for a Different Operation (One-Step Problems)

Another consideration for using this routine, before working with two-step problems, is to have students create another question that requires a different operation. This is the opposite of Variation A. This practice helps students see how information is used differently based on the question asked. In this first-grade example, students might ask how many more bikes were on the stand or how many fewer bikes were on the ground. Students don't have to rely on inverse operations for creating the new question. In third grade, students could change from addition to multiplication by asking how many bikes are in 5 stands. You could bundle this variation with the previous by having them first ask another question prompting addition and then another question for a different operation.

B

There were 9 bikes in a bike stand. There were 7 bikes on the ground. How many bikes were there?

Credit: kamisoka/istockphoto.com

Variation C: Another Question for Two-Steps (Same Operations)

You can set limitations or requirements for the question you want students to create. In this variation, the requirement is that their second question must use the same operation. So, one would subtract 36 from 105 to find the number of tacos left. To create a second subtraction step, a student might offer, "How many tacos were there to buy after 28 more were bought by second graders?" For this, one would subtract 36 for third grade and then 28 from that difference for second grade. Do know that adding another question might cause students to modify the wording slightly so that it's grammatically correct. This is completely understandable and acceptable.

C

105 tacos were made for lunch. 36 were bought by third graders. How many tacos were there for other grades to buy?

Credit: fcafotodigital/istockphoto.com

NOTES

Variation D: Another Question for Two-Steps (Different Operations)

Some students hold the misconception that you repeat an operation to solve a two-step problem, which may be inadvertently reinforced with the previous variation. So here you do the opposite. Have students first work to solve a two-step problem. During discussion, stress the operations used, such as multiplication and then multiplication again. Then, have students ask another question that would change one of the steps from multiplication to a different operation. For example, this problem might change to "There are 6 rows of 4 apps on each screen. How many apps does Deryn have after deleting 8 of them?" Now, the problem calls for multiplication and then subtraction. It is critical that the class discusses how the problem, operations, and steps change in the new questions as they compare the original question.

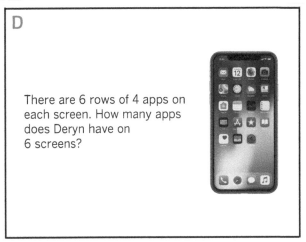

D

There are 6 rows of 4 apps on each screen. How many apps does Deryn have on 6 screens?

Credit: alexey_boldin/istockphoto.com

Variation E: A Different Question That Creates Another Step

Sometimes, students rely on the appearance of three numbers to signal that a problem is a two-step problem. In Routine 15: TMI (page 143), you'll read about how to practice with necessary and unnecessary extra information in a problem. In this variation, you start with a problem that has a bit of extra information but one that only requires one-step. After talking about the problem, have students ask another question that would change the problem from a one-step to a two-step or multistep problem. For this example, they might ask another question like, "How many more ounces are in 20 large boxes than the 20 small boxes?"

E

A large popcorn is 12 ounces, and a small popcorn is 8 ounces. There are 20 boxes of each. How many ounces of large popcorn are there?

Credit: Ljupco/istockphoto.com

NOTES

_____

_____

_____

_____

_____

_____

Variation F: Extend to More Than Two Steps

At first glance, students might think this problem has many steps because there are so many numbers. As you know, it is a simple multiplication problem with extra information. However, you can use this routine to practice problems with more than two steps by having students ask another question that uses more of the information. They can even use a one-step problem like this as a springboard to that new question. For example, other questions that cause multiple steps include:

- How many fewer ounces of cheese is needed for 13 tacos than 13 enchiladas?

- How much cheese is needed for 13 of each item?

- How much cheese is needed for a dinner that has one of each item?

F

A taco gets 2 ounces of cheese. A burrito gets 4 ounces of cheese. An enchilada gets 6 ounces of cheese. How many ounces of cheese are needed for 13 tacos?

Credit: fcafotodigital/istockphoto.com

Variation G: Provide Teacher Questions for Diverse Problem Types

This variation is more of a reminder than a different approach to the routine. The thing to note is that it's very important to change the problem types or structures as you use these routines. Certain problem types, such as start unknowns, aren't practiced enough. They are naturally more challenging to create and even more so when students have little experience with them. Because of this, you can choose to provide another question rather than have students create them or you can pose your own after they have had a chance. This move helps ensure students are exposed to and work with diverse problem types. The problem from the original offering of this routine is used as an example. Below are two examples of another question you could ask. In both, students have to grapple with a likely familiar equal groups problem and then a possibly less familiar compare, difference unknown problem.

G

A full cooler at the supermarket can hold 18 rows of 8 bottles. How many bottles are in the full cooler?

Credit: non_Pichit/istockphoto.com

A full cooler at the supermarket can hold 18 rows of 8 bottles. An older cooler held $\frac{1}{2}$ of the bottles that the new cooler holds. How many did the old cooler hold?	A full cooler at the supermarket can hold 18 rows of 8 bottles. An old cooler held 200 bottles. How many more did the old cooler hold than the new cooler?

TMI

About the Routine

The simple appearance of too much information can stop problem solving before it even gets started. Students can get hung up in the number of numbers, the complicated backstory of a problem's context, the many names in a problem, and other elements. This overwhelms, confuses, and frustrates. The problem is too big and unwieldy, challenging students' abilities to put it into their own words, share something they know about the problem, begin to draw a picture of it, or even isolate what the problem is asking. Now, mix in proper nouns and contexts that are unfamiliar, and failure is likely.

This routine, TMI (Too Much Information), is an opportunity for students to experience wordy, overly complicated problems. It helps them identify what a problem is asking and what information is needed and what isn't. Like all other routines, it is a communal experience where students share and listen to ideas. In this routine, that is especially important because there are aspects of a problem that individuals might struggle to deem unimportant.

Roni and Roxi were 10-year-old twins. They liked to go to the carnival. They went there for a party. The first thing they did was play skee ball because it was their favorite. They played 6 games. Roni made 4 balls in the 30-point ring and 2 balls in the 50-point ring. Roxi made 5 balls in the 40-point ring and 2 balls in the 30-point ring. How many points did Roni score?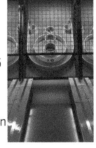

Credit: Lori Butcher/istockphoto.com

When introducing this routine, you can have students independently note an important detail and something unnecessary on separate sticky notes. During group discussion, you can sort their ideas and post them on the board in two columns: one for important information and one for unimportant information. And you can use this approach as you use new variations of the routine.

 All routines can be downloaded for your use at
https://qrs.ly/3cemjnt

How This Routine Helps With Problem Solving

This routine builds problem-solving skill by providing opportunities for students to

- think critically about what is and isn't needed to solve a problem,
- make decisions about what information to use in a problem (agency),
- become comfortable ignoring information in a problem (identity),
- identify the question to answer in a problem, and
- make arguments for important and unimportant information in a problem.

What to Do

1. Pose a problem with unnecessary information, having students read and think about it independently.
2. Have partners discuss what the question is in the problem.
3. Bring the group together to confirm agreement about the question.
4. After agreement, have students reexamine the problem to identify important and unimportant information.
5. Have partners discuss their ideas about the information.
6. Hold a second group conversation about the information in the problem
7. Optional: After the question and important information is determined, have students work to represent and solve the problem. Note that while finding a solution is an important aspect of solving a problem it can distract from the purpose of this routine, which is to only identify the question and important information.

SOMETHING TO THINK ABOUT: READING THE PROBLEM TOGETHER

Reading a problem together as a class has merit. But doing so can lead you to think that students understand a problem better than they do. Instead of reading a problem to students or reading it as a class, you can give students an opportunity to read the problem on their own first. After they read it, ask if they have any questions about it or have them retell it in their own words. At this time, you should be able to discern how well they understood what they read. Then, if you deem necessary, you can read the problem together or even read it to them. Having them read first sends a message about your confidence in them. It fosters independence. Rereading a second time models what you want them to do on their own when they don't understand a problem after a first reading.

NOTES

_____

_____

_____

_____

_____

_____

TMI (VARIATIONS): EXTRA INFORMATION COMES IN MANY FORMS

There are all sorts of things that change within problems that students must navigate as they solve a problem. Too much information in a problem is a perfect example of something they must work through. This variable, like others, can become a significant obstacle when students don't have enough experience with it. Yet even when students do get to practice too much information, the experience may only be with too much context or backstory, as shown in the opening example. Those students may not be prepared for too many numbers, too much information in tables, too many digits, or distracting number types. Those are some of the options you want to incorporate into your use of the routine, and they are captured in the following variations. But don't stop there. Look for other aspects of problems that are tricky for your students. Work those into your own variations of the routine.

Variation A: Too Many Numbers

Students who rely on plucking numbers from a problem and doing something with them as their go-to problem-solving strategy are severely compromised when there are too many numbers in the problem. In this variation, you pose a problem with extra context and information but, most importantly, it contains too many numbers. In retelling the problem, students might get caught up trying to remember all of the numbers instead of summarizing the problem in general. Have them focus on the question, using it to guide what information they need in the problem and that which they can discard. During discussion of this board game problem, you want students to share that they isolated players 4 and 5 and ignored the rest. You might hear them say that there were a lot of numbers and that so many made the problem seem really hard at first. Some might say that it was helpful to know how many turns each player had taken, which you can acknowledge but note that it isn't fully necessary for solving the problem.

> **A**
>
> 6 friends were playing a board game after school. Player 1 had 39 points after 5 turns. Player 6 had 17 points after 4 turns. Player 5 had 24 points after 4 turns. Player 4 had 53 points after 5 turns. Player 3 had 27 points after 5 turns. Player 2 had 61 points after 5 turns. How many points does player 5 need on their next turn to equal player 4?

Credit: jsolie/istockphoto.com

NOTES

_____

_____

_____

_____

_____

Variation B: Too Many Numbers in a Table

This variation is like the former example with too many numbers, but the data is presented in a table rather than a paragraph. Because of this, it may be easier for students to go right into the problem and pull out the information they need for the question. Though the provided question requires them to sift through one column of data, there are situations in which little work is needed to identify necessary information. A question like, "How many kilograms heavier is Chaser at 12 months than when she was 6 months?" wouldn't need much work to find the necessary information. When these questions come up, be sure that students can tell you and their classmates why they ignored certain parts of the table. Knowing that tables make it easier to find (and eliminate) information, you should consider starting here first and then moving to a problem that is written as a paragraph (Variation A). In fact, you could use the information in the table for one or two experiences and then write a word problem that captures all of the same information and use it for the next few experiences with the routine. Note that this problem would be perfect for early grades by changing the decimals to two-digit whole numbers and kilograms to pounds.

B

Dog Weights in Kilograms

Dog	3 months	6 months	9 months	12 months	24 months
Wagster	6.5	7.5	10.5	14.2	23.8
Rex Wiggles	2.6	3.25	4.1	5.3	6
Chaser	3.9	7.4	12.3	14.2	27.9
Barksalot	1.75	2.8	3.1	5.8	7.6
Squirrel	6	10.3	13.5	26.7	32.1
Not Spot	4	7.4	10.5	13.8	16.75

At 6 months, how much more was the largest dog than the smallest dog?

Credit: 101cats/istockphoto.com

Variation C: Just a Little Extra

As students work with this routine, you may find that they begin to rely on long problems or those with many numbers as an indication that there is something in the problem to ignore. This variation is an example of how you can account for that by giving a problem with just one bit of extra information. This might not seem very complicated, but you might find that a little extra information creates as much challenge as a lot of extra information once did. This happens because they have been "trained" to look for too much. With that element seemingly gone, they struggle to figure out how to use the extra information because it seems important. You could begin with this variation and work your way up to examples that have a lot of extra information like that in the original offering. If you do so, be sure to circle back to less complicated, extra information problems like this to be sure such an oversight doesn't take root.

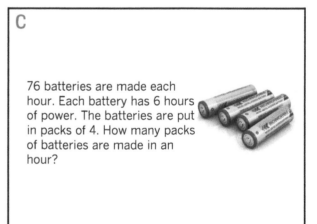

C

76 batteries are made each hour. Each battery has 6 hours of power. The batteries are put in packs of 4. How many packs of batteries are made in an hour?

Credit: scanrail/istockphoto.com

Variation D: A Distracting Outlier (Number)

A third number in a problem can seem conspicuous to the novice problem solver who interprets it as a sign of a two-step problem. This is especially so if that third number is different from the other numbers in the problem. In the top example, one number is three digits while the others are two digits. In the below example, a mixed number mingles with whole numbers. Students can be compelled to use or ignore a number that stands out from the others. In both examples, the outlier doesn't play a role in the solution but that could be easily changed. The idea here is that you provide a problem with an outlier number and charge students to determine what information is and isn't needed to solve the problem. At first, you're likely to find that students are drawn to that outlier for the wrong reasons. Through practice and discussion, you want them to talk about what the problem is asking, what is needed to answer the question, and what isn't needed, rather than rely on the characteristics of a third number. Note that you could even add a second distractor with a similar quality (e.g., two mixed numbers).

D

Jake scored 47 points and Scott scored 73 points. The game took 120 minutes to play. How many more points did Scott score?

D

8 pieces and 3 dice are needed for a game that takes $2\frac{1}{2}$ hours to play. How many pieces are needed for 6 sets of the game?

Credit: jsolie/istockphoto.com

NOTES

Variation E: Distractor Has Nothing to Do With the Problem

This skee ball problem is rife with challenge for a fourth grader who is still learning to make sense of problems rather than make use of unreliable characteristics of them. There are three numbers, which may trigger thoughts of a two-step problem. 200 is a multiple of both 5 and 10, which may disrupt ideas about which combination of numbers to use (200 and 5, 200 and 10, 5 and 10). 10 and 5 have a basic relationship that may seem too obvious to overlook leading to "solutions" of a 2 (10 ÷ 5 = 2) or 50 (10 × 5 = 50). And these are just a few of the possible missteps. Like Variation C, this version has a little extra information. The difference here is that it has absolutely nothing to do with the problem to solve. The number in the distractor is cleverly selected to see if students avoid obvious relationships between numbers and instead focus on the context, meaning, and question within the problem.

E

Min scored 200 points on his first 5 rolls. He played skee ball for 10 minutes. Each roll scored the same number of points. How many points did Min score on each roll?

Credit: Lori Butcher/istockphoto.com

Variation F: Is There Enough Information?

There are many ways you can go about this variation that is the opposite of too much information. You might use a problem like the one on the top that is seemingly void of all that's needed. In that example, there is enough information assuming that each puppy has four legs. Granted, you might have students who argue that you can't be sure and so they would note that you don't have enough information. Either argument is reasonable. On the bottom, it seems like there is a problem to be solved. It has context, different numbers, and a question. Some students will be compelled to do something with the problem. Some will be quick to tell you what isn't needed, especially if they have experienced the first few versions of this routine. But now, the point of the routine is to determine if there is enough information to solve a problem, which in this example there is not. As you use this variation, be sure to mix things up by offering both brief and longer problems that both have and don't have enough information. Do this to force your students to make sense of the problem rather than rely on its length or how many numbers are within it.

F

How many legs are in a litter of 6 puppies?

F

There are 6 puppies in a litter. Each puppy sleeps for 3 hours and plays for 2 hours before sleeping again. Then it eats and plays for another 2 hours. How many hours does each puppy sleep?

Credit: 101cats/istockphoto.com

Variation G: Middle School Example

This temperature change problem is filled with useless information and all sorts of distractions. It starts with a possible elapsed time question. It spotlights a negative number. It mentions a rate. Not to mention, it is absurd! So much of the context isn't needed. In fact, students could enter this problem "backward" by starting at the question and going back through the problem to find the important information. Often, unnecessary information isn't as conspicuous. It's usually just one or two added details. Starting with wild examples like this is good for middle schoolers (and other students) to experience the idea of too much information. From there, you can start to whittle away at the details until you present more conventional examples.

> **G**
>
> A plane takes off at 7:05 AM. Takeoff was scheduled for 6:42. Temperature changes –5.4° F for every 1,000 feet. In the plane, the temperature is 73° F and there are 184 people on board. The plane climbs at 20 feet per second and will cruise at 40,000 feet. At takeoff, what could the pilot expect the temperature at 25,000 feet to be?

Credit: sharply_done/istockphoto.com

NOTES

IT CAN'T BE

About the Routine

Making sense of an answer starts with making sense of the problem and ultimately reasoning about the operation needed to solve the problem. This can be a challenge when students simply rely on the order of numbers or certain words to select operations. In this example, students might subtract because a larger number comes before a smaller number. Or students might subtract because they notice the word *left* and recognize it as a keyword for subtracting. But when students make sense of the problem, they know that the problem is talking about the number of jackets left on a playground over 2 months. They know that the two quantities are being combined. And they should anticipate that the solution will be the result of adding the two quantities.

Once students have determined a solution path, they need to compute, which can lead to a whole new slew of challenges. In this routine, the challenge of computing is eliminated. One of the offerings *is* the solution. This allows students to focus on sense making. The routine further develops their reasoning as they disqualify possibilities. Thinking about what an answer can and can't be is a powerful way of thinking. In fact, repeatedly thinking what an answer can't be, and why it can't be, can help students find a viable solution path (Burger & Starbird, 2012).

43 jackets were left on the playground last month. This month 38 jackets were left on the playground. How many jackets were left on the playground in two months?

Credit: Green_Leaf/istockphoto.com

43	81
125	5

All routines can be downloaded for your use at
https://qrs.ly/3cemjnt

In this routine, students can ignore the challenge of exact computations so that they can focus on what is happening. They are charged with thinking about what the solution is and most importantly, why it is what it is. In the jacket problem, students should say the solution can't be 43 because that is an amount in the problem. They should argue it can't be 5 because they are combining the number of jackets on the playground, and combining those numbers will make a number greater than 5. With 81 and 125 remaining, students confront a different reasoning challenge. Both are greater, which could be the logical result of combining. Now, students might argue that it can't be 125 because they are adding two numbers less than 50 and 125 is more than 100. Others might argue that adding the ones place results in 11, so 125 couldn't be an option. And of course, some will argue that it can't be 125 because they know it is 81.

How This Routine Helps With Problem Solving

This routine builds problem-solving skill by providing opportunities for students to

- focus on strategy and operation by removing the need to calculate,
- anticipate what a solution might be to a problem based on sense making,
- determine the reasonableness of their solutions (agency),
- make arguments about why certain possibilities can't be solutions (agency), and
- listen to the arguments of others about possibilities and solutions.

What to Do

1. Pose a problem and give students time to think about it.

2. Reveal possible solutions to the problem. Note that you should select distractors intentionally, using numbers in the problem, the wrong operation, and so on.

3. Have students talk with a partner about which of the possibilities is the solution and which possibilities it (the solution) can't be.

4. Bring the class together. Poll students to see how many votes there are for each possible solution.

5. Choose one of the "can't be" possibilities and ask students if they think it can or can't be the solution to the problem. Listen carefully to their justifications. Probe student thinking during discussion to ensure that their justifications are relative to sense making and reasoning about the problem and its features. Optional: Instead of choosing a "can't be" have students identify a possibility that can't be.

6. Discuss the other possibilities in a similar fashion.

7. Choose the solution and discuss it with the class. Incorporate thoughts and disagreements from the discussion of the other possibilities. Be sure that as you and the class discuss the solution you highlight what is happening in the problem and why this number is reasonable to expect.

8. Optional: After coming to agreement about the solution, have students create an equation for the problem that includes the solution.

Something to Think About: Calculators Can't Think

Determining the reasonableness of solutions plays a critical role in finding solutions. At first glance, this seems obvious and straightforward. After all, reasonableness plays a role in calculating accurately (Bay-Williams & SanGiovanni, 2021), and this is needed for a correct answer to a problem. Often, teachers have students use calculators to support their accuracy with the goal of better problem solving. Yet, calculator use doesn't necessarily lead to better results for different reasons. Students' developing number sense doesn't enable them to recognize a faulty solution when they punch the wrong numbers into the calculator. Using a calculator correctly with the wrong solution path yields an accurate calculation but the wrong answer. Students can even begin to think that the calculator is always correct and that simply using it, without processing the problem, is quick and accurate. Calculators can't think. That's why routines like this and the others in this book that provide practice with thinking and reasoning are so powerful and necessary.

IT CAN'T BE (VARIATIONS): POTENTIALLY UNDEREMPHASIZED PROBLEM TYPES

Routines are good for practicing things that sometimes slip into the cracks. These are skills and concepts that get less attention due to how they appear in curriculum standards and even because they are hard to teach and practice. Counting and skip-counting backward is an example within number concepts. For problem solving, comparison problems for either set of operations is a good example. Some of the following variations show how you can work these into this routine as well as others.

Variation A: Focus Only On the Operation (Action)

In this first variation, you pose a problem and the four operations. Students talk about which operations can't be used to solve the problem and why. This variation is yet another step removed from spotlighting a solution. It is solely about the operation needed to solve the problem. In subtraction and division situations, you will have students argue that the operation can be addition or multiplication, respectively. In some problems, students might argue that they can add the unknown to solve a subtraction problem. Using inverse operations is viable, but they, too, can cause errors. For example, in this problem a student with such a misconception might swap 24 ÷ 3 with 24 × 3 instead of 3 × ? = 24. They can act, giving little thought about their course because they "know" either operation works. When this comes about, work to connect discussions to the problem, the action, and thinking about what the problem "looks like." In primary grades, addition and subtraction are the only operations used in this version of the routine because the other operations have not yet been taught.

There are 24 tomatoes. There are 3 tomatoes in a bunch. How many bunches are there?

Credit: dlerick/istockphoto.com

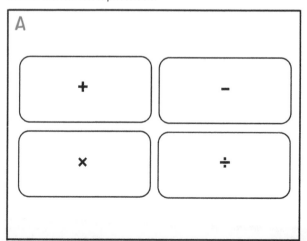

Variation B: Subtraction Version With Answers

Subtraction problems are perfect for this routine. Subtraction can be challenging for students when they only understand it as taking something away. Comparison problems, like the one shown here, can then prove quite difficult. But make no mistake, students understand the notion of comparing two things because they do it every day. Using this variation of the routine provides good opportunities to practice these types of problems. In this example, you should expect your students to be quick to eliminate 790 because it is the weight of the mother and 412, which is how much less the cub weighs. The other two options should contribute to a more robust conversation about sense making and reasoning. You want students to home in on the question, noting that it is asking about the cub. They should note that 1,202 can't be the weight of the cub because that number is greater than the mother's weight. You might hear students say that 790 + 412 = 1,202 and so the solution must be 1,202. If they do, poke their reasoning. Ask them about why they are combining the weights of the bears. Ask them to look at the question and restate what they are trying to figure out.

B

A mother polar bear weighs 790 pounds. Her cub weighs 412 pounds less. How much does her cub weigh?

Credit: bazilfoto/istockphoto.com

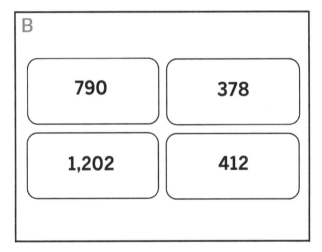

B

| 790 | 378 |
| 1,202 | 412 |

NOTES

Variation C: Division Versions With Answers

Like subtraction, division can be challenging for students to reason about because of the different meanings or interpretations of division. Partitive is finding the number of groups that can be made. Quotative or measurement is finding the number in each group. Also, like subtraction, it's possible that your students have more experience with one of the interpretations, and so problems that feature the other are difficult to make sense of. When comparisons are being made, like in this problem, productive problem solving can crumble. This problem is not the best place to begin when using division in the routine. It is here to remind you of the challenges and opportunities within the routine. You should begin with problem types that center on equal groups and arrays or area. In time, fourth and fifth graders will be ready for the comparisons shown here. And when they are, be ready for them to fall for the word *times* as an indicator to multiply!

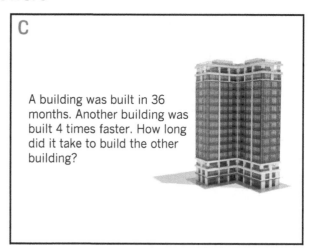

C

A building was built in 36 months. Another building was built 4 times faster. How long did it take to build the other building?

Credit: Maxiphoto/istockphoto.com

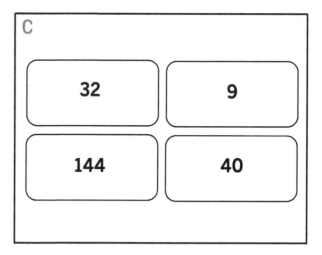

C

32	**9**
144	**40**

NOTES

_____

_____

_____

_____

_____

_____

_____

_____

_____

Variation D: Fractions and Decimals

Fractions and decimals have the potential to gum up the problem-solving works. They can be unsettling when students see them in a word problem. They can distract students from focusing first on making sense of the problem. This is when understanding the problem and question become even more important. In a problem like that in the example, you want students to think about the pencil getting smaller and how it would compare to when it is new. The solution can't be $11\frac{3}{4}$ or $11\frac{1}{2}$ because that would mean the pencil is getting longer. The other two options do require conceptual understanding of adding and subtracting fractions. That is, even a student who understands the problem might think incorrectly about the solution. Think carefully about whether you would want these two options present in early offerings of this routine with fractions. You might simply want to offer $3\frac{1}{4}$ and $11\frac{3}{4}$ at first. Also, know that it is a good idea to introduce this routine with more simple numbers at first before moving to fractions and decimals.

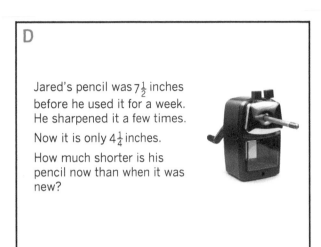

D

Jared's pencil was $7\frac{1}{2}$ inches before he used it for a week. He sharpened it a few times.

Now it is only $4\frac{1}{4}$ inches.

How much shorter is his pencil now than when it was new?

Credit: SimoneN/istockphoto.com

D

$3\frac{1}{2}$	$3\frac{1}{4}$
$11\frac{3}{4}$	$11\frac{1}{2}$

NOTES

Variation E: Students Identify What It Can't Be

As mentioned in the opening, repeatedly thinking about what a solution can't be and why it can't be helps students narrow in on what the solution or solution path is. This is a good strategy for attacking problems when one is stuck. It is a good counter to asking what one knows about a problem or what one would like to know about the problem. In this variation, you simply give students a problem like the one shown. Then, you have them create one possibility it (the solution) can't be and why. You have them share their thinking with a partner and then discuss as a class. After discussing a few of their "can't be" answers, have students begin to talk about how they would solve the problem and what the solution can be. At the end, debrief with students on how thinking about what a solution can't be could help them when they are stuck or when they start to solve a problem.

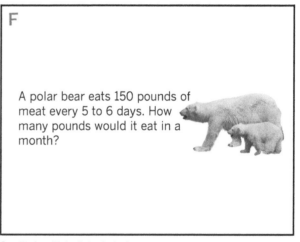

One tower had 975 residents and the other tower had 1,128 residents. The building has a limit of 2,250 residents. How many more residents could the building house?

Credit: Maxiphoto/istockphoto.com

Variation F: Two-Step Problems

This example is a two-step version of Variation A. Here, students examine a problem and think about what combination of operations they would use to solve the problem. In the example, a pathway for solving the problem would be to divide 30 days by 5 or 6 to find how many times the bear could eat. Then, they would multiply that number by 150. This variation works well because, again, it focuses students on the process of solving a two-step problem. Your students might go directly to the correct process, which is fine. When that happens, be sure to discuss the other possibilities and why they can't be the solution paths.

F

A polar bear eats 150 pounds of meat every 5 to 6 days. How many pounds would it eat in a month?

Credit: bazilfoto/istockphoto.com

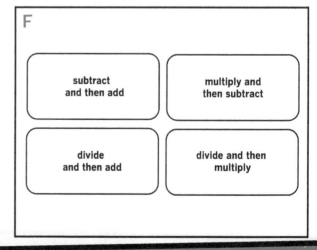

F

subtract and then add	multiply and then subtract
divide and then add	divide and then multiply

Variation G: Two-Step Problems With Solutions

This variation shows how the routine uses two-step problems with the answers instead of the process. With these problems, students, confused by extra information, might choose to grab numbers and do something with them just to get the problem over with. The distractors capture that. $5.97 is 3 groups of $1.99 or 3 × $1.99. $16.99 is the result of adding all three numbers in the problem, and $13.99 is the result of adding the last two numbers. These might seem obvious but should still lead to interesting discussions. You also have options for incorporating two-step distractors. For example, you could subtract each number from 12 or you could multiply 3 and 12 then subtract $1.99.

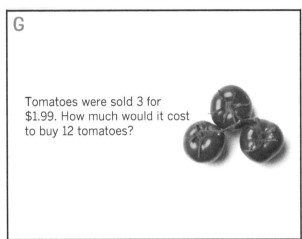

G

Tomatoes were sold 3 for $1.99. How much would it cost to buy 12 tomatoes?

Credit: dlerick/istockphoto.com

G

$5.97	**$7.96**
$16.99	**$13.99**

NOTES

IS IT REASONABLE?

About the Routine

Imagine a student who adds the prices in the example and forgets the decimal, therefore finding a sum of $2,897. They check their work by adding again and confirm that $2,897 is "correct." They don't recognize how absurd their answer is because there aren't many, if any, elementary students who pay the bill at a restaurant. Therefore, they can't call on their life experiences to determine reasonableness and catch their error.

Determining the reasonableness of an answer is a significant skill that takes time to develop. It is multifaceted. It is related to understanding numbers in context, which is acquired through life experience and practice with number routines like Big or Small (SanGiovanni, 2020). That understanding would have helped the student figure out that the meal was ridiculously expensive.

Yet, even as adults, there are problems with contexts and numbers that are unfamiliar or hard to fathom. In those situations, one can call on their number sense, computational estimation, and understanding the effect of operating on

The four people in Andrea's family went to dinner. There was an adult meal for $14.99 and two kid meals for $6.99. How much was the bill for these three meals?

Credit: DNY59/istockphoto.com

numbers. This routine takes aim at all those situations by posing problems with estimated solutions for students to deem reasonable or unreasonable. And when possible, like this restaurant problem, you can also incorporate discussions about wildly wrong answers by giving students insight into what a realistic bill might be.

All routines can be downloaded for your use at
https://qrs.ly/3cemjnt

How This Routine Helps With Problem Solving

This routine builds problem-solving skill by providing opportunities for students to

- deepen their understanding of reasonableness,
- anticipate what a reasonable solution might be,
- practice considering the reasonableness of a given solution so that they can apply such thinking to their own solutions,
- listen to others' ideas about how to determine if a solution is reasonable, and
- practice estimating in different ways.

What to Do

1. Pose a problem and ask students to think about the operation they need to solve it.

2. Have partners talk about the problem, the operation they would use to solve it, and an estimate for the solution.

3. Bring the class together for a brief discussion about their ideas.

4. Then, share a number and ask if it is a reasonable solution to the problem.

5. Give students a moment to consider the reasonability of the number you shared as a solution.

6. Facilitate a discussion about their thinking. Use questions like:
   - » How do you know that this number is (or isn't) a reasonable solution?
   - » How did friendly numbers help you think about how reasonable this number could be as a solution?
   - » How did you know that the number was unreasonable?
   - » What would be a more reasonable solution?
   - » How does estimating a solution help you make sense of your work?

7. Optional: Give the exact answer after discussion and note how it compares to the number the class discussed.

As an alternative, you can use student-generated estimates instead of posing a number you select. With this option, you should solicit two or three numbers from the group and record them on the board. Ask students which they think are reasonable or which is the most reasonable. Point out how close or far apart the numbers are. Ask if others thought about numbers that are close to those on the board. Or you can begin the discussion by asking students what they notice about the estimates of their classmates and what questions they want to ask about the numbers.

Something to Think About: Estimation

Skill with estimation comes about through experience and discussion. Too often, estimation is distilled into a process of rounding to a certain place value. It becomes procedural with focus on correct estimates instead of reasonable estimates. This is not to say you shouldn't teach rounding. But you also want to be sure that students learn about and practice different approaches to estimation, including front-end estimation, finding ranges, and using compatible numbers.

You have been practicing estimation and reasonableness for years. You might take it for granted. Be patient with your students' emerging estimation skills. Remember, it is truly about thinking and reasoning, which takes time. Estimate as much as possible and do it with both word problems and naked computations. Have students predict an answer, find an exact, and then compare their predictions to the exact. Try to avoid "correct" estimates, and instead focus more on how close estimates are to the exact answers. And remember, it's never too early to start estimating. Primary students might begin by estimating quantities with things like marbles in jars, but they can, and should, begin to estimate sums and differences as soon as possible. For example, a first grader might estimate whether 7 + 9 will be more or less than 10 or 20.

IS IT REASONABLE? (VARIATIONS): WHAT SHOULD BE CONSIDERED?

It is critical that students practice reasonableness as problems and numbers become more complex. They'll need practice selecting close, friendly numbers and alternate approaches to estimate and reason about their solutions. Students can practice thinking about unreasonable possibilities that can't be solutions. In addition to this, students can even practice thinking about the reasonableness of the strategies and representations they'll use to solve a given problem. After all, sometimes a certain strategy or a detailed representation is unreasonable because it is inefficient or ineffective. For example, a detailed drawing of a problem with large quantities isn't as reasonable as using a simpler part-part-whole or bar diagram. The upcoming variations give you some ideas about how you can approach reasonableness through this routine.

Variation A: A Reasonable Picture

You never want to discourage student drawings and diagrams as viable solution paths. But you do want students to use representations purposefully, effectively, and reasonably. In this variation, you pose a problem and ask students to draw and talk about a reasonable representation they could use to solve the problem. You want to point out how representations connect to the problem and how certain intricacies can slow the problem and lead to both distraction and frustration. In the example, you might have students who attempt to draw every butterfly, which isn't reasonable. This might also happen with multiplication and division problems that use larger numbers. Yet even in problems with small numbers, students might try to create detailed representations of each butterfly's wings, legs, antennae, and so on when a simple circle would work just as well.

A

Ms. Hill's class released 81 monarch butterflies. Mr. Santos's class released 35 butterflies. How many more did Ms. Hill's class release?

Credit: Liliboas/istockphoto.com

Variation B: Choosing Good, Friendly Alternatives for Reasonableness

As numbers become more and more complex, it is important to think about them in friendly, even simpler, ways. It helps one estimate a solution for problems with fractions, decimals, or whole numbers in the millions, as shown. In this variation, students identify useful alternatives for the numbers in a problem to gauge the reasonableness of their exact solutions. In this fifth-grade example, students could use 5 (for 2022), 3 or 4 (for 2021), and 1 (for 2020). Adding these numbers establishes that a reasonable solution should be around 9 or 10 million, which is all too helpful when some sort of calculation error comes about. It's likely that you will need to model this with students a few times before they work with the idea on their own. A table-based problem could be useful for this because you can keep the large numbers the same and simply swap out the questions you use.

B

Year	Vehicles
2022	5,230,989
2021	3,675,801
2020	1,018,032
2019	4,912,945
2018	3,845,226

How many vehicles crossed the bridge in the past 3 years?

Credit: MasaoTaira/istockphoto.co

Variation C: Is the Operation Reasonable?

Discussions about the operation used to solve a problem are invaluable to the novice problem solver. Thinking about what makes sense or what is reasonable softens the discussion about how a student selects an operation for solving a problem. In this second-grade example, you pose a problem and simply ask whether it is reasonable to add or subtract the two numbers. Let students talk with each other about which makes sense and why. Then, have the class discuss their ideas. For the fourth-grade teacher, this exact problem has utility, especially after students have been working with two-digit multiplication and have started to simply multiply everything without thinking or even reading the problem. Using this problem, that fourth-grade teacher would ask whether it is reasonable to add, subtract, multiply, or divide to solve the problem.

C

Leo's tower was 28 bricks tall. Izzy's tower was 43 bricks tall. How tall were the two together?

Credit: ivanastar/istockphoto.com

Variation D: More or Less and Why

A useful approach to estimating is to determine if a result will be more or less than a certain value. This variation is the word problem equivalent to More or Less (SanGiovanni, 2020). First, pose a problem and have students come to an agreement on how it can be solved. For this problem, one would multiply. Then, have students independently think about how the solution compares to a number. For example, one might say the solution will be less than 530 because $10 \times 53 = 530$ and they are only multiplying 8×53. Another might say that it will be more than 400 because $8 \times 50 = 400$ and 53 is more than 50. And it works just as well with addition, subtraction, or division. Pretend for a moment that this problem was $53 + 18$, which is a regrouping problem that could cause issues in second grade. Those students could reason that the solution would be more than 63 because $53 + 10 = 63$ and they are adding 18, or they could reason that it is less than 73 because $53 + 20 = 73$.

D

Monarch butterflies are shipped to schools in packs of 8. Recently, 53 packs were shipped. How many butterflies were shipped?

Credit: Liliboas/istockphoto.com

Variation E: It Can't Be

Another good way to think about the viability of an answer is to determine what a solution can't be. And by thinking of different impossibilities, a solution path can come into focus (Burger & Starbird, 2012). In this variation, you don't ask students to think of a reasonable answer for the problem. Instead, you ask them to think of something that isn't reasonable and why it isn't reasonable. It's similar to Routine 16: It Can't Be (page 150). The subtle difference is that you want students to incorporate friendly numbers or operation selection, when possible, into their creations. In this problem, an idea about friendly numbers might sound like, "It can't be 200 because $800 \div 4$ is 200 so it has to be less than 200." A student thinking about operations might say, "It's unreasonable to subtract because you're finding the number in each set. So, it can't be 716 because $720 - 4 = 716$."

E

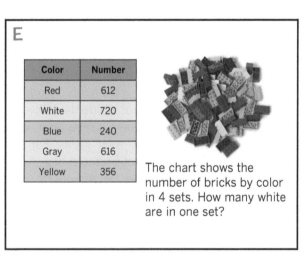

Color	Number
Red	612
White	720
Blue	240
Gray	616
Yellow	356

The chart shows the number of bricks by color in 4 sets. How many white are in one set?

Credit: ivanastar/istockphoto.com

Variation F: Multiple Numbers to Consider

The opening example calls for you to give one number for students to consider. In this variation, you offer more than one. You can have the class discuss each one separately but ideally you would pose all at the same time and let students determine which is reasonable. This variation can be good for helping students see that there can be more than one reasonable estimation. In this problem, most will likely use 2,000 for 2,135, finding 12,000 (2,000 × 6) to be a reasonable estimate. But it's possible that a student might think of 2,000 × 5 making the case for 10,000 to be reasonable. And it's OK if this happens. Acknowledge that 10,000 is reasonable, and have all students consider the viability of these two different numbers. Also talk about why 1,200 and 120 are not reasonable estimates for this problem, but both were intentionally selected because of their similarity with 12,000.

F

2,135 cars crossed a bridge each hour for 6 hours. How many cars crossed the bridge?

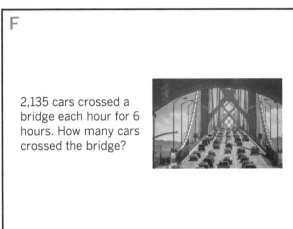

F

10,000	1,200
120	12,000

Credit: MasaoTaira/istockphoto.com

NOTES

Variation G: Reasonable With Multistep Problems

Using friendly numbers to anticipate reasonable solutions is quite useful for solving multistep problems that incorporate multidigit numbers. After students have had a few moments to work with this problem, you might ask whether it is reasonable to have about $20 left. Hopefully, students will be quick to dismiss $20 as reasonable. Then, you might ask if $10 left is reasonable. Students who miss the amount tipped could argue that $10 is reasonable because $60 – $50 (estimate for $48.76) is $10. A third offering might ask if $2, $50, or even $60 is reasonable. Know that as the first offering is discussed, other possibilities might not be needed because they might be discounted during the conversation. When that happens, move back to the solution path and substitute friendly numbers, and then offer a second, final estimate for students to think about. In this example, that might sound like, "The bill was about $49 then a $10 tip was added and that was all paid for, or subtracted from, $60, so a reasonable answer is about $1."

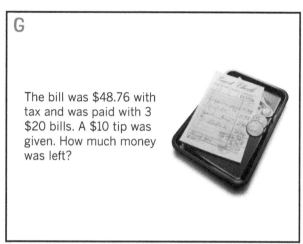

G

The bill was $48.76 with tax and was paid with 3 $20 bills. A $10 tip was given. How much money was left?

Credit: DNY59/istockphoto.com

NOTES

STICKY PATTERNS

About the Routine

Mathematics is the study of patterns (Fried, n.d.). Looking for and using patterns is a mathematics practice for making sense of the world and solving problems (NGA & CCSSO, 2010). If you think about it, finding and completing a pattern is problem solving itself. To do so, you must make sense of the terms in the pattern, look for relationships, think about what is being repeated, question your thinking, and try new terms to see if they fit the pattern. And though students might not call on their patterning skills for many word problems, they will call on their thinking and reasoning skills. This routine serves to further develop both of those.

Sticky Patterns is a routine that takes patterning and problem solving to a whole new level. You record a pattern on the board and cover it with sticky notes. You reveal one term in the pattern and have students create a pattern that would have the matching term. In the example, 2 was revealed first. So, a student could create a pattern like 2, 4, 6, 8, 10; another student could create a pattern of 2, 12, 22, 32, 42; and a third student might create 2, 7, 12, 17, 22. Students share their creations, and you discuss some of them noting the different possibilities. Then, a second term is revealed (20 in the example). Students with patterns that don't have the same term, in the same position, must work to create a new pattern that would match. Students who do have 20 in the correct position keep their pattern. This continues until the full pattern is revealed. In the example, the pattern adds 6 each time (2, 8, 14, 20, 26).

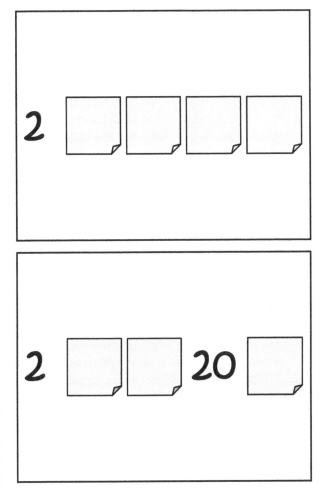

How This Routine Helps With Problem Solving

This routine builds problem-solving skill by providing opportunities for students to

- look for patterns,
- think critically about relationships between terms in a pattern,
- think flexibly,

- build perseverance as their attempts to identify new patterns are unsuccessful (agency),
- create their own patterns (identity and agency),
- recognize that others' have viable solutions even if they are different, and
- demonstrate their mathematical brilliance (identity).

What to Do

1. Record a pattern on the board and cover each term in the pattern with a sticky note.

2. Remove the first term in the pattern. Have students predict what the next four terms in the pattern might be based on the first term.

3. Have students share their pattern and its rule with a partner. Solicit a few patterns to record on the board. Briefly discuss the similarities and differences within the patterns.

4. Remove a second sticky note to reveal the next term in the pattern. Students with patterns that have a matching second term do nothing. Those who don't have a matching second term create a new pattern and share it. Note: The second term you reveal doesn't

have to be the second term in the pattern. As shown in the example, the second term revealed was the fourth term in the pattern.

5. Students discuss their new patterns, and you can record some of their new creations while eliminating those that no longer work.

6. Repeat the process with third and fourth terms in the pattern.

7. Celebrate their success.

Note that you don't have to record a new series of patterns after every term is revealed. But it is important to pause and discuss some of the differences within their creations. Each time you do, be sure that they see how the patterns are different.

Something to Think About: Reframe Problem Solving

The possibilities of a problem, from structure and situation to numbers, contexts, and wording are endless. There is no foolproof method for solving every problem. That's what makes problem solving really hard to teach. You can model it, but students think differently. You can share methods or procedures, but any of those can prove faulty as new problems are encountered. Tips like highlighting important information and circling numbers in a problem don't necessarily yield results. And each of these teaching moves, among others, add layers of complexity that contribute to students' anxiety about solving problems and math in general.

You want problem solving to be an engaging and rewarding experience even when solutions aren't

found. Immerse them in it throughout the lesson and the week. Vary the ways that they engage with it using routines like these, high-quality tasks for teaching concepts, as well as games and centers (page 59). Stay patient along the way because it takes time to gain a lot of experience with a variety of problems and situations. Try to lessen fear and anxiety by approaching problem solving in clever ways. Avoid framing problems with comments like, "This is going to be really hard." In short, help students be curious as they encounter problems. Unpack setbacks along the way. Model joy in working with problems, trying new approaches, and the sense of accomplishment when finding a solution.

STICKY PATTERNS (VARIATIONS): "HIDDEN" STANDARDS

There are skills in math that help students find success. Some of those skills aren't always clear in curriculum standards; you might think of them as "hidden" standards. For example, skill with counting backward and skip counting backward aids in subtraction and division. Yet, counting backward may not be explicitly stated. Skill with doubling numbers and halving numbers is useful for all sorts of applications and fluencies, but it's not something that is often taught or practiced beyond basic facts.

And there are some topics, such as patterning, that are in mathematics curricula but fall behind other, more major concepts like addition or fractions.

Clever use of routines, including this one, provides valuable experience with these hidden standards while also practicing thinking and reasoning to become productive problem solvers. The following variations highlight some of those, but there are always more for you to consider.

Variation A: Patterns With Shapes

Sticky Patterns is perfect for practicing repeating patterns with shapes in primary grades. It will also give insight into your students' mathematical brilliance. In the example, after the first term is given you might expect something like circle, square, circle, square (repeating AB pattern). But you're likely to hear complex, creative patterns like a three-term repeating pattern (ABC) that goes circle, square, rectangle. When the triangle is revealed next, a new repeating pattern (circle, triangle, circle, triangle) could be shared, but so could circle, square, triangle, triangle. This exposes students to the many possibilities within just one pattern. It stokes their curiosity and playfulness. It deepens their understanding, thus better positioning them for noticing and using patterns.

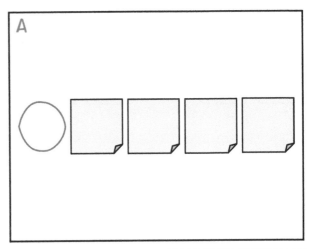

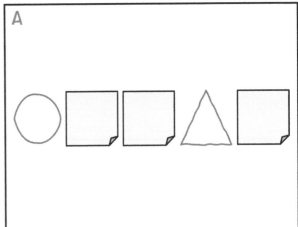

Variation B: Patterns That Skip Count Backward

Skip counting is a great choice for this routine. The example is a reminder that the first term you reveal doesn't have to be the first in the pattern. Here, the middle term is offered first, setting up all sorts of possible patterns, which should yield good discussions about the patterns students create. The example also suggests some other things you should consider when doing skip counting patterns. For one, include skip counts that count backward. Skill with skip counting backward by tens and hundreds help students apply strategies to multidigit subtraction and division. Another idea here is to practice skip counts that begin with numbers other than 0 or a number that is the interval of the skip count (e.g., 5, 10, 15, 20). This, too, helps with computation when students solve problems like 98 – 43, enabling them to count back 10 or even 40 from 98 and then counting back 3 more.

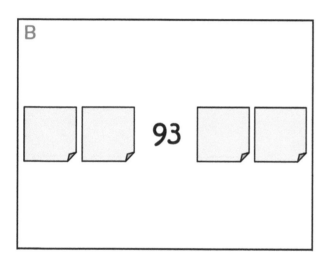

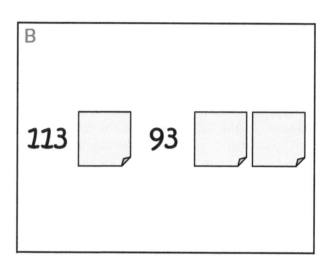

Primary students aren't the only ones who benefit from practice with forward and backward skip counts. In this second example, the pattern counts backward by 2.5. It should prove to be a worthy challenge. Before presenting it, explore patterns that skip count forward and backward by negative numbers. The routine can evolve to patterns that multiply by a negative number each time (e.g., 4, −12, 36, −118) or subtract negative fractions (e.g., −12, −9$\frac{1}{2}$, −7, −4$\frac{1}{2}$,). Doing this disguises dull, but needed, computation practice with an engaging activity grounded in patterning and reasoning.

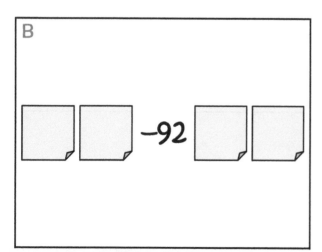

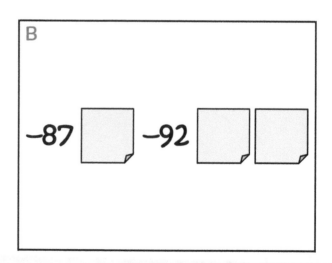

Variation C: Patterns That Double

As noted, doubling is a very useful skill. It has obvious applications to finding multiples but also supports computation strategies of doubling and halving. It is more than a basic fact strategy. In this example, each term is doubled. Again, it first shows something other than the first term in the pattern. Even revealing the second term won't necessarily determine the pattern. A rule for the pattern could be that each new term is found by adding two more than the previous. Here, that would be 6, 14 (6 + 8), then 24 (14 + 10). Accuracy with computations become more and more important as you introduce doubling, halving, quadrupling, and so on. This creates a challenge for students still developing their fluency. Your move is not to withhold these patterns from them but to instead shift the focus on the pattern rather than the computation. Providing tools like fact charts and calculators can help tremendously.

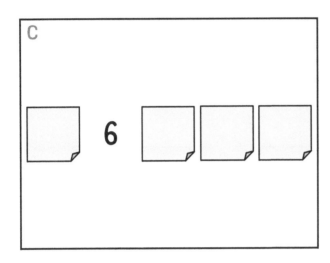

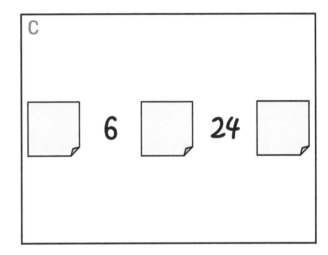

Skill with doubling has all sorts of applications. In the middle school example above, each ratio in the pattern is equivalent. Each number in the ratio is doubled as you move from left to right and term to term. Remember, you can give as much or as little information as you like before kicking off the routine. You might say that this pattern features equivalent ratios or you might say nothing at all. The actual pattern featured in this example is 5:6, 10:12, 20:24, 40:48, and 80:96. Again, each number is doubled and so each ratio remains equivalent. This isn't necessarily obvious to students, and so it becomes a worthy practice. You could change from doubling to tripling, quadrupling, and so on.

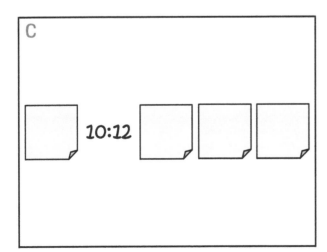

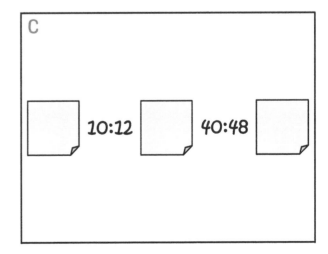

Variation D: Patterns With Fractions

Sticky Patterns is a good way to incorporate necessary practice with skills without relying on worksheets. In this fourth- or fifth-grade example, students practice adding and subtracting fractions. Though you could incorporate unlike denominators, it's likely best to stick with common denominators. However, do note that including mixed numbers is a very good idea. In fact, you could easily change this pattern so that the second term is $1\frac{4}{6}$. Eventually, you should use patterns like $3\frac{1}{4}$, $3\frac{3}{4}$, $4\frac{1}{4}$, $4\frac{3}{4}$, which not only includes a mixed number in each term but also adds $\frac{1}{2}$ though none of the denominators are 2. And like skip counting, remember to have fraction patterns count backward (subtract). Depending on your students' skill and comfort with fractions, you could even work in patterns that multiply fractions each time.

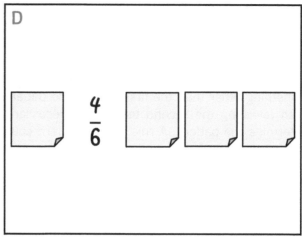

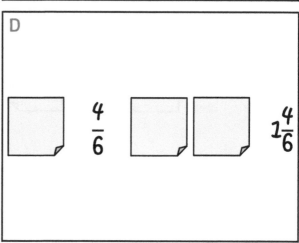

NOTES

Variation E: Patterns With Decimals

This variation speaks to the clever practice you can incorporate as mentioned. Here, the pattern subtracts 0.12 each time. If you were to reveal 2.51 first, you should expect students to create patterns that count by ones (1.51, 2.51, 3.51), tenths (2.41, 2.51, 2.61), or hundredths (2.51, 2.52, 2.53). This is fine! More importantly, it provides yet another opportunity for practice.

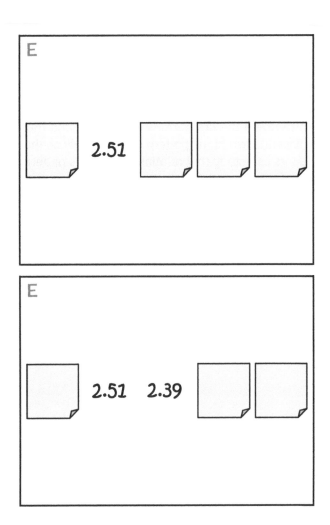

NOTES

Variation F: Patterns With Two-Step Rules

Two-step rules, like two-step problems, are simply more challenging. Patterns with two-step rules or functions aren't typically introduced until fifth grade. You might find that your students are ready for them sooner. If you use this variation, you should plan to reveal the first term in the pattern and then the second term in the pattern consecutively so that students can study that relationship. In this pattern, the rule is to multiply by 2 then add 3. Often, students will need the third term and possibly the fourth before they even consider two steps unless you make them aware upfront. Be patient with their progress. Don't give up on the variation if it doesn't go smoothly the first few times but also move on from it if you find that it is becoming overly frustrating for your students.

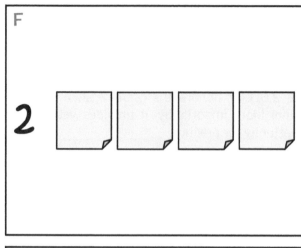

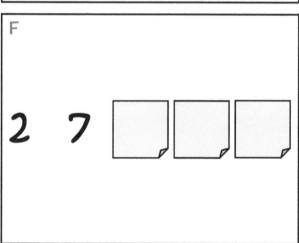

NOTES

_____

_____

_____

_____

_____

_____

_____

_____

Variation G: Patterns That Are Student Created

An easy way to get a sense of how well developed your students' patterning skills are, is to have them create the patterns to use for the routine. You'll see if they rely on using 0 when they skip count, and then you'll know to move them forward by using skip patterns that don't start with 0. You'll see if they prefer patterns that count up or add, and then you will know that you need to infuse patterns that subtract or divide. Note that you should expose them to different possibilities within the routine before having them create examples. Without doing so, the lack of diversity in their patterns may be due to what they think they are supposed to create rather than what they can create. You can even put restrictions on the types of patterns you want them to create. You might ask them to create a pattern that shows multiples. The example shows what a student might create in response to that. Having them create the pattern for the day's routine has other benefits. It lessens your planning burden. You can have everyone make a pattern, which you collect and use in later offerings of the routine. Most importantly, it positions them as doers and creators who are meaningful contributors to their math class.

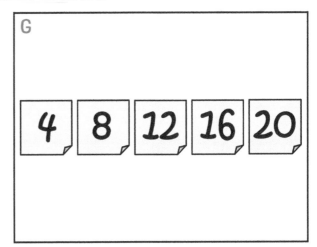

NOTES

LOTS AND LOTS

About the Routine

Traditionally, word problems form the bulk of what is problem solving in the elementary mathematics class. As such, most of the routines in this book are geared toward helping students build skill with solving word problems. But as you know, there are all sorts of other ways to provoke thinking and discussion. A good, open-ended question does just that while holding the potential to deepen student understanding through the problem (Kaplinsky, 2020; Small, 2010; Sullivan & Lilburn, 2005). Good questions have powerful potential.

Open-ended questions help students see that there is possibly more than one right answer for a given situation. This has value because it challenges conceptions about a single right answer in math. These questions create multiple entry points so that any student can engage with a problem in their own way. Good questions naturally lead to good discussions about what is possible, and during those discussions students are exposed to diverse ideas. And, when you record their ideas carefully (see note in the directions), lots and lots of answers can uncover patterns within math that students can use for solving new problems.

This routine is about one good question that yields lots and lots of possible answers (hence

> Two numbers have the same sum as
> 37 + 24.
>
> What could those numbers be?

the name). It might seem like such an open question with so many possibilities will take an entire class period to investigate and discuss. But it won't. You want to pose an open question, have students engage with it, and then discuss. As with other routines, keep it to 5 to 10 minutes. And remember, this routine might take a bit longer the first few times you use it, but that's true with any routine. A real challenge that you face with this routine is that some of your students may have acquired a narrow view of math and right answers. It might be hard for them to process an open-ended question with many possibilities. But they can see math differently and be better off for it.

All routines can be downloaded for your use at
https://qrs.ly/3cemjnt

How This Routine Helps With Problem Solving

This routine builds problem-solving skill by providing opportunities for students to

- experience problem solving without a traditional word problem;
- consider more than one possibility;
- see patterns and relationships within computations, problems, and solutions;
- practice slowing their approach to prompts to think more deeply;

- continue to think about a problem after a solution is found (when this ability is transferred to closed problems it helps students reexamine the problem and their solution after finding one);
- create their own solutions to a problem (identity); and
- think critically about their solutions as they listen to the ideas of others.

What to Do

1. Pose an open prompt.
2. Have students find a possible solution.
3. Have partners share their solutions with each other.
4. Bring the group together to solicit different ideas. Record those ideas on the board.
5. Discuss their ideas. Ask questions like:

   » How are these related?
   » How are they different?
   » What would happen if _____?
   » Based on what you see, what can't be a solution to this problem?

Note: When recording student ideas, try to organize their answers so that patterns can be more apparent. In the example, you might record 31 + 30 above 30 + 31, above 29 + 32, above 28 + 33, and so on. Doing so will help them see that one more is being given from the first addend to the second addend each time. That pattern is easier to see when the expressions are written above one another. Also note that it takes practice to do this well. A tip for beginning this work is to anticipate what students might say so that you know the different possibilities. Then, visualize what they might look like on the board so that when they give you one of those possibilities you have a decent idea where to record it.

Something to Think About: Creating Open Questions

Creating open questions can be challenging at first. With practice, you'll get the hang of it. In fact, you're likely to find that your questioning in general shifts from more closed questions to more open questions. But until then, you may be wondering how to create an open question or prompt. In short, you want to take any closed problem, find the answer, and then write a new problem that starts with the answer.

A good way to create an open prompt is to find and solve a closed prompt. The example in the opening was taken from 49 + 12. After finding the

sum, another expression (37 + 24) was identified and used to create the open question. That doesn't mean that the goal is for a student to come up with the original 49 + 12. It was simply used as a starting point. A similar, open question could have been, "The sum of two numbers is 61, what are they?" The only difference now is that students don't have to find the sum before creating the possible addends. Keep in mind that there is no wrong way to ask an open question. The original problem is included with the following variations so you can get a better sense of how to do this.

LOTS AND LOTS (VARIATIONS): KEEP IT JOYFUL

There is joy in doing math, or at least there should be. Routines are a way to keep things fun by providing bite-sized problem-solving engagements for each student. Enjoyment comes from both being challenged and finding success more often than not. You want to vary routines so that they provide just enough challenge, yet many students are likely to find success with. You want them to be accessible with multiple entry points like those offered in an open-ended prompt. Your variations can ratchet up the rigor and challenge but if you find yourself with a version that is creating frustration, stop doing it no matter how clever it is. That's not to say you should stop at the first sign of struggle. But you do need to keep a pulse on your students' tone and mindset. Disengagement can be perceived as a lack of interest, but it might be the result of feeling overwhelmed and incompetent (SanGiovanni et al., 2020).

Variation A: Base Ten Number Creations

Having students create examples provides good insight into their understanding and possible misconception. Take this variation for example. It started with a prompt asking students to write the number shown with 3 sticks and 7 dots (37). Some young students think that the only way to represent a number with base ten blocks (sticks and dots) is by showing the tens and then the ones. They might not understand that 7 dots followed by 3 sticks is also 37. Asking for a third representation might cause more challenge, even for those who know that the order of the sticks and dots can be reversed. Here, a third example might be 2 sticks, 2 dots, 1 stick, and 5 more dots, but 2 sticks and 17 dots is also a viable option. First-grade students exposed to these diverse representations will soon recognize that it's not about the order of the images but rather what value those images represent. This is a significant precursor to decomposing numbers abstractly. Three- and four-digit numbers can be included by using squares (hundreds) and cubes (thousands) in later grades.

A

Use sticks and dots to show 37 in three different ways.

Variation B: Equivalent Expressions

The concept of equal and the meaning of the equal sign is an essential understanding in primary grades. Students need to understand that the sum or difference can appear on the left side of an equation and that two different expressions with the same operation (e.g., 5 + 5 and 6 + 4) can be equal as well. This example shows a new challenge in which students need to create an addition problem that is equal to a subtraction problem. In first grade, it might look something like 4 + 5 = 10 – 1. Students in second and third grade are likely to use two- or three-digit numbers, though at first their problems may simply use friendly numbers (e.g., 40 + 50 = 100 – 10. Fourth- or fifth-grade students could work with very different operations, such as subtraction and multiplication (e.g., 45 – 3 = 6 × 7). Remember to start with comfortable situations, lift up connections, and slowly progress to more challenging situations as your students show that they're ready for them.

> **B**
>
> An addition problem and a subtraction problem are equal. What might they be?

Variation C: Representing Fractions

This prompt is like Variation A in that students are asked to create different representations of a given number. It was inspired by a worksheet that asked students to identify the fractions shown. The obvious difference here is that students are to create fractions. But there are two other differences. First, students aren't told how many examples to create. Asking for an exact number of examples is fine but leaving that number open can help keep students engaged who might have met their quota faster than their classmates. That openness can push student thinking, increasing the likelihood of unique creations that spark great conversation. A more important difference here is that students are asked to create examples or nonexamples of the fraction. This interesting twist lays the foundation for conversation and debate between partners and within the class. For instance, some examples might have three shaded parts, yet some nonexamples might have three shaded parts (with unequal partitions). The presence of both creates an environment for both a good conversation and ultimately deeper understanding.

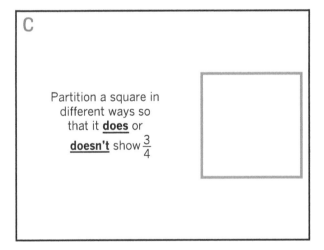

> **C**
>
> Partition a square in different ways so that it **does** or **doesn't** show $\frac{3}{4}$

Variation D: Restrictions

Comparing fractions to benchmarks is a good use of this routine. The example on the top is completely open, inspired by a problem asking students to identify which of two fractions was greater. The problem on the top is a good place to begin. Over time, you might notice that your students find convenient shortcuts or go back to the same numbers repeatedly. So, you can adjust your prompt to put a restriction on what they create. For the top prompt, students might be quick to say, "done!" after naming $\frac{5}{8}$, $\frac{6}{8}$, and $\frac{7}{8}$. Acknowledge their quick recognition of these correct examples. Ask how they decided so quickly, and have them describe the common relationship between the numerators and the denominators in each of them. The next time you pose the prompt (possibly right after discussion of the top example) use the one below to move student thinking forward. Primary teachers can swap out fractions with whole numbers, asking first graders about numbers between 50 and 100 or asking second graders about numbers between 500 and 1,000.

D

Three different fractions are between $\frac{1}{2}$ and 1. What might those fractions be?

D

Three different fractions are between $\frac{1}{2}$ and 1. But none have a denominator of 8. What might those fractions be?

NOTES

Variation E: Create–Share–Create

In this variation, students create a possible solution. They share their solution with a partner and give their partner feedback. Then, each student creates a new example and then shares that with a different partner. This can be repeated two or three times before having the group discuss. During that discussion, ask students to share a partner's solution and what they liked or noticed about it. Ask if any partner's ideas helped them rethink the possibilities. Ask if any partners had the exact same solutions. The two examples here offer new ideas about what you might do with the routine. But for this create-share-create variation, the one on the top would be problematic because it calls for five examples. To maintain a good pace for this variation, use prompts that require just one example.

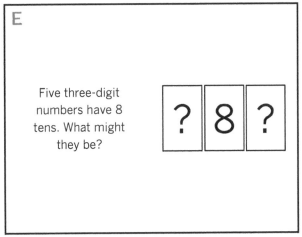

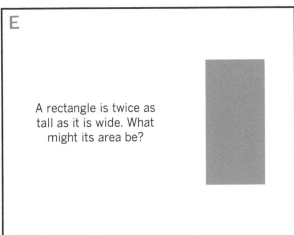

NOTES

Variation F: Time and Money

Time and money are two examples of topics or standards that hold the potential to hijack your instructional time. Both seem like significant topics, but in the grand scheme of elementary mathematics they aren't (Student Achievement Partners, n.d.). Teaching these can become traps that take time and energy from more essential skills and concepts. This variation of Lots and Lots gives two examples of how you might incorporate needed practice with these while continuing to move through your curriculum scope and sequence. You want to be sure that your open questions create just the right challenge for your students so two examples for each topic with varying degrees of challenge are shown. The top left shows an elapsed time problem that might be used in third or fourth grade and the bottom left shows a telling time problem that first or second graders would benefit from. Notice the subtle difference between the two money problems. The lower example would be good for students' early work with counting money, whereas the top could be used later that year or any grade after.

F

Ebony's favorite movie is 1 hour and 55 minutes long. What might be her start and stop times for watching it?

F

Amy has 7 coins in her pocket, and they aren't all the same. How much money might she have in her pocket?

F

The minute hand is pointing to 9 on the clock. What time might it be?

F

Cole has 5 of the same coin. How much money might he have?

Credit: clock image from kyoshino/istockphoto.com; coins image from NoDerog/istockphoto.com

Variation G: One Solution for Different Open Prompts

Variation E shows a solution to different open-ended prompts. In first grade or second grade, the variation could be as simple as 14 with one prompt being, "It is the sum of these two numbers," and the other being, "It is the difference of these two numbers." In this seventh-grade example, −14 is the result of all four operations. However, you could stick with the same operation prompting that −14 is the sum of these two numbers, the sum of these three numbers, and the sum of these four numbers. There is no limit. The idea is for students to see patterns, relationships, and possibilities. Your goal is to help students see that math is more than just one right answer.

G

- Sum of three different integers . . .
- Difference of two different integers . . .
- Product of these two integers . . .
- Quotient of these two integers . . .

$$-14$$

NOTES

THE SWAP

About the Routine

What do the numbers in the example have in common? Clearly, each is a three-digit number, but you could also say that each is less than 1,000 or that all of them are between 200 and 950. Did you notice that? What's different about them? Better yet, what's different about one of them in particular? Well, you likely noticed that 738 is the only number that doesn't have 1 ten in it. You might have noticed that 217 is the only number less than 500. You might have thought about one being even or odd before you caught that another shared the same trait. Though sticking with that idea, you might have thought that 917 is the only one where each digit is an odd number. Now, regardless of the characteristic you considered, what is a new number you could create to swap out for the number you disqualified?

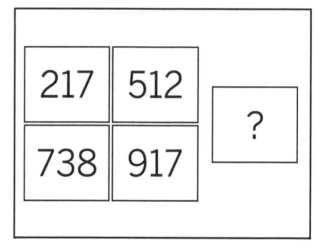

This routine, The Swap, might remind you of Which One Doesn't Belong (Danielson & Danielson, 2016) or the instructional activity Eliminate It (O'Connell & SanGiovanni, 2013). It is similar with one notable difference. In this routine, not only are there often different interpretations of the relationships, but students are also charged with creating new examples that fit the pattern they identify. This is powerful and extremely important because it taps into student creativity, while increasing cognitive demand. It also spotlights the potential for many, many possibilities, which is an important consideration

for students who are beginning to perceive math as strict and procedural.

You might also be wondering how this routine fits in a book about problem solving. It fits because it is about looking for patterns and relationships, which is a recognized problem-solving strategy, especially for nonroutine or nonword problems. More importantly, it charges students with thinking and reasoning, which is an essential ingredient for becoming productive problem solvers. The Swap also incorporates practice for comparing and contrasting, which is a problem-solving skill baked into other routines, such as Routine 7: Same and Different (page 76).

 All routines can be downloaded for your use at
https://qrs.ly/3cemjnt

How This Routine Helps With Problem Solving

This routine builds problem-solving skill by providing opportunities for students to

- practice problem solving without a word problem,
- compare and contrast characteristics of numbers (and other concepts),
- look for patterns within numbers,
- think critically about relationships,
- use patterns to find solutions,

- examine numbers and other concepts through a variety of lenses,
- create their own examples that fit patterns (identity),
- consider multiple possibilities after one relationship and/or solution has been determined,
- use patterns to create new examples, and
- listen to the perspectives of others and consider how their ideas are viable.

What to Do

1. Pose four numbers or concepts. Three of those should share a certain characteristic.

2. Have students examine the items independently before talking with a partner about the relationships they see.

3. Discuss student thinking about the four items. Be prepared to accept more than one possible relationship.

4. Record noted relationships on the board.

5. Have students create a new example that they could "swap" with the example that doesn't fit.

6. Record new examples under the noted relationship you recorded on the board.

7. Optional: You can adjust the directions by asking students to generate more than one example for one of the noted relationships. You can have students identify an example for each of the noted relationships. Another option is to have students create a new example that doesn't fit the relationship. In the example, 738 doesn't fit if you see a pattern within how many tens are in each number. A new example that doesn't fit could be 456 (5 tens), 349 (4 tens), 802 (no tens), and so on.

Something to Think About: Logic Games

Obviously, working with word problems is a good way to develop students' problem-solving skills. But, at its core, problem solving is about thinking and reasoning. Both are developed in all sorts of ways. In short, you want to "train the brain" to think strategically, self-question, predict, maneuver, and adjust. Strategy games and logic puzzles are great ways to do this. These activities are games like Blokus, Othello, Mancala, Nine Men's Morris, and so many others. Tangram puzzles and the like make great centers. The point is that these activities are rich in reasoning and breed engagement. They also develop other useful problem-solving skills like perseverance and productive struggle.

But logic games are often left behind for basic fact games, number centers, and fluency worksheets. The suggestion here is to work logic games and puzzles into your center and independent practice rotation. Feature them at Back-to-School and Family Math Nights. Assign them for homework from time to time. And don't forget to talk about the games after students play them to memorialize their thinking and reasoning. Ask questions like, "What did you try that worked?" "What didn't work?" "What would you do differently next time?" or "What questions do you have for your opponent about the moves they made?"

THE SWAP (VARIATIONS): INTRODUCING A SKILL OR CONCEPT

The Swap works with every skill or concept that you teach. The following variations give you a sense of what it could look like with some of those across different grades. And while routines, in general, are intended to practice ideas that have been taught, this is the one routine that you might leverage to introduce a topic. Posing examples and asking students how they are related before teaching a concept gives you insight into their perceptions and could expose understanding that they already have, though it may not have been taught or formalized. At the very least, it is another opportunity for them to observe and think critically.

Variation A: Dot Card Numbers

The Swap is perfect for any grade level, and quite frankly it's never too early to introduce. This variation shows what it might look like in kindergarten. In this example, numbers are shown on ten frames. Students might exclude the bottom left example because it is the only one with its first ten frame empty. They might exclude the top left because its second ten frame is empty. While both are viable, you really want them to think about the number (8) represented in each example. Then, they should make a new example of 8 to swap out for the 18 in the upper right. Ten frames are just one representation to use. You can include dot cards, dominoes, base-ten blocks, and so on. You can even mingle representations by showing 8 with a ten frame, a dot card, and a domino.

NOTES

Variation B: Even and Odd Numbers

Using even and odd numbers is probably an obvious example. The variation is shared for two distinct reasons. First, recognizing even and odd numbers is one of those standards that sometimes fades into the background as instruction focuses on other, more critical skills and concepts. But, identifying even and odd numbers with automaticity plays an important role in students' number sense and computational fluency. This variation also shows how you can naturally extend a concept to deepen student understanding. The top example shows the basic expectation of identifying even or odd with two-digit numbers. While that may be the limit of an instructional standard at a given grade level, it's perfectly fine (and wise) to push students further when they show they're ready. The bottom example does this by presenting three-digit numbers. A clever transition between these two examples could be to mix three, two-digit numbers with a fourth, three-digit number (e.g., 24, 88, 39, and 324) before mixing two of each (e.g., 24, 89, 622, and 156).

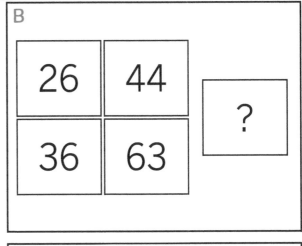

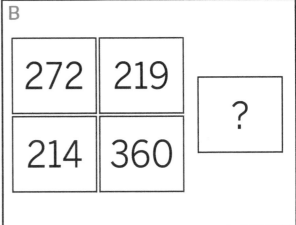

Variation C: Basic Facts

Learning basic facts through strategies creates significant performance and retention advantages (Baroody et al., 2009; Henry & Brown, 2008; Hiebert & Carpenter, 1992; Hiebert & Lefevre, 1986; Jordan et al., 2006; Thornton, 1978). Of course, quality practice with these strategies is critical for students' utility and application of them (Bay-Williams & SanGiovanni, 2021). You can use this routine to practice both critical thinking and basic fact strategies. In this example, students might think that 8 – 4 should be swapped out because it is the only fact with a single-digit minuend. While viable, they should also consider removing 18 – 10 because that is the only subtraction problem that doesn't represent a double (addition) or halve (subtraction) fact. A new fact they could swap out for it could be something like 20 – 10 or 6 – 3.

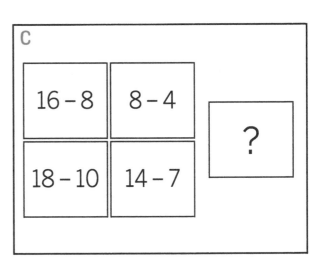

Variation D: Reasoning Strategies for Fluency

Building on the basic fact example in the previous variation, this routine could be easily tooled for practicing computational strategies like adding on, making ten, compensation, and partial sums. It would also work well with multiplication and division strategies. The goal here is not to find the sum but to instead focus on the reasoning strategy that might be used to solve each. In this example, the lower left problem lends itself to a count on strategy. The others could be solved by counting on, but it's likely more efficient to use a make ten strategy. That is, 69 + 13 could be thought of as 69 + 1 + 12 or 29 + 17 could be thought of as 29 + 1 + 16. In each of these, one addend is decomposed to make a ten so that the other addend is easier to work with. Again, the point is to focus on the thinking not the solution. After coming to an agreement about the strategy the three have in common, students could create new expressions like 59 + 24 or 26 + 39.

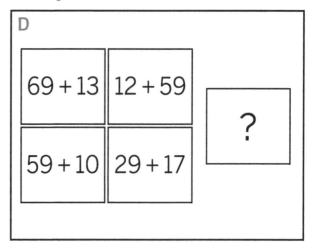

Variation F: Fraction Concepts

This routine is perfect for practicing concepts of fractions. This example focuses on representing $\frac{1}{4}$. Notice that there are some unique examples that are likely to challenge student thinking. Because many students experience fractions through squares, circles, and pizzas the lower right triangle might be hard to make sense of. The triangle and the square counter prevalent shading practices in which the numerator is always the shaded amount. But in these two (upper left and lower right), $\frac{1}{4}$ is not shaded. The lower left exposes misconceptions about equally partitioning shapes. In short, this one seemingly simplistic example goes a long way toward realizing the deep understanding of fractions our students must have. As a side note, many of the routines in this book are intended to be done as mental practices, rich with discussion, requiring no writing. However, this example would require that.

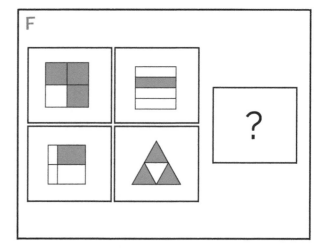

Variation G: Compare to Benchmarks

Sticking with the fraction theme, The Swap is a good routine for practicing benchmark comparisons. On the top, students might think about the size of the denominator, noting that $\frac{2}{12}$ is the only one with a two-digit denominator. Others might argue that $\frac{1}{4}$ has the smallest denominator. Still others might argue that $\frac{1}{8}$ is the smallest fraction. Each of these arguments work fine. But it would also be good to hear that $\frac{6}{8}$ is the only fraction greater than $\frac{1}{2}$. New examples could then be any fraction greater than $\frac{1}{2}$. Know that students might not come up with this reasoning, which is fine. If they don't, be sure to share something (this benchmark comparison) that you noticed. The bottom example is similar because comparisons would be made to one whole. In it, $\frac{8}{10}$ is the only value less than one. It serves as a reminder to work in mixed numbers with fraction practice as often as possible.

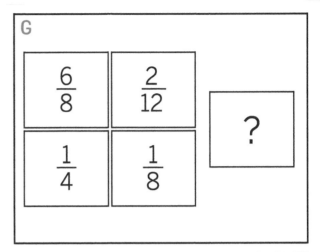

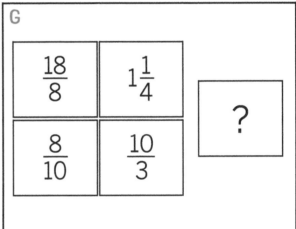

Variation H: Geometry

This variation shows how you can move beyond number into concepts like geometry and measurement. This example pokes students to count the number of sides or to recognize quadrilaterals. To grow the possibilities, change the color, orientation, and size of the shapes. In primary grades, mix in nonpolygons, irregular figures, or even three-dimensional shapes. In later grades, you can use other geometric concepts like angle measure or composite figures. As for measurement ideas, in upper elementary grades, you could show figures that have equal area or perimeter.

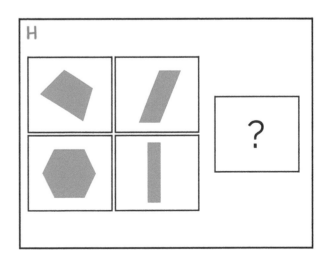

Variation I: The Swap in Middle School

The ideas shared in the different variations easily transfer to middle school content. For example, you could swap out even and odd numbers with fractions that convert to terminating or repeating decimals. Variation D could morph into sums or integers that are either negative or positive. In this example, all but the upper right are examples of triangle measurements that represent a 3–4-5 right triangle. Examples of other content that work with this routine include equivalent ratios, sets of equivalent values (e.g., 38% of 100, 19% of 200, and 50% of 76), examples of transformations, symmetrical versus nonsymmetrical figures, or possibly square numbers. As mentioned in earlier routines, The Swap is perfect for students to create during independent time or for homework. You can then use their creations for your routine nurturing student voice, identity, and relevancy.

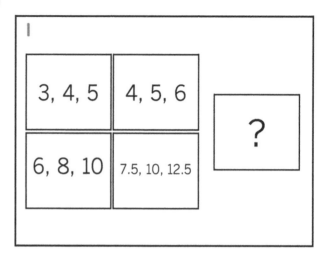

NOTES

PART 3

WHERE TO GO NEXT

You are now armed with understanding how routines can develop student skill with solving problems. You hopefully see how they can engage your students. You have examined a host of examples and modifications ready to implement in your classroom. So where do you go next?

MAKE A PLAN

Using routines in your mathematics classrooms might be considerably different than what has been done previously. To be successful, you need to craft a plan that addresses fundamental considerations. First, identify the problem-solving content or big ideas you want to focus on with your students. Next, determine which routines you think will work best. Think about a rotation of routines and whether you will change routines out daily or if you will work with one routine for a few days before moving to the next. You can find success with either approach, though the latter, sticking with the same routine for a week or so, is probably the better option. There are a few other details you need to think about to plan your routines with intention and purpose.

Identify Content for Routines

Routines are not intended as first instruction. You want students to be engaging in rich discussion with content that they have been introduced to already. These routines are chances to practice problem-solving skills. The number types and problem situations that you select are relative to where your students are. For example, if your students are just beginning to work with three-digit numbers it's best for the problems in your routines to be two-digit numbers. If your students are just learning about comparison problems, avoid including those in your problem-solving routines for a bit. And know that it is OK for classrooms in the same grade to be at different places. The goal is to advance all students' reasoning and problem-solving skills from where they are currently.

Identify Routines

It's likely that you prefer certain representations, strategies, or instructional techniques in general. The same can probably be said about your preference of routines. It's also likely that your preferences are different than those of your colleagues. This collection of routines offers choice so that you can find the ones that suit you and your students best. Some may be simply more appealing than others. You have options. Do not feel compelled to use a specific sequence of routines or to "cover" or "complete" all of the routines.

Choose a few routines that you want to master first. You might make your selection based on students' interests or academic needs. You might choose Imagine That (page 111) or Match the Equation (page 118) because your students need practice with representing problems. You might choose What's the Question? (page 50) or Asked and Answered (page 57) because understanding the question has proven difficult to your students. Or you might choose Sticky Patterns (page 165) or The Swap (page 182) because you want your students to better see patterns and relationships.

Determine Your Rotation

Doing the same routine each day will become mundane quite quickly. Think about which routines you will rotate through, including the order of them. You might start with one that is about retelling a problem, followed by one that focuses on the question in a problem, followed by Match the Equation, which practices how a problem can be represented. It's OK to be unsure at first. It's OK to deviate from a planned sequence. You might find that you need to circle back to a certain routine before continuing on with your rotation.

It's important to realize that you don't have to dedicate a specific number of days or class periods to a routine before rotating to another. The time spent with two different routines may not be equivalent. You can plan the amount of time you spend with a routine based on students' needs, engagement, interest, and excitement for it. However, even if you spend a few extra days with a certain routine, you should plan to move on from it so that it doesn't become stale. You should be mindful of those routines that students truly enjoy and plan to come back to them throughout the year.

Give It Time

Thinking, reasoning, and discussion may be unchartered waters for some of your students. It's possible that many of your students haven't had many opportunities to work with problem solving on a day-to-day basis. Some may not have had opportunities to think and reason on their own when problem solving. Their lack of experience may mean that they are hesitant to share their thinking because they lack confidence or because they aren't sure how to talk about their thinking. Give them opportunity and time. When well nurtured, you will find that you can't stop them from sharing their ideas and looking for new ways of solving problems. That number of students probably diminishes further when you factor in opportunities for discussion and justification of reasoning and number sense.

This may be unchartered waters for you too. Many teachers have little training in effective problem-solving instruction. They rely on their own experiences and perceive the goal of the activity to be getting the right answer. When students struggle, teachers can be compelled to stop the process and show them how to be successful. In short, your first routine, or two, may flop because of you and your students' unfamiliarity. That is fine. It should be expected. Be patient. Stick with it. Reflect on what happened, what surprised you, and how you might go about it differently. Try it again for the next day and the next. Work to find a rhythm. But also know that some routines just might not work for you or your students. That's another reason why there are so many to choose from. If you find that one isn't hitting the mark after a few days of practice, toss it out and start with a new one.

Set Goals

You can offset the challenges with goals, but be sure to keep your goals reasonable. At first, you might set the goal of doing a routine three times a week or mastering a specific routine over the course of two weeks. You might set a goal to use three different routines over the course of a month or five different routines in a marking period.

You can think about setting goals for students as well. You might want to develop how well they retell a problem. You might want them to work with justifying their thinking or determining operations and writing equations. You can measure those goals in all sorts of ways. One way might be to revisit a routine from early in the year with the exact same problems or numbers later in the year and compare student performance. In other situations, it might make sense to measure growing student proficiency on a brief written assessment. You can also measure student dispositions, behaviors, communication skills, and confidence. A simple set of survey questions like those below could be a good place to start.

- I can solve problems.
- I have ideas about how to solve new problems.
- I have different strategies for solving problems that I know how to use.
- I like solving problems.
- I know how to show problems.
- I can usually tell if my answer makes sense when I solve a problem.
- I know what questions to ask myself when I try to solve problems.

ADJUST TO THEIR ADJUSTMENTS

Throughout the day, you naturally respond to student thinking and reasoning. You ask questions to challenge student ideas. You push back on your students' strategies. You ask them to clarify. You'll need to leverage all of those same teacher moves during these problem-solving routines. You'll also need to keep in mind that as students work with routines, they'll begin to adjust their reasoning. They may begin to favor specific strategies or approaches. When they do, you'll need to respond by changing the numbers, skills, and/or the routine that you use.

FURTHER MODIFY ROUTINES

Each of the routines here are creations or adaptations of activities used in real classrooms. They have served real students very well. There are directions and procedures for implementing them; but those directions are not set in stone. In fact, many of the routines presented are variations of the first offerings. There are ideas for modifying presented throughout, but more can be changed. You should feel free to change how a routine is carried out. Change the starting point, the process, or how students interact. Modify these routines to make them their own.

DESIGN YOUR OWN ROUTINES

These routines are all built to go after the difficulties students have when they encounter problems. Each routine is an opportunity for students to discuss and defend their reasoning. You can modify almost any instructional activity to become a routine. As you become more comfortable with routines, you can begin to develop your own based on games and activities you use during instruction. You can look for routines online. You might even investigate number sense routines and incorporate them in your own instruction.

Students might even take the next step and create their own examples from the various routines. When students create, producing new or original work, they are working at the highest cognitive level (Anderson & Krathwohl, 2001; Bloom, 1956).

WORK COLLABORATIVELY AND SHARE THE LOAD

Sometimes your students' creative thinking will inspire new possibilities or new routines. Keep in mind that your colleagues are also an excellent creative source for generating examples. When teachers plan together, they learn about others' perspectives, experiences, and mathematical insights. They learn about how others think and reason about numbers and computation. The exchange of ideas with your colleagues can help you reinforce and grow your own ideas. It helps you prepare. It helps you facilitate student reasoning through discussion.

Leveraging insights from other teachers and students is also a great way to share the workload. For example, four teachers on a team could each create four sets of prompts for a routine. If those four teachers share their four, each teacher would have a routine planned for 16 days, or a little more than three weeks. Each of those teachers could also have students create examples of their routine. If so, they could select four student examples and rotate them as well. In doing so, a teacher who created four examples could wind up with 32 days ready to go.

USE JUMP-START ROUTINES FOR PROFESSIONAL LEARNING OR PLCS

Routines are the perfect focus for professional learning or a professional learning community (PLC). In fact, many of the routines offered in this book are the result of ongoing collaborative conversations, dabbling, and reflection. In a PLC about routines, you might first learn about what routines are, why they matter, and the instructional challenges they intend to solve. You and your colleagues can then begin to learn about specific routines, try them out, and share your experiences. The steps below are a helpful framework for investigating and learning about routines in a PLC.

1. **Learn About the Routine:** Colleagues select a routine that they all want to focus on. They read about it and discuss what it might look like or how it might be adjusted for their students.

2. **Identify Content for the Routine:** Colleagues discuss what problem situations and number types they would feature in the routine and why.

3. **Create Examples:** Colleagues select or create examples of the routine for use with their students. One way to do this is to make use of collaborative software, such as Google Slides, in which each teacher can craft some examples of the routine they intend to use with their students. A collaboration tool allows those teachers to have a record of their work for future use as well as providing a way to share examples between them. And, sharing examples also helps lessen the workload.

4. **Predict What Might Happen:** After making examples of the routine to use with students, colleagues anticipate what their students will do. They might share the strategies that students will use, the misconceptions they might show, or the questions that the teachers themselves might ask.

5. **Do Them:** Members of the PLC do the routines with their students.

6. **Reflect:** Individuals jot down notes or capture reflections about the routine. Those reflections are brought to the next meeting in which colleagues share their experiences and consider what went well and what they might do differently in the future.

These six steps are then started again with a new routine. There are no rules as to how this must proceed. There is logic in exploring the same routines with your colleagues. However, the PLC can play out just as well if you all select your own routines to use.

The work of the PLC might be strengthened through peer observation and feedback. To do this, you simply visit one another and look for how routines are being implemented. Then, you give and receive feedback from your colleagues about how things went. Peer observations can be supported with a "look for" tool. It's possible that colleagues don't have the time to visit each other during the day. Another option might be for you to make a video of your routine for others to view and offer feedback.

Problem Solving Look-For

A look-for tool helps guide a visit to a colleague's classroom as they do a routine. Some of those ideas are below, but the list is not exhaustive.

The classroom environment is conducive to a routine.

- Student proximity to the teacher is appropriate.
- Student arrangement promotes discussion between students and as a class.
- Respectful behaviors are established.
- Students are comfortable sharing ideas.

The routine is appropriate.

- The purpose of the routine is clear.
- The problem type is appropriate.
- The selected numbers are appropriate.
- The routine focuses on reasoning and sense making.

Multiple solutions/rationales are investigated/discussed.

- Student ideas and insights are solicited first before the teacher shares their ideas.
- Strategies are recorded and/or discussed.
- Thinking is recorded accurately.
- More than one solution pathway is investigated (as appropriate).

Communication is prevalent.

- Students share their reasoning.
- Students listen and react to the reasoning of others.
- Teachers react to student reasoning by asking questions.
- Representations (e.g., drawings, equations) are connected to the problem by the student and/or teacher.

Discussion promotes reasoning.

- More than one perspective is featured.
- Teacher asks students to justify their thinking and most attempt to do so.
- Teacher questions overly complicated or highly inefficient strategies.

JUMP-START MATHEMATICS ENGAGEMENT

A routine is an opportunity to jump-start engagement, problem solving, and reasoning. They might work best at the beginning of a lesson (SanGiovanni, 2020) but can work well at any point during the math block. Routines are quality tasks for working with a wide range of problem-solving skills. They are opportunities for promoting engagement through novel prompts, interesting situations, and discussion. They are opportunities to play with problem solving and for making student thinking and reasoning routine!

APPENDIX

TITLE	BRIEF	TARGETED PROBLEM-SOLVING SKILL	PG
#1 I Would Say	Students practice restating problems in their own words.	Making Sense: Retelling	24
#2 3Qs	Students practice with a variety of questions so that they can determine how to make sense of a problem, identify the question, and think about a strategy for solving it.	Making Sense: Asking Questions	33
#3 Asked and Answered	Students learn to think carefully about a question by grappling with questions that can, and cannot, be answered.	Questions: Understanding the Question	41
#4 What's the Question?	Students practice problem solving by creating questions and problems that yield a given solution.	Questions: Identifying Questions	50
#5 Same Data, Different Question	Students practice thinking and reasoning as questions change from day to day.	Questions: Identifying Questions	57
#6 How Do You . . .?	Students are presented with situations and then a question. Students determine how they would find the solution.	Reasoning: Solution Pathways	68
#7 Same and Different	Students compare and contrast two problems to analyze the changing nature of contexts, numbers, and questions.	Making Sense: Problem Elements	76
#8 What's the Sitch?	Students develop a process for analyzing different problem-solving situations (structures).	Making Sense: Analyzing Problems	86

TITLE	BRIEF	TARGETED PROBLEM-SOLVING SKILL	PG
#9 They Did What?	Students examine strategies and solutions of worked examples.	Reasoning: Reasonable Solutions/Pathways	94
#10 This Number, That Number	Students practice the strategy of solving a simpler problem by working with identical problems that have different number complexities.	Reasoning: Simpler Problems	103
#11 Imagine That	Students practice visualizing problems and generating useful representations to solve them.	Making Sense: Representing	111
#12 Match the Equation	Students practice representing problems with equations.	Making Sense: Representing	118
#13 And Then . . .	Students experience two-step problems in an engaging way through a narrative that they control.	Making Sense: Two-Step Problems	126
#14 Another Question	Students simply ask "another question" that generates another step resulting in more two-step problem practice.	Making Sense: Two-Step Problems	136
#15 TMI	Students practice identifying important information as well as extra or irrelevant information in problems.	Making Sense: Relevant Information	143
#16 It Can't Be	Students confront possible solutions to a problem and make arguments about why some of those possibilities can't be the solution.	Reasoning: Reasonable Solutions/Pathways	150
#17 Is It Reasonable?	A problem is posed. Students estimate the solution and discuss how they arrived at their estimates.	Reasoning: Reasonable Solutions	158
#18 Sticky Patterns	Students build skill with looking for and using patterns to solve problems.	Reasoning: Using Patterns	165

TITLE	BRIEF	TARGETED PROBLEM-SOLVING SKILL	PG
#19 Lots and Lots	Students practice finding more than one right answer as they solve open-ended problems.	Reasoning	174
#20 The Swap	Students examine a set of numbers and determine why they think a certain number doesn't belong. Then, they create a new example that would fit the relationship.	Reasoning	182

SOMETHING TO THINK ABOUT SECTIONS OVERVIEW

Problem solving intersects with so much of what is learned and taught in mathematics. Some of those important considerations are unpacked throughout this book in the Something to Think About sections. These brief passages give you something to think about as problem solving comes about in your classroom. A brief overview is included in the table that follows.

Avoid Proceduralizing Problem Solving (Routine 1: I Would Say)	There is no set of procedures that will solve any problem a student encounters. Be careful not to invest instructional time in a "foolproof" method for problem solving.
Rereading (Routine 2: 3Qs)	Rereading is important for making sense of a problem and getting unstuck. There is no set number of times a student should reread.
Where Do You Get the Data? (Routine 3: Asked and Answered)	It takes time to find authentic data for problems, tables, and charts. How can you do this efficiently?
What to Listen For (Routine 4: What's the Question?)	What sorts of things should you listen for as students solve problems to understand how well they are doing?
Using Routines for Centers and Homework (Routine 5: Same Data, Different Question)	Centers and homework are good opportunities for practicing skills reinforced during routines.
Problem Solving Can't Be Rote (Routine 6: How Do You . . .?)	Problem solving can't be a procedure. But thinking itself can't be rote. Instructional practices that ask students to mimic teacher thinking don't work.
Scaffolding a Routine (Routine 7: Same and Different)	Problem solving is for each and every student. Scaffolds help students access problems. Scaffolds are temporary.

Whole School Agreements (Routine 8: What's the Sitch?)	Approaches to teaching problem solving should be consistent across grades and schools.
More Than Just the Right Answer (Routine 9: They Did What?)	Right answers do matter in math. However, when students are learning math, right answers aren't the only thing that matters.
Why So Many Routines? (Routine 10: This Number, That Number)	There are different problem-solving skills to practice, and they need to be practiced in different ways. A variety of routines promotes transfer of skills while aligning to preferences and strengths of students and teachers.
Representations Match Situations (Routine 11: Imagine That)	Representations powerfully aid problem solving. Representations should align with what is happening in the problem.
Use What You Know (Routine 12: Match the Equation)	Leverage routines to target skills that students need to practice more.
Introducing a Routine (Routine 13: And Then . . .)	Take time to introduce a routine so that it functions well in your classroom.
Bundling Routines (Routine 14: Another Question)	Use routines in tandem or in a certain sequence to maximize instructional impact.
Reading Problems Together (Routine 15: TMI)	Be mindful of reading problems together. You can be misled about how well students are independently making sense of problems.
Calculators Can't Think (Routine 16: It Can't Be)	Tools help students. But tools don't think. Students think. They use the tool for better accuracy.
Estimation (Routine 17: Is It Reasonable?)	Estimation helps determine reasonableness of solutions to problems. Be careful that estimation isn't another procedure within problem solving.
Reframe Problem Solving (Routine 18: Sticky Patterns)	Change the problem-solving narrative from one of fear and anxiety to one of enthusiasm and joy.
Creating Open Questions (Routine 19: Lots and Lots)	Good questions prompt thinking. They can be included in every lesson. How do you write them?
Logic Games (Routine 20: The Swap)	Logic games and puzzles are other great ways for practicing thinking, reasoning, and problem solving. They can be a good addition to your centers collection.

REFERENCES

Aguirre, J. M., Mayfield-Ingram, K., & Martin, D. B. (2013). *The impact of identity in K–8 mathematics: Rethinking equity-based practices*. National Council of Teachers of Mathematics.

Anderson, L. W., & Krathwohl, D. R. (2001). *A taxonomy for learning, teaching and assessing: A revision of Bloom's taxonomy of educational objectives* (Complete ed.). Longman.

Barlow, A. T., & Cates, J. M. (2007). The answer is 20 cookies. What is the question? *Teaching Children Mathematics*, 13(5), 252–255. https://pubs.nctm.org/view/journals/tcm/13/5/article-p252.xml

Baroody, A. J., Bajwa, N. P., & Eiland, M. (2009). Why can't Johnny remember the basic facts? *Developmental Disabilities Research Reviews*, 15(1), 69–79.

Bay-Williams, J. M., & SanGiovanni, J. (2021). *Figuring out fluency in mathematics teaching and learning, grades K–8: Moving beyond basic facts and memorization*. Corwin.

Berry, R. (2018). *Thinking about instructional routines in mathematics teaching and learning*. National Council of Teachers of Mathematics. https://www.nctm.org/News-and-Calendar/Messages-from-the-President/Archive/Robert-Q_-Berry-III/Thinking-about-Instructional-Routines-in-Mathematics-Teaching-and-Learning/

Bloom, B. S. (1956). *Taxonomy of educational objectives handbook 1*. Longman.

Boaler, J. (2015). *Mathematical mindsets: Unleashing students' potential through creative math, inspiring messages, and innovative teaching*. Jossey-Bass.

Burger, E. B., & Starbird, M. (2012). *The 5 elements of effective thinking*. Princeton University Press.

Bushart, B. (n.d.). *Numberless word problems*. Numberless Word Problems. Retrieved September 1, 2022, from https://numberlesswp.com/

Carpenter, T. P., Fennema, E., Franke, M. L., Levi, L., & Empson, S. B. (2014). *Children's mathematics: Cognitively guided instruction* (2nd ed.). Heinemann.

Danielson, C., & Danielson, C. (2016). *Which one doesn't belong? A shapes book*. Stenhouse Publishers.

Dweck, C. (2006). *Mindset: The new psychology of success*. Penguin Random House.

Journal of Adolescent & Adult Literacy 42 Edwards, S. A., Maloy, R. W., & Anderson, G. (2009, June 30). *Reading coaching for math word problems*. Literacy Coaching Clearinghouse. Retrieved April 25, 2022, from https://eric.ed.gov/?q=SOLVING%2BMATH%2BWORD%2BPROBLEMS&id=ED530295

Egan, M. (1999). Reflections on effective use of graphic organizers. *Journal of Adolescent & Adult Literacy, 42*, 641–645.

Fosnot, C. T., & Dolk, M. (2001). *Young mathematicians at work: Constructing multiplication and division*. Heinemann.

Fried, M. N. (n.d.). *Mathematics as the science of patterns – Mathematics as the science of patterns*. Mathematical Association of America. Retrieved May 20, 2022, from https://www.maa.org/press/periodicals/convergence/mathematics-as-the-science-of-patterns-mathematics-as-the-science-of-patterns

Gladwell, M. (2008). *Outliers: The story of success*. Little, Brown and Company.

Henry, V. J., & Brown, R. S. (2008). First-grade basic facts: An investigation into teaching and learning of an accelerated, high-demand memorization standard. *Journal for Research in Mathematics Education*, 39(2), 153–183.

Hiebert, J., & Lefevre, P. (1986). Conceptual and procedural knowledge in mathematics: An introductory analysis. In J. Hiebert (Ed.), *Conceptual and procedural knowledge: The case of mathematics* (pp. 1–27). Lawrence Erlbaum.

Hiebert, J., & Carpenter, T. P. (1992). Learning and teaching with understanding. In D. A. Grouws (Ed.), *Handbook of research on mathematics teaching and learning* (pp. 65–97). Macmillan.

Jordan, N. C., Kaplan, D., Olah, L., & Locuniak, M. N. (2006). Number sense growth in kindergarten: A longitudinal investigation of children at risk for mathematics difficulties. *Child Development*, 77(1), 153–175.

Kaplinsky, R. (2020). *Open middle math: Problems that unlock student thinking, 6–12.* Stenhouse Publishers.

Karp, K. S., Bush, S. B., & Dougherty, B. J. (2014). 13 rules that expire. *Teaching Children Mathematics*, 21, 18–25.

Karp, K. S., Dougherty, B. J., & Bush, S. B. (2021). *The math pact, elementary: Achieving instructional coherence within and across grades.* Corwin.

Kelemanik, G., Lucenta, A., Creighton, S. J., & Lampert, M. (2016). *Routines for reasoning: Fostering the mathematical practices in all students.* Heinemann.

Land, T. J., Drake, C., Sweeney, M., Franke, N., & Johnson, J. M. (2014). *Transforming the task with number choice kindergarten through grade 3.* National Council of Teachers of Mathematics.

McGinn, K. M., Lange, K. E., & Booth, J. L. (2015). A worked example for creating worked examples. *Mathematics Teaching in the Middle School*, 21, 26–33.

Merseth, K. K. (1993). How old is the shepherd? An essay about mathematics education. *Phi Delta Kappan*, 74(7), 548–554.

Moore, S. D., Morrow-Leong, K., & Gojak, L. (2020). *Mathematize it! Going beyond key words to make sense of word problems grades 3–5.* Corwin.

Morrow-Leong, K., Moore, S. D., & Gojak, L. (2020). *Mathematize it! Going beyond key words to make sense of word problems grades K–2.* Corwin.

National Council of Teachers of Mathematics (NCTM). (n.d.). *Problem solving.* NCTM. Retrieved April 27, 2022, from https://www.nctm.org/Research-and-Advocacy/Research-Brief-and-Clips/ProblemSolving/

National Council of Teachers of Mathematics (NCTM). (2014). *Principles to actions: Ensuring mathematical success for all.* NCTM.

National Governors Association Center for Best Practices & Council of Chief State School Officers (NGA Center & CCSSO). (2010). *Common core state standards for mathematics.* NGA Center & CCSSO.

O'Connell, S., & SanGiovanni, J. (2013). *Putting the practices into action: Implementing the Common Core Standards for mathematical practice, K–8.* Heinemann.

Parrish, S. (2014). *Number talks: Helping children build mental math and computation strategies, grades K–5.* Math Solutions.

Renkl, A. (2014). Learning from worked examples: How to prepare students for meaningful problem solving. In V. Benassi, C. E. Overson, & C. M. Hakala (Eds.), *Applying science of learning in education: Infusing psychological science into the curriculum* (pp. 118–130). http://teachpsych.org/ebooks/asle2014/index.php

Rowland, T. (1999). Pronouns in mathematics talk: Power, vagueness and generalisation. *For the Learning of Mathematics*, 19(2), 19–26. http://www.jstor.org/stable/40248295

SanGiovanni, J., Katt, S., Dykema, K. J., & Larson, M. (2020). *Productive math struggle: A 6-point action plan for fostering perseverance.* Corwin.

SanGiovanni, J., Katt, S., Knighten, L., & Rivera, G. (2021). *Answers to your biggest questions about teaching elementary math.* Corwin.

SanGiovanni, J. J. (2020). *Daily routines to jump-start math class: Elementary school.* Corwin.

Small, M. (2010). *Good questions: Great ways to differentiate mathematics instruction.* Teachers College, Columbia University.

Smith, M. S., & Sherin, M. G. (2019). *The 5 practices in practice: Successfully orchestrating mathematics discussions in your middle school classroom.* Corwin.

Smith, M. S., & Stein, M. K. (2018). *5 practices for orchestrating productive mathematics discussions* (2nd ed). National Council of Teachers of Mathematics.

Star, J. R., & Verschaffel, L. (2016). Providing support for student sense making: Recommendations from cognitive science for the teaching of mathematics. In J. Cai (Ed.), *Compendium for research in mathematics education*. National Council of Teachers of Mathematics.

Stauffer, B. (2022, March 17). *What are 21st century* skills? AES. Retrieved April 22, 2022, from https://www.aeseducation.com/blog/what-are-21st-century-skills

Student Achievement Partners. (n.d.). *Mathematics: Focus by grade level*. Achieve the Core. Retrieved May 25, 2022, from https://achievethecore.org/category/774/mathematics-focus-by-grade-level

Sullivan, P., & Lilburn, P. (2005). *Good questions for math teaching why ask them and what to ask, grades K–6*. Math Solutions.

Thornton, C. (1978). Emphasizing thinking strategies in basic fact instruction. *Journal for Research in Mathematics Education*, 9(3), 214–227.

Van de Walle, J. A., Karp, K. S., & Bay-Williams, J. M. (2019). *Elementary and middle school mathematics: Teaching developmentally* (10th ed.). Pearson.

William & Mary School of Education. (n.d.). *Graphic organizers: Guiding principles and effective practices considerations packet*. Retrieved April 27, 2022, from https://education.wm.edu/centers/ttac/documents/packets/graphicorganizers.pdf

Woodward, J., Beckmann, S., Driscoll, M., Franke, M., Herzig, P., Jitendra, A., Koedinger, K. R., & Ogbuehi, P. (2018). *Improving mathematical problem solving in grades 4 through 8: A practice guide (NCEE 2012–4055)*. National Center for Education Evaluation and Regional Assistance, Institute of Education Sciences, & U.S. Department of Education. http://ies.ed.gov/ncee/wwc/publications_reviews.aspx#pubsearch/

INDEX

Addition and subtraction situations, 12 (figure), 72, 74, 123

Agree/disagree with retelling, 31

Anchor charts, 16–17, 26

And Then routine, 126
    builds problem-solving skill, 127
    comparing student questions, 133–134
    creativity, 128–135
    multistep problems., 132
    new question with same/different operation, 128–129
    problems and questions, 131
    process, 127
    similar question, 135
    variations, 128–135
    whole-class math lesson, 127
    younger grades, 130

Another Question routine, 136
    bundling routines, 138
    different question for same/different concept, 139–140
    diverse problem types and, 142
    problem-solving skill and, 137
    process, 137
    for two-steps (same/different operations), 140–141
    variations, 138–142

Answers to Your Biggest Questions About Teaching Elementary Math (SanGiovanni), 96

Asked and Answered routine, 41
    builds problem-solving skill, 42
    data, 42–43
    picking between two questions, 45
    process, 42
    questions can't be answered, 46
    with rating, 49
    students generated questions, 47
    using charts, 47
    variations, 43–49
    without data tables, 44

Base ten number creations, 176

Beginning, middle, and end organizer, 30

Benchmark comparisons, 187

Best question, selection of, 38

Big idea and details for retelling, 29

Bundling routines, 138

Calculators, 151–152

Changing the operation, 78

Charts, 47

Classroom-ready routines, 13–14

Comparing and contrasting. *See* Same and Different routine

Comparing two different samples, 102

Confidence, 10

Content/concepts in routines, 16

Contextual information, question, 59

Creating question, 51–52

C-U-B-E-S, 4–5

Different question for same/different concept, 139

Distracting outlier (number), 147–148

Diverse problem structures, 11

Division structures, 13, 90, 154, 160

Dot card numbers, 184

Doubling, sticky patterns routine, 169

Drawing/diagraming problems, 111

Dweck, C., 10

Effective instructional strategy, 94

Efficiency, focus on, 116

Equal sign
    concept of, 177
    misconception of, 123

Equations with unknowns, 121

Equivalent expressions, 177

Estimation, 159–160

Even and odd numbers, 185

Failure, 10

Finding partner problems, 73

Formal reasoning/formulating proofs, 8

Fractions and decimals
    It Can't Be routine, 155
    question routine, 55, 109
    sticky patterns routine, 170–171
    Swap routine, 186

Geometry, 187

Gladwell, M., 9

Gradual release of problem solving, 6

Graphic organizers, 115

Growth mindset, 9–10

Higher-order thinking, 43, 47, 51

How Do You routine, 68
    changing the process, 70
    finding partner, 73
    keyword approach, 69
    mixed list, 74

operation (+/−), comparison of, 71–72
percent change problems, 75
problem solving skill and, 69
process, 69
single problem, 70
using tables, 71–72
variations, 70

Imagine That routine, 111
building agency, 113–117
drawing/diagraming problems, 111
focus on efficiency, 116
graphic organizers, 115
integers, 117
large numbers, 115
picture for discussion, 114–115
with problem solving, 112
process, 112
representations, 113, 116
variations, 113–117
Incorrect examples, samples of, 99
Inequalities and equations, comparisons, 85
Instructional hazards, 4–6
Integers, 117
Is It Reasonable routine, 158
alternatives for, 161
builds problem-solving skill, 159
estimation, 159–160
more or less than certain value, 162
with multiple numbers, 163
with multistep problems, 164
picture, 160
process, 159
variations, 159–172
It Can't Be routine, 150–151
builds problem-solving skill, 151
calculators, 151–152
division, 154
fractions and decimals, 155
operation (action), 152
process, 151
solution/solution path, 156
subtraction problems, 153
two-step problems, 156–157
variations, 152–157
I Would Say routine, 24
avoid proceduralizing, student thinking and reasoning, 25–26
beginning, middle, and end organizer, 30
big idea and details, 29
graphic organizers, 26
Know-What-Solve organizer, 26
with problem solving, 25

process, 25
retelling strategy, 24
Three Asks for, 28
Three-Read organizer, 26
variations, 26–32
See also Retelling strategy

Jump-start routines
addition and subtraction situations, 12 (figure)
classroom-ready routines, 13–14
diverse problem structures, 11
implementation, 11–19
multiplication and division situations, 13 (figure)
Number Talks, 11
problem solving and, 1
students understanding of, 11
timing of, 14–15
See also Routines

Keyword strategy, 5, 69
Know-Want-Learn (K-W-L) chart, 26
Know-What-Solve (K-W-S) organizer, 26

Language comparison, 80
Large numbers, 115
Learning basic facts, 185
Listen for charts, 17
Logic games, 183
Look-for tool, 193–194
Lots and Lots routine, 174
base ten number creations, 176
builds problem-solving skill, 175
create-share-create variation, 179
equivalent expressions, 177
open-ended questions, 174, 175
process, 175
representing fractions, 177
restrictions, 178
solution to different open prompts, 181
time and money, 180
variations, 174–181

Match the Equation routine, 118
builds problem-solving skill, 119
changing numbers, 124
changing problem types, 122
equal sign, misconception, 123
equations with unknowns, 121
more than one equation, 120
process, 119
target with routine, 120–125
two-step problems, 125
variations, 120–125

Mathematical reasoning, 8
Mathematics engagement, 194
Mental problem-solving activities, 16
Middle school example, 149, 188
Mixed list problems, 74
Mnemonics, 4–5
Monitoring practice, 18
Multiplication and division situations, 13 (figure), 90
Multiplication samples, 97
Multistep problems., 132

Notice and Wonder strategy, 6
Number complexity, reversing order of, 105
Number pluckers, 10–11
Number routines, 111
Number Talks, 11
Number types/measurement units, 3Qs, 39

One-step and two-step problems, 83
Open-ended questions, 174
Operation (+/−), comparison of, 71–72
Outliers (Gladwell), 9

Partially completed samples, 100
Percent change problems, 75
Personal tools, 17
Picture for discussion, 114–115
Picture, reasonable, 160
Planning routines, 189
    determining rotation, 190
    goals, 191
    identifying content, 189–190
    thinking, reasoning, and discussion, 190–191
"Problem-attack" skill, 76
Problem solving
    C-U-B-E-S, 4–5
    defined, 2
    Friday, 5–6
    gradual release of, 6
    instructional hazards, 4–6
    jump-start routines for, 1, 7–8
    keyword strategy to, 5
    mnemonics, 4–5
    Notice and Wonder strategy, 6
    routines, 7
    rule-based approaches, 10
Problem-solving routine. *See* Routines
Problem-solving situations, 12–13, 12 (figure), 13 (figure)
Problems without numbers, 106
Professional learning, 192–193
Professional learning community (PLC), 192–193

Quality practice, 8–9

Rating question and answer, 49
Reasonableness of answer, 158
    alternatives for, 161
    operation and, 161
    See also Is It Reasonable routine
Reasoning strategies, 8, 18, 186
Representations, 113, 116
Retelling strategy, 24
    beginning, middle, and end organizer for, 30
    big idea and details for, 29
    Know-What-Solve organizer for, 26
    solving linear equations, 32
    students agree/disagree with, 31
    Three Asks for, 28
    Three-Read organizer for, 26
    two-step problems and choice, 32
    See also I Would Say
Routines, 7, 195–198
    Another Question, 136–142
    Asked and Answered, 41–49
    collaborative/sharing work, 192
    confidence, 10
    connecting strategies and concepts, 19
    content/concepts, 16
    designing, 192
    growth mindset, 9–10
    guidelines, 14
    Imagine That, 111–117
    Is It Reasonable, 158–164
    It Can't Be, 150–157
    I Would Say routine, 24–32
    look-for tool, 193–194
    Match the Equation, 118–125
    mathematics engagement, 194
    meaningful discourse, 17–19
    modifying, 192
    personal tools, 17
    plan for, 16–19
    prevent/rehabilitate number pluckers, 10–11
    for professional learning/PLCS, 192–193
    quality practice and, 8–9
    reasoning and, 8
    Same Data, Different Question, 57–67
    selection of, 15, 16, 18
    sequencing student ideas, 18–19
    shape of, 14
    Sticky Patterns, 165–173
    support language and discussion, 16
    The Swap, 182–188
    And Then, 126–135
    They Did What, 94–102
    thinking and reasoning, 190–191
    This Number, That Number, 103–110
    TMI (Too Much Information), 143–149

tools to support, 16
What's the Question, 50–56
What's the Sitch, 86–93
working process, 8
Rule-based approaches, 10

Same and Different routine, 76
changing the operation, 78
inequalities and equations, comparisons, 85
language comparison, 80
modifying possibilities, 78–85
number types, changing, 81
one-step and two-step problems, 83
with problem solving, 77
process, 77
same problem, different contexts, 79
scaffolding routines, 77
students creating own comparisons, 84
three problems, 82
variations, 78–85
Same Data, Different Question routine, 57–58, 61
builds problem-solving skill, 58
for centers and homework, 59
contextual information, 59
number types, 62
perceptions, 57
primary examples, 63
process, 58–59
questions that can't be answered, 65
revisiting and reviewing, 67
student's question, 66
with traditional word problems, 60
two-step problems, 64
variations, 59
Scaffolding routines, 77
Sentence starters, 16–17
Shapes, sticky patterns routine, 167
Single digit to two digit, 107
Single problem, 70
Skip counting, sticky patterns routine, 168
Smith, M. S., 18
Solving linear equations, 32
Stein, M. K., 18
Sticky Patterns routine, 165
builds problem-solving skill, 166
with decimals, 171
doubling, 169
with fractions, 170
"hidden" standards, 167–173
process, 166
reframe problem solving, 166
with shapes, 167
skip counting, 168
student created patterns, 173

with two-step rules, 172
variations, 167–173
Student created patterns routine, 173
Student creativity, 43–49
Students choice, question routine, 56
Students generated questions, 47
Subtraction problems, 153
Support language and discussion, 16
The Swap routine, 182
benchmark comparisons, 187
builds problem-solving skill, 183
dot card numbers, 184
even and odd numbers, 185
fraction concepts, 186
geometry, 187
learning basic facts, 185
logic games, 183
in middle school, 188
process, 183
reasoning strategies, 186
skill/concept, 184–188
variations, 184–188
Symbols, 108

Tables, 71–72
They Did What routine, 94
builds problem-solving skill, 95
comparing two different samples, 102
effective instructional strategy, 94
incorrect examples, samples of, 99
multiplication samples, 97
partially completed samples, 100
process, 95
right answer, 96
two-step problems, 101
variations, 97–102
worked examples, 94, 97–102
wrong answer, right process sample, 98
This Number, That Number routine, 103
builds problem-solving skill, 104
changing challenging problems, 110
fractions to decimals, 109
grade level context, 105–110
number complexity, reversing order of, 105
numbers selection, 110
problems without numbers, 106
process, 104
single digit to two digit, 107
using symbols, 108
variations, 105–110
3Qs (Question, Question, Question) routine, 33
best question, selection of, 38
with different number types/measurement units, 39

essential questions, 33–35
  fitting category of problem, using question, 37
  problem solving and, 33
  process, 35–36
  purpose of, 35
  right question, starting with, 39
  Three-Read protocol, 36
  with two-step problems, 40
  variations, 36–40
Three Asks for retelling, 28
Three problems, 82
Three-Read organizer for retelling, 26
Three-Read protocol, 36
Timing of routines, 14–15
TMI (Too Much Information) routine, 143
  builds problem-solving skill, 144
  distracting outlier (number), 147–148
  middle school example, 149
  process, 144
  reading a problem together, 144
  in table, 146
  too many numbers, 145
  variations, 145–149
Traditional word problems, 60
Two-step problems in retelling, 32

Vocabulary anchor charts, 16

What's the Question routine, 50
  answers without images, labels, or both, 54
  builds problem-solving skill, 51
  creating question, 51–53
  fractions and decimals, 55
  operation/condition requirement, 52
  process, 51
  students answer, 54
  students choice, 56
  variations, 52–56
  What Can't Be the Question, 53
What's the Sitch routine, 86
  builds problem-solving skill, 87
  different number types, 93
  focus on one problem type/structure, 89
  four operations, 91
  multiplication and division structures, 90
  process, 87
  Thinking Chart, 86, 87 (figure)
  variations, 88–93
  whole-school agreements, 88
Whole-school agreements, 88
Word problems, 2
  challenges, 2–4
  structures, 12–13
  See also Problem solving
Wrong answer, right process sample, 98

NOTES

NOTES

NOTES

NOTES

NOTES

Supporting TEACHERS | *Empowering* STUDENTS

PETER LILJEDAHL

14 optimal practices for thinking that create an ideal setting for deep mathematics learning to occur.

Grades K–12

CHASE ORTON

A guide that leads math teachers through a journey to cultivate a more equitable, inclusive, and cohesive culture of professionalism for themselves.

Grades K–12

KIMBERLY RIMBEY

Much-needed guidance on how to meet the diverse needs of students using small group math instruction.

Grades K–5

BETH MCCORD KOBETT, FRANCIS (SKIP) FENNELL, KAREN S. KARP, DELISE ANDREWS, LATRENDA KNIGHTEN, JEFF SHIH, DESIREE HARRISON, BARBARA ANN SWARTZ, SORSHA-MARIA T. MULROE

Detailed plans for helping elementary students experience deep mathematical learning.

Grades K–1, 2–3, 4–5

LOU EDWARD MATTHEWS, SHELLY M. JONES, YOLANDA A. PARKER

A resource for designing inspiring learning experiences driven by the kind of high-quality and culturally relevant mathematics tasks that connect students to their world.

Elementary, Middle and High School

JOHN J. SANGIOVANNI, SUSIE KATT, KEVIN J. DYKEMA

A guide for empowering students to embrace productive struggle to build essential skills for learning and living—both inside and outside the classroom.

Grades K–12

To order, visit corwin.com/math

**JENNIFER M. BAY-WILLIAMS,
JOHN J. SANGIOVANNI,
ROSALBA SERRANO,
SHERRI MARTINIE,
JENNIFER SUH, C. DAVID WALTERS**

Because fluency is so much more
than basic facts and algorithms.
Grades K–8

**ROBERT Q. BERRY III, BASIL M. CONWAY IV,
BRIAN R. LAWLER, JOHN W. STALEY,
COURTNEY KOESTLER, JENNIFER WARD,
MARIA DEL ROSARIO ZAVALA,
TONYA GAU BARTELL, CATHERY YEH,
MATHEW FELTON-KOESTLER,
LATEEFAH ID-DEEN,
MARY CANDACE RAYGOZA,
AMANDA RUIZ, EVA THANHEISER**

Learn to plan instruction that engages
students in mathematics explorations
through age-appropriate and culturally
relevant social justice topics.
**Early Elementary, Upper Elementary,
Middle School, High School**

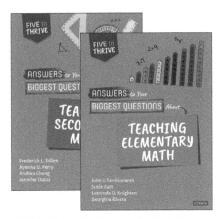

**JOHN J. SANGIOVANNI, SUSIE KATT,
LATRENDA D. KNIGHTEN,
GEORGINA RIVERA,
FREDERICK L. DILLON,
AYANNA D. PERRY,
ANDREA CHENG, JENNIFER OUTZS**

Actionable answers to your most
pressing questions about teaching
elementary and secondary math.
Elementary, Secondary

**SARA DELANO MOORE,
KIMBERLY RIMBEY**

A journey toward making
manipulatives meaningful.
Grades K–3, 4–8

A SAGE Publishing Company

Helping educators make the greatest impact

CORWIN HAS ONE MISSION: to enhance education through intentional professional learning.

We build long-term relationships with our authors, educators, clients, and associations who partner with us to develop and continuously improve the best evidence-based practices that establish and support lifelong learning.